W9-CPF-957

NER EYAL

SAMSON RAPHAEL GRUNFELD

A GUIDE TO
THE LAWS OF SHABBAT
AND FESTIVALS IN SEDER MOED

H er earliest recollections always revolved around family; the stories recalling the traditions created by her parents for their children. Her music was the background to our life. Her laughter bespoke a serenity, a calm that permeated our home. Her tears gave us an understanding of her purity and self sacrifice. Her compassion showed us by example, continuously; her friendship to others knowing no bounds.

R ose Shisgal Schwartz was a woman whose message was clear: She mastered the role of an Aishes Chayal from the very beginning, dedicating her life, her time and all her resources to her family. As a child, she traveled with her parents from Russia to Pawtucket, R.I., where her father led a small outpost of Yiddishkeit during the Depression years. He returned to Williamburg only so that his children could attend the proper Torah institutions and to lead a congregation on the Lower East Side — the Sneir/Vilner Congregation, also known as the Pink Shul, on Montgomery Street. There Raizel, as she was known to all, began her career as a teacher that took her from the halls of Bais Yackov and other Hebrew day schools, to being a dedicated social worker for the elderly and all who needed help. Working as a team with David, her husband of almost 50 years, they carried the beauty of those values to the wider world, pioneering vibrant Orthodox communities in towns and villages, from Lawrence, to Highland Park, to West Hempstead and then back to New York. She gave so much of herself to others, without sacrificing her warmth and love for her children. She loved each and every one of us and let us love her in return. We remember the patience of her guidance; the way she welcomed each new member into the family, the way she emphasized the important things in life. Now it is our turn to honor her, to take her gifts to us and make them our gifts to others, to our time, to the ones we love.

W e dedicate this book to her memory, with thanks to Raphael Grundfeld who has worked steadfastly during the year of Kaddish. Raphael, visited our mother while she was struggling with her illness. There are many people who will always remain close to her but none more then Irwin and Lily Chanales, they stood vigil and offered support each and every day. To Rabbi Mat and Vivian Kanig who showed strength and courage to her and have devoted out of love an enormous amount of time in the editing and thoughts of this book To Israel and Natalie Friedman her life long friends who shared in her joys her tears and her dreams. They all offered more than they could have known, and may they be blessed both in this world and in Olam Habah.

T he guiding theme and wisdom throughout this book is based on the teachings of the Gadol Hador Rabbi Moshe Feintein, father-in-law of Rabbi Eliyahu Moshe Shisgal, Raizel's brother, a Tzadik and Gadol in his own right and father of Rebetzin Faye, sister-in-law, friend and source of support throughout her life.

This volume is dedicated
in memory of

Rose Schwartz ע"ה

רייזל בת הרב אברהם יצחק זצ"ל

וטשארנא ע"ה

David H. Schwartz

Elliot and Judy Schwartz **Susan and Danny Sklarin**

Jenny, Rachel and Harris Yigal, Tammar and Eli

Donna and Robert Ashheim

Mayer, Cara and Rebekah

ISBN: 0-615-11899-2

Printed in New York by ArtScroll Printing Corp.

For Daniela, Ishai and Itai.

This book is dedicated in loving memory
of our first born son,
Eyal Baruch Chaim Grunfeld ז"ל

ספר זה מוקדש במלואו
לבנינו הבכור
אייל ברוך חיים גרונפלד ז"ל
שנכנס לעולם ביום ד בניסן תשל"ג
ויצא מן העולם עם נר דלוק על ראשו ביום טז בכסלו תשל"ד

ACKNOWLEDGEMENTS

I am deeply grateful to my dear friend, David Schwartz, who coached and coaxed me into this book.

In loving memory of David's unforgettable wife, Rose Schwartz ז״ל.

To my beloved teacher and Rav, Rabbi Abraham Weiss of the Hebrew Institute of Riverdale, for his profound knowledge of Halachah which he translates daily into Tikun Olam, and to his wife, Tobi Weiss, the remarkable Rebbetzin of our community.

To Elliot Schwartz and his wife Judy for making this book happen.

To my beloved wife, Daniela, whose love and support allowed me to open a Sefer and whose wisdom and insight gave me a better understanding of what was written within.

To our beloved sons, Ishai and Itai, for the hours spent together learning and discussing the Halachic concepts in this book and for the time they devoted to getting it into print.

To my Chavruta, Hillel Jaffe, whose keen insights and constant support made it easier to get up each morning for our early hours of learning that fed this book, and to his wife, Madeline for encouraging him along the way.

To Michael Horen and his wife Marilyn for the superb artwork that graces the cover.

To Rabbi Emmanuel Vinas, the Sofer of Riverdale, and his wife, Erica Vinas, for giving light and life to the Hebrew letters of the title.

To Professor Harold Fisch for his encouragment and constructive criticism.

To Els Bendheim and Charles Bendheim ז״ל for their helpful input on the section on Eruvin.

To Dr. Vivian Krohn-Kenig for her diligent work in editing the manuscript.

To Judge Henry Guttman, Robert Kalfus, and Hillel Jaffe for their time and patience in reviewing the manuscript.

To Tzipora Levine for her hard work and effort in producing this book.

To Haya Gordin, Chief Librarian of the Yeshivah University Library, for locating many of the books cited in this work.

To Dr. Elli Kranzler, Leon Wildes and Avery Steinberg for the hours spent learning together.

To Rabbi Barry Gelman for igniting the spark.

To Rabbi Dov Weiss, Rabbi Dov Linzer, Rabbi Shmuel Herztfeld, Rabbi Aaron Frank, Rabbi Jeffrey Fox and Rabbi Adam Starr whose Talmudic and moral support helped fan the flame.

To Rabbi Mayer Twersky and Rabbi Levi Shemtov, for illuminating some of the more obscure texts.

To Dr. Jonathan Sarlin for discussing with me the Halachic rulings of Rabbi Ovadiah Yosef.

To Yosepha Sarlin for her kindness in facilitating the review of the manuscript.

To Kenneth Dubin for his technical support and computer savvy.

To Shimi Kaminetski, Beverly Muller and Kurt Frankfurter for their dedication, every Friday, week after week.

To Rabbi Yaacov Elman for his advice on the footnotes.

I should also like to express my grateful thanks to the following participants of the Tuesday night Daf Yomi Shiur:
Stanley Langer, Paul Klein, Dr. Avraham Teller, Milton Honig, Professor Eric Schon, Dr. Lewis Bernstein, Haim Glickman, David Eiseman, Ronnie Nussbaum, Mark Frisch, Larry Rothbaum, Noah Rothbaum, Peter Singer, Paul Blank, Jonathan Blank, Mark Baker, Stephen Oppenheimer, Murray Rudnick, Herbert Lowenstein, Kenneth Dubin, Paul Pizem, Dr. David Pulver, Michael Zimet, Professor Jeffrey Gurock, Bernie Horowitz, Dr. Ronnie Schechter, Dr. Judah Schorr, Moshe Margalit, Vitali Gutman, Avraham Dubin, Joey Brender and Dr. Mark Levy.

In loving memory of Dr. Herman Kugelmann ז''ל, Recha Kugelmann ז''ל, Miriam Brassloff ז''ל, Isidor Wohlfarth ז''ל, Johanna Wohlfarth ז''ל, Dr. Martin Purley ז''ל, Ilse Purley ז''ל, Shmuel Purley ז''ל and Ruth Wohlfarth ז''ל.

In memory of Yitzchak Maas ז''ל, Rozalia Maas ז''ל and Halina Maas ז''ל, who perished in Lvov and whose noble spirit lives on in Cecilia Maas who devotes her life to Chesed Shel Emet.

I hope this book can repay a little of the debt to my beloved parents Dayan Dr. I. Grunfeld ז''ל, and Dr. Judith Grunfeld ז''ל, whose love of Torah, each other, and their children warmed our hearts and those of so many others.

To my sisters Dr. Anne Cohn and Naomi Grunfeld and to my brother Rabbi Shemayah Grunfeld for continuing in their tradition.

To Professor John Cohn for his kindness and integrity and helpful comments on this work.

And to you, my brother Akiva Yosef, ז''ל who knew everything that we are still continuing to learn, may your beautiful נשמה reap the rewards of the joy you gave to others.

PREFACE

The resident of the building next to Carnegie Hall heard the music night after night, year after year. It formed pleasant background noise as he moved through his apartment, preoccupied with his daily activities. Yet he never knew what was playing or who was performing.

So he bought a ticket, read up on the composer and conductor and listened to the CD. Then, he went to the concert. And though the music was familiar to him, he felt he was listening to it for the first time.

How many times have we heard the same chapters read from the Torah week after week, year after year, and all we get is the chant of meaningless words?

If we invest time, however, in the Oral Law, the Midrash, Talmud and Halachah, each word will soon strike a note and engage us in a live performance.

The Halachah is the distillation of the Torah as it applies to our lives. It is God's bottled prescription for our well-being. We need to be able to read it to understand its instructions.

Too many people, however, feel locked out by the esoteric and involved language in which Halachah is sometimes written.

This book attempts to enhance our appreciation of the Halachah by conveying it in simple language, tying it to everyday experience and introducing us to its technical terms.

It does not purport to decide Halachic issues. It is intended, rather, to assist in identifying them. Just as the business person knows when to consult a professional, so the reader will learn when to consult a Posek, (a Halachic authority).

Samson Raphael Grunfeld
New York April 19, 2001

TABLE of CONTENTS

CHAPTER ONE - SHABBAT

CHAPTER TWO - ERUVIN

CHAPTER THREE - PESACH

CHAPTER FOUR - YOM TOV

CHAPTER FIVE - THE THREE WEEKS and TISHA BE'AV

CHAPTER SIX - SHEKALIM

CHAPTER SEVEN - MEZUZAH

CHAPTER EIGHT - OTHER TOPICS in SEDER MOED

SUMMARY DESCRIPTION of CONTENTS

CHAPTER ONE - SHABBAT

CHAPTER TWO - ERUVIN

CHAPTER THREE - PESACH

טעם כעיקר, the importance of taste in Halachah in determining whether food and utensils are Kosher during the year and Kosher for Pesach / The way in which utensils that have absorbed the taste of forbidden food can be restored for use during the year and for Pesach / The way the vessel absorbs the food determines the way it is Kashered / Different methods of Kashering / By means of a white hot flame, ליבון / By means of a flame just hot enough to ignite straw, ליבון קל / By immersion in boiling water, הגעלה / By pouring boiling water over utensils, עירוי / By soaking them in cold water, שטיפה / The application of these different forms of Kashering to the different ways the vessels have absorbed the forbidden flavors / Whether and to what extent the different methods of Kashering are interchangeable.

List of substances that qualify for Kashering / Controversy whether glass can be used without Kashering / How to Kasher glass / Controversy regarding vessels made of synthetic materials such as plastics and nylon, Pyrex, Duralex and Corningware / How to Kasher tabletops and other surfaces used for Chametz / Controversy over whether dishwashers with plastic walls can be Kashered / How to Kasher gas stoves and electric ovens / How to Kasher microwave ovens / Whether mixers, blenders, coffee percolators and whisky glasses can be Kashered.

The requirement to immerse certain vessels owned by non-Jews into natural water gathered in a Mikveh before they are used by Jews / The reasons for and source of this requirement / List of substances that are exempt from Tevilah / The blessing recited prior to Toveling / Persons eligible to perform Toveling / Toveling of vessels used to prepare food but not used to eat with / Whether Tevilah is required in cases where the non-Jew retains ownership of the utensils such as when they are rented / Preparation of vessels for Toveling / How to tovel electrical appliances such as a coffee percolator / Whether one may Tovel vessels in the sea, river or snow / Differences between Kashering and Toveling and instances in which the same vessels require both procedures.

The definition of Chametz / Various opinions about the length of time it takes for flour and water to ferment into Chametz / The three prohibitions, not to eat, not to possess and not to derive enjoyment from Chametz on Pesach / Whether the prohibitions and which of the prohibitions apply to mixtures which contain decomposed Chametz not usually eaten / The concept of נפסל מאכילת כלב - Chametz that is not fit for human consumption / Whether one may take medicine on Pesach which contains Chametz / Whether coated tablets, liquid medicine, isopropyl alcohol, ethyl alcohol, creams and ointments containing grain alcohol, toothpaste, body soap and liquid dishwashing soap may be used on Pesach, and what level of supervision is required for such products.

בטל בשישים, בטול ברוב, the concept of the majority overcoming the minority and the concept of the ratio of 60 units of permitted food to one unit of prohibited food during the rest of the year /

חמץ במשהו Chametz which became mixed with Kosher LePesach food on Pesach renders the food prohibited irrespective of the ratio of the permitted to the prohibited / Reasons for this stringency on Pesach - דבר שיש לן מתירין , לא בדילי מיניה / Certain combinations of Chametz and non Chametz products that were mixed before Pesach are subject to the permitting ratios / Application of this rule to לח בלח, mixtures that blend together / The concept of חוזר וניעור, the reawakening of the prohibited substance in the mixture on Pesach / Applications of these principles to various foods such as granulated sugar, table salt, instant coffee, tea, tea bags, cocoa and milk, club soda, seltzer, juices, vegetables, plastic tablecloths, paper plates, aluminum foil, frozen fruits, brown sugar, sugar substitutes, spices, condiments, cheese and more.

Commencement of the Chametz prohibition according to the Torah / Cut off times for eating, possessing and deriving benefit from Chametz imposed by the Rabbis / The time for burning and nullifying Chametz on Erev Pesach / Why it is necessary to sell Chametz that has been nullified / The terms and conditions that are necessary for an effective sale of Chametz to a non-Jew before Pesach / חמץ שעבר עליו הפסח - The status of Chametz that remained in the possession of a Jew during Pesach / Selling or renting to a non-Jew the place in the house in which the Chametz resides / Buying back the Chametz from the non-Jew after Pesach / Return of deposit and forgiveness of loan / Empowering the Rabbi to sell Chametz for the community by means of signing a power of attorney / Whether the power of attorney can be given orally / Whether the sale of the Chametz by the Rabbi covers those members of the community that did not empower the Rabbi to sell their Chametz / Times for selling Chametz residing in one's home when one is away for Pesach in a different time zone.

Case study of Kosher food prepared in the vicinity of non-Kosher food / Dispute between Rav and Levi whether the aroma of non-Kosher food contaminates Kosher foods / The position of the Halachah / The aroma of pungent non-Kosher foods and their ability to contaminate Kosher food in the vicinity / Isolating Kosher food from pungent non-Kosher food in the vicinity by means of a lid on a pot or wrapping the food in foil / Whether aromas conveyed through wet steam have the power to contaminate Kosher food / Cooking a milk dish in a pot without a lid in the same oven as a meat dish / Whether one may eat meat and fish together / חמירא סכנתא מאיסורא, health concerns and the stringency of health considerations in Halachah / The accepted practice of how to separate fish from meat.

The Biblical source of the prohibition / The three prohibitions, איסור בישול, the prohibition to boil meat and milk together, איסור אכילה, the prohibition to eat meat and milk together, and איסור הנאה the prohibition to derive benefit from meat and milk together / The application of the prohibitions to domesticated and undomesticated animals and to fowl / The extension of the prohibition to forms of preparing meat and dairy together / Possible reasons for the prohibitions / Laws that apply to the consumption of milk after meat / Length of the waiting period and reasons for the waiting period between meat and milk.

CHAPTER FOUR - YOM TOV

The difference between Rosh Hashanah and the other Festivals in terms of the time available to the emissaries to reach outlying districts and advise them that the previous month was a חדש חסר of 29 days / Confusion in the Temple arising out of the tardiness of the witnesses bearing testimony as to the sighting of the moon / The decree of the Rabbis rendering the testimony inadmissible if the witnesses arrived late in the afternoon of the 30th and declaring the 31st day of the month Rosh Hashanah / The decree of the Rabbis merging the 30th day with the 31st to prevent people from working late into the afternoon on the 30th day / The different status of the two days of Rosh Hashanah and the two days of the other Jewish Festivals / Practical ramifications arising out of this distinction / The decree of Rabbi Yochnan Ben Zakkai following the destruction of the Temple to once again admit the testimony of witnesses arriving late afternoon on the thirtieth day / The situation in the Diaspora after the destruction of the Temple / Why Rosh Hashanah is celebrated for two days in Israel after the destruction of the Temple / Why today, in the era of the calendar, despite knowing for certain which day is Rosh Hashanah and which is not, we continue to celebrate two days Rosh Hashanah.

Description of the Service of The High Priest in the Temple on Yom Kippur / The significance of the phrase ברוך שם כבוד מלכותו לעולם ועד on Yom Kippur / The recital of Yizkor on Yom Kippur / The closing נעילה - Neilah prayer.

The reason for the commandment to dwell in Succot / Why Succot is celebrated in the month of Tishrei and not in the month of Nissan, in which the Exodus occurred / Debate between Rabbi Eliezer and Rabbi Akiva whether the Succot of the desert were booths or clouds / The explanation of the Netziv / The relationship between the laws of Succot and the laws of Eruvin / The Biblical requirement to eat in the Succah on the first two nights of Succot / The requirement to eat regular meals in the Succah on the other days of Succot / How to fulfill the Mitzvah of Succah when it rains on Succot.

The Succah cannot primarily be built as an invalid structure and then be corrected and made valid / Origin of this rule / How to remedy a Succah that is built under a tree / How to lay down the Sechach on a Succah equipped with a rain roof / Other examples of the principle of תעשה ולא מן העשוי.

The four species mentioned in the Torah as interpreted by the Rabbis / The proper way of binding and holding the four species / Waving the Four Species in four directions and the reason thereof /

Connection between the Mitzvah of the Four Species and reciting Hallel / The days of Succot on which the Mitzvah of the Four Species applied in the Temple Era and after the destruction of the Temple / The minimum requirements of a Kosher Etrog / Features which add beauty to an already Kosher Etrog / The status of an Etrog that lost its Pitam / The minimum requirements of the הדס, myrtle / The minimum requirements of the ערבות - willows / Minimum requirements common to all the Four Species / The order of the blessings recited upon picking up the Four Species / Why the Etrog is inverted when the blessings are recited / Why the Four Species are not used on Shabbat.

The meaning and Scriptural source of Hallel / The days on which Whole Hallel is recited / The blessing recited before Hallel / When it is recited and when it is not recited / Why Hallel is not recited on Rosh Hashanah and Yom Kippur / The difference between Whole Hallel and Half Hallel / Why Half Hallel is recited on the last 6 days of Pesach / When Half Hallel is recited / Half Hallel as a Minhag on Rosh Chodesh and other days that do not qualify for Whole Hallel / Whether a blessing may be recited when performing an act, which is a Minhag / Whether Hallel should be recited on days of national celebration for recent miracles / Hallel on יום העצמאות Yom Haatzmaut / Following the custom of one's Synagogue.

The reason for the celebration of one day Yom Tov in Israel and two days Yom Tov outside Israel / חדש מלא, a month of 30 days and a חדש חסר, a month of 29 days / The critical importance of determining which month is מלא and which is חסר / How the status of the month in terms of מלא or חסר is determined today and how it used to be determined before the establishment of the Jewish calendar / The testimony of witnesses before the Jerusalem Court of Law testifying to the sighting of the new moon on the 30th day of the month / What happens if there were no witnesses / How the news of a חדש חסר reached outlying districts / How people in outlying districts who would not hear the news of a חדש חסר on time protected themselves against a possible violation of Yom Tov / Why we continue to keep two days Yom Tov outside Israel, even though no doubt remains as to whether the month is מלא or חסר / Practical Halachic ramifications arising out of the two days of Yom Tov celebrated in the Diaspora.

The prohibition of cooking on Yom Tov for a meal the next day / Whether one may cook on Yom Tov for the next day Shabbat / Reasons why it is permitted by Torah law to cook on Yom Tov for the next day Shabbat / The reason of Rabbah, הואיל - Ho'il / The reason of Rav Chisdah / The Rabbinical requirement of Eruv Tavshilin before one may cook on Yom Tov for the next day Shabbat and the reasons therefor / How and when the Eruv Tavshilin ceremony is conducted / The blessing recited over Eruv Tavshilin / Whether people who eat out on Yom Tov are required to perform the ceremony of Eruv Tavshilin / Whether the Eruv ceremony allows one to cook on Thursday for Shabbat when the first day of Yom Tov is Thursday / When the Challah used for the Eruv Tavshilin ceremony should be eaten / What to do if one remembered at Minchah time in the Synagogue on Erev Yom Tov that one forgot to perform the Eruv Tavshilin ceremony / Whether one may rely upon the Eruv Tavshilin ceremony conducted by the Rabbi for the entire community / The Halachic basis for somebody else performing the ceremony on one's behalf / The time by which cooking should cease on Yom Tov, Friday afternoon.

Shaving, laundering, marriages and engagements on Chol Hamoed / Similarities between the laws of Chol Hamoed and the laws of mourning.

The correct blessing recited for Havdalah when Shabbat ends and Yom Tov arrives / The concept of the נשמה יתרה, the extra soul on Shabbat / Why בשמים, spices, are not used for Havdalah when Shabbat ends and Yom Tov arrives / Why Besamim are not used when Yom Tov ends Monday night / Reason of the Tosafists and reason of the Sefat Emet.

Description of the Shiva and the Shloshim, the seven day period and thirty day period of mourning for a deceased relative / The circumstances under which the arrival of Yom Tov terminates the Shiva and the Shloshim / Whether Shabbat cancels the Shiva or the Shloshim / Mourning on Shabbat / Dispute between Rabbi Eliezer and Rabbi Gamliel as to why Yom Tov terminates the Shiva and the Shloshim / The circumstances under which the arrival of Yom Tov does not terminate the Shiva or Shloshim but shortens them.

If you are busy performing a Mitzvah you are exempt from performing another Mitzvah / Debate among Rishonim as to the application of the rule of העוסק במצוה פטור מן המצוה in cases where it is impossible to perform both Mitzvot; in cases where it is difficult yet still possible to perform both, in cases and where it is easy to perform both / Whether the rule applies when the second Mitzvah is more important, carries a harsher penalty and will be impossible to perform later / Whether the rule applies when the second Mitzvah has the power to override the first Mitzvah.

Status of a stolen Lulav on the first day of Succot / Other examples of the Torah requirement that a Mitzvah cannot be performed with stolen goods / Status of a stolen Lulav on second day Succot and stolen Matzah on the first day Pesach / Rabbinical prohibition on use of stolen books, Tefillin, Matzah and a synagogue built on stolen land / Situations in which a stolen Lulav or a stolen Matzah may be used even on the first day of Succot or Pesach / Examples include where the owner loses the right to the physical Lulav or Matzah and is relegated to monetary compensation from the thief or where there has been a fundamental change in the stolen item / The case of יאוש, renouncing hope of ever retrieving the item and its transfer to a third party / Whether a blessing may be recited over a Mitzvah performed with a stolen item in such circumstances.

Why the Talmud's description of Chanukah focuses on the miracle of the jar of oil rather than on the miracle of the military victory / זמן הדלקת נרות, the appropriate time for lighting the Chanukah lights during the week, on Friday afternoon and on Motzaei Shabbat / Whether women must participate in the Mitzvah of Chanukah lights and whether spouses may light for each other / Whether the Mitzvah of Chanukah lights is a personal obligation or an obligation which applies to the house / Whether Chanukah lights must be lit in a hotel room / Whether an electric light qualifies for the Chanukah lights / The order of lighting candles for Shabbat and for Chanukah on Friday afternoon.

CHAPTER FIVE - THE THREE WEEKS AND TISHA BE'AV

CHAPTER SIX - SHEKALIM

the Rambam and quotations from Pirkei Avot against making Torah a profession and dissenting opinions of the Rema, the Maharam of Rottenburg and Rav Moshe Feinstein on the matter.

CHAPTER SEVEN - MEZUZAH

CHAPTER EIGHT - OTHER TOPICS

inconsistencies between the conduct of our forefathers and the Mitzvot.

The relationship between the Oral Law and the Written Law. The Divine source of the Written and Oral Law / הלכה למשה מסיני - taught by Moses himself and the Thirteen Rules of Derivation - Yud Gimmel Midot / Whether one may disagree with the Rabbis' interpretation of the Yud Gimmel Midot / Whether a contemporary court of law can disagree with the interpretation of the Yud Gimmel Midot accepted by the Talmud / The answers of the Rambam and the Kesef Mishneh / Whether the decisions of the Poskim who lived in post Talmudic times are binding on subsequent Poskim / The public acceptance of certain Halachic interpreters over others / The unique status of the Shulchan Aruch / Whether subsequent Poskim may rule against a ruling set forth in the Shulchan Aruch / How to decide a dispute between two equally accepted contemporary Poskim / The duty to follow the decision of the leader of the community one lives in.

The difference between the Revelation at Sinai and the acceptance of the Torah by the Jews on Purim / Whether acts of Rabbinical legislation are enforced when the public cannot abide by them / The duty to assess the probability of public acceptance of legislative acts before the Rabbis enact them / Whether legislative acts of the Rabbis of a previous generation can be repealed by the Rabbis of a subsequent generation / Whether protective legislation accepted by the public can be repealed / The power of the previous generation of legislators to give the subsequent legislators the power to repeal their legislation / The power of the Rabbis of a subsequent generation to repeal a legislative act that is not in the category of protective legislation and the conditions under which this may be applied / The power of Rabbis of a later generation to repeal Hillel's Pruzbul / Whether a legislative act automatically expires where the stated rationale for its enactment no longer applies / The power of Rabbis to suspend any law under extenuating circumstances.

NOTE TO THE READER

Many of the Halachic questions explored in this book are decided differently by various Halachic authorities cited. In some instances, the decision of one authority, concerning one issue may be more lenient than the decision of another Halachic authority on the same issue. The Halachic decision to be adopted by the reader on any particular issue discussed should not be dictated by its leniency or its stringency but rather, by the ruling of the Halachic authority that the reader follows, in the spirit of עשה לך רב, which means, one should consistently follow one Halachic authority.

Chapter One

Shabbat

CANDLE LIGHTING TIME
זמן הדלקת נרות

The Shabbat candles must be lit by (and preferably 18 minutes before) sunset. Once it is twilight, the time between sunset and nightfall known as בין השמשות, it is too late to light.[1] Bein Hashmashot begins when the sun sets below the horizon and is no longer visible.

According to Rabbi Yehudah in Tractate Shabbat,[2] Bein Hashmashot lasts 13 1/2 minutes. The same Rabbi Yehudah in Tractate Pesachim,[3] however, maintains that Bein Hashmashot lasts 72 minutes.

In explaining the discrepancy between the duration of Bein Hashmashot according to Rabbi Yehudah in Shabbat (13 1/2 minutes) and Rabbi Yehudah in Pesachim (72 minutes), Rabbeinu Tam[4] explains that there are two separate sunsets: Sunset I, which begins immediately after the sun has sunk below the horizon and lasts 58 1/2 minutes, and Sunset II which starts thereafter when light begins to fade into darkness and lasts an additional 13 1/2 minutes until nightfall.

According to Rabbeinu Tam, the period on Friday between Sunset I and Sunset II (58 1/2 minutes) is considered weekday during which time all weekday work may be performed, and one may light candles until Sunset II, i.e. 58 1/2 minutes after Sunset I.

Many Rishonim, such as the Rambam[5] and the Gaonim disagree with Rabbeinu Tam. They maintain that for candle lighting there is only one relevant sunset, i.e. Sunset I, when the sun dips below the horizon, and candles must be lit before such time.

Although the Shulchan Aruch[6] agrees with Rabbeinu Tam and maintains that candles can be lit as late as 58 1/2 minutes after Sunset I, the Vilna Gaon, following the opinion of the majority of the Rishonim, disagrees with the Schulchan Aruch and maintains that candles must be lit by Sunset I.[7]

There is a third opinion, that of Rabbi Eliezer of Metz, according to which Bein Hashmashot begins 13 1/2 minutes before Sunset I. In his view, candle lighting time would be 13 1/2 minutes before Sunset I.

It should be noted that the 13 1/2 minute period is derived from the time it takes a person to walk 3/4 of a "mil."[8] According to most opinions, it takes a person 18 minutes to walk the distance of one mil (in which case 3/4 of a mil would take 13 1/2 minutes) but according to a stricter opinion, it takes a person 24 minutes to walk one mil (in which case 3/4 of a mil would take 18 minutes).

In view of the fact that we are dealing here with the possible violation of a Biblical Melachah, all modern day Poskim agree that one must adopt the strictest of all approaches, namely, that of Rabbi Eliezer of Metz and that of those that say it takes 24 minutes to walk a mil.[9] Therefore, we light candles 18 minutes before Sunset I. To know when this time is, one should consult a local newspaper or a reputable Jewish calendar.

Rabbi Moshe Feinstein[10] writes that during the 18 minute period between candle lighting and Sunset I, members of the household that are not responsible for lighting the Shabbat candles may continue with weekday work until Sunset I, but that this should not be encouraged.

On the first night of Yom Tov, except on Shavuot,[11] candles may be lit either at the same time as on Erev Shabbat, or after returning from Ma'ariv evening prayer service, provided one lights from an existing light. On the second night Yom Tov however, as well as whenever Shabbat precedes Yom Tov, and on both days of Shavuot, candles should be lit from an existing light, after nightfall.[12]

THE DEATH OF REBBI
נרות שבת

When Rabbi Yehudah Hanasi, the redactor of the Mishnah, known as "Rebbi," lay dying, he made his sons promise him that after his death, they would set the Shabbat table and light candles for him every Friday night.

There is a connection between the righteous, the world to come and Friday night. All are invested with holiness, Kedushah. Kedushah is synonymous with peace. Shabbat is synonymous with peace. Shabbat Shalom. Peace is a state of harmony between body and soul when they no longer fight each other and no longer pull in different directions. Perhaps nobody suffered more from this internal strife than King David. Abigail's words of farewell to King David as he lay dying were, "May your soul be bound up in the bundle of life" (Tehei Nafsho Tzrura Betzror Hachaim).[1] In the world to come, when the body is separated from the soul, there is eternal peace.

The soul, having left the body, settles in its eternal resting-place under God's heavenly throne. This, however, does not happen immediately. For the first twelve months after death, the soul wanders restlessly between heaven and earth, trying to reunite with the body.[2] The life long partnership with the body, however volatile it may have been, is not easily terminated. It is only when the soul has reached the eternal level of holiness that it finally comes to rest in the presence of God. Hence, the Kaddish is recited during the first eleven months of restlessness to assist the soul in its quest for peace. On Friday night, we rest in peace from the physical toil of the week and have a taste of the world to come, וינוחו בה ישראל. Indeed, Shabbat is referred to as a mirror of the world to come - מעין עולם הבא - Me'eyn Olam Habah.

Few people have managed to live in eternal peace during their own lifetime. One such person was Rebbi, who lived in the second century. As he lay dying, he lifted his ten fingers toward heaven and said, "You know that I toiled with my ten fingers in the study of Torah. May it be Your wish that there be peace in my place of eternal rest."[3] "The Torah is a tree of life to those that cling to it. Its roads are harmonious and its ways are peaceful." No wonder then, that Rebbi, who toiled his whole life in the streets of Torah, found peace during his own lifetime. Indeed, he was known as our holy Rebbi, Rabbeinu Hakadosh.

It seems that Rebbi was so content in this world that he did not want to leave. "Why are you crying?" asked Rabbi Chiyah, the disciple of Rebbi. "You know that it is a good omen to die with a smile." "I am crying on account of the Torah that I will no longer be able to study and the commandments that I will no longer be able to perform," answered Rebbi.[4]

Rebbi's disciples also did not want him to leave. Neither, of course, did his "maidservant" (Amtei deRebbi). So they decreed the day a public fast and gathered around Rebbi's home in the mountain village of Tzipori and prayed for his recovery. "Anybody," they warned "who breaks the news of Rebbi's death will himself be put to death." And as long as they prayed, Rebbi did not die. But he suffered terribly. And his "maidservant" could see him suffer no more. So she ascended to the roof, carrying an earthenware jug. She turned her eyes heavenward and cried out, "The angels seek to take Rebbi and the people seek to keep Rebbi. May it be Your wish that those above overcome those below." But the disciples would not stop praying and would not release Rebbi from his suffering. So Rebbi's "maidservant" held the earthenware jug aloft and cast it down into the street below where the disciples stood praying. The crash of the earthenware on the street below silenced their prayers for an instant and Rebbi's soul departed. "Bo Beshalom," come in peace, the angels greeted him.

The soul of Rebbi was equally at peace, both in this world and the next. His soul did not suffer the distress of the wandering souls. And so we are told, each Friday night when Boi Beshalom was recited, he would return home, sit at the Friday night table and say Kiddush for his family. One Friday night, however, a neighbor saw him. Fearing that those who saw him would elevate him in their minds above his peers, he departed and was never seen again.[5]

THE THIRTY NINE MELACHOT AND THEIR DERIVATIVES
ל"ט מלאכות

Thirty nine primary activities which served to construct the Sanctuary in the desert are known as - אבות מלאכות - Avot Melachot and are Biblically prohibited on Shabbat.[1] Other similar activities which were not part of the construction of the Sanctuary but which fit into the categories of Avot Melachot are also prohibited Biblically on Shabbat and are called - תולדות - Toldot. In addition, the Rabbis enacted protective legislation - גזירות - Gezerot, designed to restrain us from performing many acts on Shabbat which, although not Melachot in themselves, resemble or lead to Melachot.

What follows is a list of the Avot Melachot ("AM") with practical examples of Toldot ("T") and Gezerot ("G") included in their category:
1) Ploughing the earth (AM) including digging (T) and leveling out a mound of earth (G);
2) Sowing seeds in the earth (AM) including watering the lawn (T) and placing cut flowers in water (G); 3) Reaping with a scythe (AM) including hand picking fruits from trees (T) and eating fruit fallen from a tree on Shabbat (G); 4) Sheaf Making in the field (AM) including stringing figs together (T) and making a bouquet of flowers (G); 5) Threshing (AM) including separating food from its natural container e.g. shelling nuts (T) except for immediate consumption and pressing out the juice of oranges to drink (G); 6-8) Winnowing, Selecting ("Borer"), Sifting, (AM) including removing less desirable food from more desirable food with a utensil specifically designed for such activity (T) and removing more desirable food from less desirable food (G) except by hand or silverware for immediate consumption; 9) Grinding natural products (AM) including pounding substances in a mortar (T) and grating vegetables with a grater (G), 10) Kneading (AM), including mixing water and substance to form a paste, such as mixing water with potato powder to make mashed potatoes (T); 11) Baking (AM), including cooking (T) and drying wood in an oven; 12) Sheep Shearing (AM), including cutting nails (T) combing hair (G) other than with a soft brush; 13) Bleaching (AM) including washing clothes (T) and brushing clothes (G); 14) Combing raw materials such as raw wool (AM) including disentangling threads (G); 15) Dyeing (AM) including painting (T) and adding coloring matter to food (G) except for immediate consumption, 16) Spinning (AM) including rope-making (T) and re-twisting a thread; 17,18 and 19) Weaving Operations (AM) including knitting (T) and braiding hair (G); 20) Separating into threads (AM) including unpicking a knitted garment (T) and separating a twisted thread into strands (G); 21-22) Tying and Untying a knot designed to last for seven days (AM) including tying a double knot (T) and tightening such a knot (G); 23) Sewing (AM) including stapling papers together (T) and pulling and winding a thread around a loose button to tighten it(G); 24) Tearing for reconstructive purposes (AM) including undoing stitches (T) and tearing apart and turning joined pages of a book (G);

25) Trapping (AM) including fishing (T) and trapping flies and bees (G); 26) Slaughtering (AM) including killing insects by spraying directly at them, rather than around them (T); 27) Skinning or Flaying (AM) except skinning chicken for immediate consumption which is permitted; 28) Tanning leather (AM) including softening leather (T) and salting meat to kosher it on Shabbat (G); 29) Scraping to smoothe material (AM) including polishing shoes (T); 30) Marking out i.e. impressing lines on a surface as preparation for cutting, 31) Cutting to size (AM) including sharpening a pencil (T); 32) Writing two letters (AM), including typewriting (T) and drawing with a finger on a moist window pane (G); 33) Erasing two letters (AM) including writing over existing writing (T) and tearing through letters on a food wrapper (G), unless contents are urgently required; 34) Building (AM) including fixing a broom handle into a broom end (T) and opening an umbrella (G); 35) Demolishing for reconstructive purposes (AM) including demolishing a utensil (T) unless necessary to access food for immediate consumption; 36) Kindling a Fire (AM) including switching on a light (T) and traveling in a vehicle operated by a non-Jew (G); 37) Extinguishing a Fire (AM) including switching off a light (T) and opening a window where the draft might extinguish a flame (G); 38) Putting the Finishing Touch to any manufactured article (AM) including sharpening a knife (T) and dipping (Toveling) utensils in the Mikveh and 39) Carrying from a private to a public domain, or vice versa (AM) including throwing from domain to domain (T) and wearing in the street (in the absence of an Eruv) such articles as one may inadvertently take off and carry.

There is much discussion among contemporary Halachic authorities "Poskim" whether an umbrella, even if opened before Shabbat, may be used on Shabbat. Some of the factors considered are whether opening an umbrella is considered part of building (see AM 34 above) or whether it is part of a more general category of not detracting from the aura of Shabbat, Uvda Dechol.[2]

MELACHOT AND INTENT
דבר שאין מתכוין

The juxtaposition in the Torah of the laws of Shabbat and the Sanctuary, Mishkan, not only serves to identify the 39 Melachot which are prohibited on Shabbat,[1] but also determines the conditions that must exist before one can be held liable for performing a Melachah. One of these conditions is intent. Like the Mishkan, Melachah requires carefully planned work - מלאכת מחשבת - Melechet Machashevet.[2] There are various states of mind which may lack the intent necessary to perform a Melachah. In some cases, such a state of mind results in one being Biblically exempt from the consequences of one's act, although the act remains Rabbinically prohibited. In other cases, the lack of requisite intent means that the act is permissible on Shabbat in the first place.

A person who is aware of the act he is performing but forgot that today is Shabbat or that the act is prohibited on Shabbat, is called a - שוגג - Shogeg. In the Temple era, the Shogeg had to bring a sin offering, a Chatat, to atone for the act.[3] A person who intended to perform a permitted act such as retrieving a knife out of a shrub and in so doing, unwittingly performed a different act which is a Melachah, such as cutting the shrub when lifting out the knife, is called a - מתעסק - Mitasek. The Mitasek, unlike the Shogeg, had no intention of performing the Melachah and is, therefore, entirely exempt.[4]

An act which is permissible in itself on Shabbat, but which may, possibly, but not inevitably, cause an unintended Melachah to occur, is called a - דבר שאין מתכוין - Davar She'ein Mitkaven. For example, dragging a garden chair across the lawn, which is an act permissible in itself on Shabbat, may cause grooves to form in the earth which, if performed intentionally, would constitute the Melachah of ploughing. Or, simply walking on the grass, which is permissible in itself on Shabbat, may result in the uprooting or tearing of grass, which, if performed intentionally, would constitute the Melachah of Reaping. Whether or not a Davar She'ein Mitkaven is permitted is a Tannaic dispute between Rabbi Shimon who permits it in the first place and Rabbi Yehudah who prohibits it.[5] The Halachah adopts the more lenient view of Rabbi Shimon.[6] A person cannot, however, claim the exemption of Davar She'ein Mitkaven where the Melachah was an **inevitable** result of the permitted act. For example, if the chair is so heavy that it must form a groove in the earth, or, if one washes one's hands (in itself a permitted act) over one's own lawn, causing its inevitable watering (constituting the Melachah of Planting), one cannot claim that one did not intend the Melachah. This is because the result is so inevitable as to impute to one the intent to perform the Melachah in the first place. Such an inevitable result is called a פסיק רישא - Psik Reishe.[7] Note however, that if the inevitable Melachah arising from the permitted act is of no use to its performer, such as where one washes one's hands over a stranger's lawn, the act is Biblically permitted in the first place and is called a - פסיק רישא דלא ניחא לה -

Psik Reishe Delo Neecha Lei.[8] Such an act, though Biblically permitted, would according to most opinions,[9] be Rabinically prohibited, unless certain extenuating circumstances exist. Such circumstances are the threat of severe financial loss, or when the performance of a מצוה is involved.[10]

Based upon the above principles, Rabbi Moshe Feinstein[11] permits one to open the door of a thermostat-controlled, lit oven on Shabbat, even though the resulting intake of air may cause the thermostat to kick in and turn up the flame. Rabbi Feinstein's reasoning is that one's intent is merely to open the oven door. This will not inevitably result in the thermostat kicking in, and it is, therefore, not in the category of Psik Reishe, but rather, a Davar She'ein Mitkaven. As such, it is permitted in the first place.

THE PURPOSE OF THE MELACHAH
מלאכה שאינה צריכה לגופה

The link between the laws of Shabbat and the Mishkan, the Sanctuary, not only defines the 39 Melachot, but also determines the conditions for liability. As we have seen,[1] one of these conditions is intent. The other is **purpose**. The Melachah must be performed for a similar **purpose** as the act performed in the Mishkan. Accordingly, one might intentionally perform the same act performed in the Mishkan, and yet be exempt from Biblical liability, if it did not have a similar purpose. For example, digging, (a derivative of Ploughing), was performed in the Mishkan for the use of the hole itself, in which tent pegs were sunk. Therefore, one who digs for earth and has no use for the hole has not performed a Melachah in the Torah sense of the term, (Melachah De'oraita).[2] Similarly, extinguishing a fire, a primary (Av) Melachah, was performed in the Mishkan to produce glowing embers needed to smelt metal. Therefore, one who turns off the light in order to sleep, or to save electricity, has not performed a Melachah De'oraita. Such an act is known as a - מלאכה שאינה צריכה לגופה - Melachah She'eina Tzericha Legufa.[3] Although Biblically exempt from liability once performed, a Melachah She'eina Tzericha Legufa is Rabinically prohibited, a Melachah Derabanan and should not be performed in the first place.[4]

What, one might ask, is the difference between a Melachah De'oraita and Melachah Derabanan if both are prohibited? The answer is that, generally, there is more room for leniency in Melachot Derabanan.[5] For example, Melachot Derabanan may, mostly, be performed during twilight, Bein Hashmashot on Erev Shabbat;[6] they may, with certain restrictions, be performed by a Jew on Shabbat to alleviate substantial pain;[7] they may, in certain situations, be performed by a Jew on Shabbat in order to avert a substantial financial loss;[8] they may, in certain circumstances,[9] be performed for a Jew on Shabbat by a non-Jew; and they are not themselves subject to protective legislation.[10]

Because the Melachah She'eina Tzericha Legufa is closest to a Melachah De'oraita in that it only lacks the element of common purpose and because there is a dispute with regard to its definition,[11] the Rabbis are less lenient with it than with other Melachot Derabanan.[12] Accordingly, it enjoys some, but not all of the flexibility described.[13] For example, a Melachah She'eina Tzericha Legufa may not be performed Bein Hashmashot. Such a Melachah may, however, for the most part, be performed by a Jew on Shabbat for the sick, even the not dangerously sick;[14] and, in certain situations, it may be performed for a Jew on Shabbat by a non-Jew.[15]

Based on these principals, Rabbi Shlomo Zalman Braun, in his work, Sha'arim Metzuyanim Behalachah, writes that sparks ignited by plugging in or out of electricity is akin to a Melachah She'eina Tzericha Legufa, in that it is a Psik Reishe Delo Neecha Lei.[16] Accordingly, to avoid substantial financial loss, one may ask a non-Jew to reconnect a well-stocked freezer that became disconnected from its electricity on Shabbat. Similarly, one may ask a non-Jew to turn off an appliance which, if left running all Shabbat, would overheat and burn out.

MOUNTAINS HANGING FROM HAIRS
פסיק רישא דלא ניחא ליה

Y ou arrive home after Shul on Friday night. All the dishes that the dishwasher washed before Shabbat are locked in the dishwasher. You have no other eating utensils and you want to retrieve them for the Friday night meal. In order to take them out you have to unlock the door by turning the lever lock to the left. The action of the lever, necessary to unlock the door, automatically turns off the panel indicator lights that advise you that the dishwashing cycle is complete. So you cannot open the door without turning off the lights. What do you do?

Clearly, the act of retrieving the dishes from the dishwasher is, in itself, a permissible act on Shabbat. The problem is that it inevitably causes the Melachah of switching off the indicator lights. This Melachah is the inevitable and unintended result of retrieving the dishes, though it is of no use to its performer. An inevitable Melachah which is of no use to its performer and which arises out of a permitted act, is known in Halachic terminology as פסיק רישא דלא ניחא ליה - Psik Reishe Delo Neecha Leh.[1] We shall refer to it as the "inevitable, unwanted Melachah." If one performed an inevitable, unwanted Melachah, one is - פטור - Patur, which means one is exempt from any Biblical liability. The question is whether one is allowed, under Rabbinical law to deliberately perform an inevitable, unwanted Melachah, such as, turning the indicator lights off in order to retrieve the dishes.

The answer to this question depends on the classification of the inevitable, unwanted Melachah and the existence or absence of any mitigating circumstances. If the inevitable, unwanted Melachah is Biblically prohibited, then according to the majority of Halachic opinions, one may not deliberately perform the permitted act that causes it. There is a minority opinion, that of the Aruch, that permits it, but the Halachah does not adopt this minority opinion.[2] Accordingly, one may not, for example, wash one's hands over a public lawn because, even though washing one's hands is permitted on Shabbat, it causes the inevitable, unwanted result of watering the grass.[3] And watering the grass on Shabbat is classified under the Biblical Melachah of Ploughing and Sowing. Similarly, one may not open a door to the street, on a windy day, when the inevitable, unwanted result of the permitted act will be that lighted candles, placed next to the door, blow out.[4] What if the inevitable, unwanted Melachah is not Biblically prohibited, but only Rabinically prohibited? Still, according to the majority of opinions, one may not deliberately perform the permitted act that causes the Rabbinical Melachah, except in a limited number of mitigating circumstances.[5] Physical pain or discomfort, or the performance of a Mitzvah are examples of mitigating circumstances that might permit one to deliberately perform the permitted act that causes the inevitable, unwanted Rabbinical Melachah. For example, trapping a bird inside one's home is Rabbinically prohibited. Yet, if a wild bird flew into one's house in winter, one would be allowed to close the windows to avoid the cold. This act is permitted even though it causes the inevitable, unwanted Rabbinical Melachah of trapping .[6] If the red berries on the Hadas, the myrtle branch, are more numerous than the myrtle leaves, the Hadas is invalid for Arba Minim. Yet, if a friend of the owner of the Hadas picks off the berries on Yom Tov for food, the owner of the Hadas would be permitted to use it for the Mitzvah of Arba Minim. Picking the berries in this way is permitted, even though it causes the inevitable, unwanted Melachah of fixing something for use, Makeh Bepatish, because it enables the performance of a Mitzvah.[7]

Is the inevitable, unwanted Melachah of turning off the dishwasher indicator lights a Biblical Melachah or a Rabbinical Melachah? The Biblical Melachah of extinguishing fire was performed in the Mishkan to produce glowing embers needed to smelt metal. Extinguishing fire for any other purpose not used in the Mishkan is called a Melachah She'eina Tzericha Legufa.[8] Although Biblically exempt from liability once performed, a Melachah She'eina Tzericha Legufa is Rabinically prohibited and should not be deliberately performed. The majority of modern Poskim agree that turning off an electric light involves the act of extinguishing fire and is, therefore, prohibited under the category of Melachah She'eina Tzericha Legufa.[9] It is further accepted that the Rabbis are less lenient with the Melachah of extinguishing fire than with other Rabbinical Melachot.[10]

What if turning off the indicator lights does not involve the Melachah of extinguishing fire? In fact, the light of most indicators installed in dishwashers is produced by light emitting diodes (LED) and not by heat. Turning off such indicators does not involve extinguishing fire. Rather, it involves the less stringent Rabbinical Melachah of - הפסקת מוליד - Hafsakat Molid (ending a creation), and, as such, can be deliberately performed under the extenuating circumstances described above.[11] In these circumstances, opening the lock in an unusual manner, such as with one's elbow, Derech Shinui, would render the Melachah a double Derabanan. I have heard from Rav Dovid Feinstein that the extenuating circumstances described above would be considered בדיעבד - Bedi'avad - after the fact, and, accordingly, one could even turn off an indicator powered by light emitting heat. Of course, it would be better to remember to leave the door open before Shabbat, or if you forgot, to have a non-Jew open it on Shabbat.[12]

MELACHOT, PERMANENCE AND UMBRELLAS
דבר המתקיים

Certain activities, such as building, tying, weaving, writing, dyeing and sewing are not prohibited unless they are made to last.[1] For example, one may tie a knot that is not tied in a professional way and that will be untied within seven days, such as shoelaces or the ribbon around the Torah scroll, on Shabbat afternoon.[2] So too, a safety pin may be used on Shabbat since it is not a form of permanent sewing.[3] Similarly, writing or painting with fluid that fades away, or writing on a substance that does not retain script is not a Melachah, in the Torah sense of the term (Melachah De'oraita), although it is Rabinically prohibited (Melachah Derabanan)[4]. For the practical differences between a Melachah De'oreita and Derabanan, see "The Purpose of the Melachah," Chapter One above.

When do the above activities become permanent and, therefore, a Melachah De'oraita? According to the Rambam, if the product lasts throughout Shabbat it is a Melachah De'oraita.[5] According to Rashi, however, it must have the ability to last forever.[6]

May one build a structure on Shabbat, if one intends to take it apart on Shabbat, shortly after its use? This question is debated between two sages in the Jerusalem Talmud.[7] Rabbi Yosi Bar Nun maintains that it is prohibited because the Mishkan, the Sanctuary itself, from which we derive the 39 Melachot, was a temporary structure. Rabbi Yosah disagrees. He maintains that it is permitted because, in his view, the Mishkan was, in the eyes of the people, a permanent structure. They never knew when God would require them to move on and, until such time, they lived their lives in permanence. Whereas the Jerusalem Talmud rules in accordance with the first view,[8] the Babylonian Talmud rules in accordance with the second and maintains that building this type of structure is not considered a Melachah at all.[9] The debate is picked up by Rishonim and Acharonim in connection with the construction of a provisional tent on Shabbat. According to the Rif,[10] this is a Melachah De'oraita. According to the Rambam, it is a Melachah Derabanan.[11] And according to Rashi[12] and the Rosh,[13] constructing a provisional tent is permissible in the first place.

Based on the above authorities that prohibit the construction of a provisional tent on Shabbat, the Noda Beyehuda[14] considers the opening of an umbrella on Shabbat a Melachah De'oraita and prohibited its use in his community, even if opened before Shabbat, because onlookers would think it was opened on Shabbat (Marit Ayin). Conversely, basing himself on the authorities which permit the construction of a provisional tent on Shabbat, the Chatam Sofer[15] maintains that using an umbrella on Shabbat is not even a Melachah Derabanan and he did not object to its use in his community. The consensus of opinion of today's Poskim prohibits the use of an umbrella on Shabbat. The Chafetz Chaim[16] prohibits it because, irrespective of its temporary nature, it is intended to be used as a tent for protection against the elements. The Chazon Ish[17] prohibits it because it makes the Shabbat look like a working day (Uvda Dechol). Rav Ovadia Yosef,[18] after summarizing all the authorities for and against, sides with the authorities that prohibit it.

MELACHAH, CREATIVE AND DESTRUCTIVE ACTS
AND THE OPENING OF CANS AND LETTERS
כל המקלקלין פטורין

Using one's creative powers seven days a week may lead one to believe in oneself as a creator. This danger is averted in Judaism by the institution of Shabbat, in which one refrains from Melachot. Melachot are acts which demonstrate one's mastery of the world by means of the constructive exercise of one's intelligence and skill.[1] For just one day a week, we are asked to lay aside our skills and acknowledge the real Creator.

Essential, then, to the definition of Melachah, is the concept of a constructive act. Any act of pure destruction, however strenuous, is not a Melachah, or, as the Talmud puts it כל המקלקלין פטורין.[2] Thus, if one were to knock down a house, simply to destroy it, one would not be performing a Melachah, in the Torah sense of the term (Melachah De'oraita), although the act would be prohibited under Rabbinical protective legislation (Melachah Derabanan). If, however, one would perform the self-same act with the objective of building a new house in its place, one would have performed a Melachah.[3]

The classification of an act as a Melachah Derabanan, rather than De'oraita, has many practical consequences.[4] Generally, whenever there is a compelling reason, the Sages are more flexible in permitting a Melachah Derabanan. Thus, for example, opening a can of food, a milk carton, or tearing open a tea bag, when such containers are to be immediately discarded, are not constructive acts and because they enhance the enjoyment of Shabbat, the Rabbis permit it. If, however, when opening a can one intends to use it afterwards as a container, the act becomes constructive, and is thereby transformed into a Melachah De'oraita which the Rabbis have no leeway to permit. It is recommended that such containers be opened, in such a way as to make it overtly clear that they cannot be used again.[5] Some Halachic authorities require one to open before Shabbat containers of food that will not spoil on Shabbat.

A constructive act includes not only physical acts but may include spiritual acts as well. For example, tearing one's clothes on Shabbat simply to destroy them would not be a Melachah De'oraita. However, tearing them on Shabbat, in a situation where the Torah would command one to do so were it a weekday, is a Melachah De'oraita. Accordingly, when confronted with the tragic news of the death of a close relative on Shabbat, one may not tear one's garment.[6]

Because the opening of a letter on Shabbat involves the destructive act of tearing up and discarding the envelope, there is discussion amongst the Acharonim whether this is or is not permitted. Why, it is argued, should this be different from the permitted act of opening a can of food on Shabbat? Indeed, the Pachad Yitzchak[7] permits the opening of a sealed envelope on Shabbat. The Chafetz Chaim, however, prohibits it other than in extenuating circumstances, when he does permit a Jew to ask a non-Jew to do it for him on Shabbat.[8] Rabbi Moshe Feinstein[9] explains that, whereas the opening of food cans is required for Shabbat itself, the opening of letters is not, and therefore remains prohibited as a Melachah Derabanan.

INDIRECT MELACHAH AND SHABBAT CLOCKS
גרם מלאכה

Whereas the Torah prohibits one from performing a Melachah on Shabbat, - לא תעשה מלאכה -, Lo Ta'aseh Melachah[1], it does not prohibit a Melachah from being performed on its own. Accordingly, a Melachah is Biblically permitted, if done indirectly - גרם מלאכה - Grum Melachah. Although Grum Melachah is not Biblically prohibited, it is Rabbinically prohibited.[2]

Because the prohibition of Grum Melachah is a Rabbinical one, there is considerable flexibility in its application. Accordingly, its application is relaxed in order to prevent financial loss or to permit the performance of a Mitzvah. Thus, one may block the path of a threatening fire by throwing up a barrier of utensils full of water, even though they will crack in the heat, spill their water and extinguish the fire; similarly, one may place a wet towel over a piece of burning furniture even if this results in extinguishing the fire, both cases being illustrations of severe financial loss.[3]

The use of Shabbat clocks set before Shabbat to indirectly turn lights on and off is generally accepted as permissible.[4] Whether Shabbat clocks may be used to turn on an appliance that will heat food is a subject of debate among modern day Poskim. According to the Chazon Ish, this is permitted on condition that the food was fully cooked before Shabbat, the appliance is covered with a Blech (such as an electric hot plate) and the food was placed on the Blech before Shabbat.[5]

Others, including Rabbi Moshe Feinstein, prohibit the use of a time switch for heating up food in this way. Rabbi Feinstein argues that, if it is forbidden to verbally instruct a non-Jew to heat food on Shabbat, how much more so should it be prohibited for a Jew to use a Shabbat clock for such purpose on Shabbat? If causing a Melachah to be performed indirectly by word of mouth of the Jew is prohibited, causing a Melachah to be performed by the indirect action of a Jew should be all the more forbidden. Furthermore, he argues, if one permits re-heating of food to be performed in this way, all Melachot should be permitted in this way and this would be disrespectful to the Shabbat. Though Rabbi Feinstein criticizes the use of time switches to turn lights on and off, he permits this activity, based on the opinion of the Rema, as well as the age old custom which permits instructing a non-Jew to turn on lights for the purpose of a Mitzvah, such as prayer or Shabbat meals.[6]

As for adjusting a time switch on Shabbat to delay or accelerate the turning on or off of the lights, Rabbi Feinstein prohibits any such interference. Rabbi Shlomo Zalman Auerbach and Rabbi Ovadiah Yosef however, permit adjusting it in such a way as to turn the lights on or off at a later time than originally set, but not at an earlier time.[7] Furthermore, according to the Rabbi Shlomo Zalman,[8] a timer may be adjusted while the electricity is off, in such a way that after it has been turned off it will switch itself on again earlier than originally set.

BATHING, WASHING AND SWIMMING ON SHABBAT
רחיצה בשבת

One may not bathe in, wash or shower with water heated on Shabbat.[1] Whether one may perform these activities with water heated before Shabbat is debated by Rav, who maintains that one may wash one's entire body, limb by limb, in such water, and Shmuel, who maintains one may only wash one's face, hands and feet in such water.[2] As with Shehiyah and Chazarah discussed below, the Rabbis restricted the ways in which one may use such water for fear that a person may reheat water on Shabbat, an act that is forbidden according to all. Indeed, this fear was grounded in experience for, as the Talmud relates, originally, one was allowed to bathe in water heated before Shabbat, but later, the Rabbis forbade it, because the bathhouse attendants would heat the baths on Shabbat and claim that they heated them before Shabbat.

The Shulchan Aruch determines the Halachah, the law, in accordance with Shmuel's opinion, whereas the Rema[3] determines the Halachah somewhere between Rav and Shmuel's opinions that one may wash one's other limbs too in such water, but not one's entire body.

May one use hot water from the tap on Shabbat? This depends on whether the water coming out of the tap was heated on Shabbat, in which case it would be forbidden, or whether it was heated before Shabbat, in which case it would be permitted, subject to the restrictions described above. But even if the initial water coming out of the hot water tap was heated on Erev Shabbat, opening it on Shabbat would be prohibited, if this would inevitably cause cold water to re-enter the boiler in the hot water's place and be heated on Shabbat. Accordingly, Rabbi Moshe Feinstein permits using water from the hot water tap on Shabbat if one turns off the boiler approximately two hours before Shabbat. Turning off the boiler guarantees that cold water re-entering the boiler will not be heated on Shabbat, neither by the fire, nor by the hot water in the boiler, which by Shabbat would have cooled down to below the temperature of Yad Soledet Bo (40° C to 70° C). This solution may be practical in a one family home but not in an apartment house.[4] One may use the Mikveh on Shabbat. It is a generally accepted custom to abstain from swimming on Shabbat.[5]

It should be noted that the Chafetz Chaim quotes Halachic sources that permit washing one's entire body in water heated before Shabbat, if not doing so would cause one to suffer on Shabbat.[6]

WARMING FOOD ON SHABBAT,
THE BLECH AND THE HOTPLATE
שהיה וחזרה

Whereas a person may not cook food on Shabbat, there is no Biblical prohibition against food cooking itself on Shabbat. Therefore, a person may place raw meat in a pot on Friday afternoon, Erev Shabbat before sunset and allow it to cook through till the following day for the Shabbat lunch meal.[1] Or, one may place partially cooked food on the stove on Erev Shabbat before sunset and allow it to cook through, so that it will be ready for the Friday night meal. The only concern the Rabbis have with this is that once Shabbat has entered one may be tempted to accelerate the cooking by turning up the flame. To eliminate this concern, the Rabbis required that the coals used in the stoves in Talmudic times be covered over with ashes - קטום - Katum, to prevent their stoking.[2] The modern day equivalent of Katum is the aluminum sheet placed over the burners popularly referred to as the "Blech."[3] Thus, as long as partially cooked food is put on the Blech on Erev Shabbat, it may remain cooking there in preparation for the Friday night meal. Leaving the food on the Blech in this way on Erev Shabbat is known as - שהיה - Shehiyah.[4]

Can food which has been left on the stove on Erev Shabbat as described by the term Shehiyah be removed from the Blech for serving and returned to the Blech on Shabbat, an action called - חזרה - Chazarah?[4] Here, the Rabbis are not concerned with turning up the flame, because the Blech is already in place. Rather, they are concerned that one should not look like one is cooking on Shabbat - מיחזי כמבשל - Mechze Kemevashel.[5] They therefore permit Chazarah where the following conditions are present: (i) the food must have originally been on the Blech on Erev Shabbat (ii) the Blech must be in place (iii) the food must be fully (not partially) cooked (iv) it must not have cooled off (v) from the time it was removed to the time it is returned to the Blech, it must have been handheld, (vi) before removing it, one must have the intention to return it to the Blech.[6] With these conditions present, the Rabbis are satisfied that Chazarah on Shabbat is no more than an extension of Shehiyah performed on Erev Shabbat and, as such, is permitted. They do not view it as an initiation of cooking on Shabbat which would be prohibited. It should be noted, however, that Chazarah with these conditions present is permitted with solids but not with liquids.

According to the Schulchan Aruch, if one of the above conditions is absent, the food cannot be returned to the Blech on Shabbat. All Poskim agree that there can be no Chazarah without the presence of the first three conditions, but many argue that some or all of the last three are unnecessary. For example, the Mishnah Berurah mentions that at a pinch, either condition (v) or condition (vi) can be waived.[7] Others, such as Rabbi Moshe Feinstein[8] waive, in addition, condition (iv) and permit food to be taken out of the fridge and put on the Blech, but away from the flame, so long as the food will not reach a temperature on

Shabbat which would burn one's hand (Yad Soledet Bo), which according to some means 100 degrees Fahrenheit (43° C), and according to others, 160 degrees F (71° C)[9]. Rav Ovadia Yosef concludes that a hot plate does not fall into the category of Mechze Kemevashel because it is not used during the week. Rav Yosef, therefore, concludes that food (not liquids) may be taken from the fridge and placed on the hot plate even if it heats up to Yad Soledet Bo.[10]

MUKTSEH ON SHABBAT AND YOM TOV
מוקצה בשבת ויום טוב

Sunday. Many of us do not go to work. There is, however, so much to do at home. How many of us would have the self-control to make Sunday a voluntary day of rest and refrain from balancing our checkbooks, paying our bills, clearing out the attic, or mowing the lawn? On Shabbat, the Torah commands us to rest - למען ינוח - Lema'an Yanuach.[1] The Rabbis, keenly aware of our workaholic tendencies, declared that all objects which are not conducive to rest are simply out of bounds and set aside - מוקצה - Muktseh. Accordingly, Muktseh objects are those that we exclude from our minds when we think of Shabbat rest.[2] Moreover, declaring a pen or an electric drill Muktseh serves to protect one from inadvertently performing Melachot on Shabbat.[3]

There are various degrees of Muktseh. Objects in the category of First Degree Muktseh are so intrusive to the Shabbat atmosphere that they may not be handled on Shabbat under any circumstances, unless they present a danger. Included in First Degree Muktseh, known as - מוקצה מחמת חסרון כיס - Muktseh Meichamat Chesron Kis, are valuable objects, which, if used for activities which are permitted on Shabbat, will become damaged. Common examples are barber's scissors, knives used for slaughtering, bank notes, rare stamps, pens and stock certificates, just to name a few.[4] Also included in First Degree Muktseh are useless objects known as - מוקצה מחמת גופו - Muktseh Meichamath Gufo such as sticks, stones, earth, sand and broken crockery.[5] Second Degree Muktseh, known as - כלי שמלאכתו לאיסור - Kli Shemelachto Le'issur, pertains to objects that are normally used for activities which are prohibited on Shabbat, but which can also be used for activities that are permitted on Shabbat. Examples include a hammer, which could be used for cracking nuts on Shabbat, or a match which, can serve as a toothpick. Second Degree Muktseh objects may be handled on Shabbat for a permitted use, and may also be moved, if they are in the way.[6] Third Degree Muktseh, known as - בסיס לדבר האסור - Busis Ledavar Ha'asur, applies to objects which, although permitted for use on Shabbat, were used at the commencement of Shabbat to hold or support a Muktseh object, for example, a drawer containing money. Even if the money were removed on Shabbat by a non-Jew, the drawer without the money would still remain Muktseh, because it was Muktseh at the inception of Shabbat.[7] If, however, the drawer contains BOTH money and a Siddur, or any other permitted object which is more important to the owner than the Muktseh object, it may be handled on Shabbat.[8]

Precious candlesticks are First Degree Muktseh, Mechamat Chesron Kis, because they are valuable and used exclusively for lighting Shabbat candles, an activity which, of course, is prohibited on Shabbat.[9] Accordingly, they may not be moved, even if they are in one's way. Furthermore, any surface on which they are placed before Shabbat may also not be moved because the surface becomes a Busis Ledavar Ha'asur. They can, however, be removed if they are placed on a tray before Shabbat together with an object which is not Muktseh, such as a Siddur, or a piece of Challah. The tray with the candlesticks and the permitted item may then be removed on Shabbat.[10]

There is also an additional category of Muktseh, applicable mainly to food on Yom Tov, known as "Muktseh Mechamat Hachanah," which means Muktseh because one had no intention on Erev Yom Tov to eat such food on Yom Tov. For example, the owner of a delicatessen may not eat food on Yom Tov that was part of his stock in trade and intended for sale, nor may one use food on Yom Tov that was stored away for use after Yom Tov. Similarly, on Yom Tov one may not eat the meat of an ox ordinarily used for ploughing or a chicken ordinarily used for laying eggs and not for food. This prohibition is based on the principle known as הכנה דרבה.[11] Hachanah De'Rabah requires that before Yom Tov we specifically designate in our minds the food that we will use on Yom Tov. It is considered disrespectful to Yom Tov to postpone plans for Yom Tov meals to Yom Tov itself. This type of Muktseh Mechamat Hachanah applies on Yom Tov but not on Shabbat.[12] This is because on Shabbat one is not allowed to cook and, therefore, one naturally plans Shabbat meals before Shabbat, whereas on Yom Tov, one is allowed to cook and might postpone such plans to Yom Tov itself. Included in the category of Muktseh Mechamat Hachanah is food one could not have intended on Erev Yom Tov to eat on Yom Tov because such food only came into existence on Yom Tov. This type of Muktseh is known as נולד, Nolad. Thus, for example, an egg which was laid on Yom Tov, and, according to some opinions, milk taken from a cow on Yom Tov, would be prohibited for use on Yom Tov. Whether or not food in the category of Nolad is Muktseh on Shabbat is a matter of Halachic debate. The Rema prohibits it, but the Magen Avraham permits it.[13]

Although Muktseh objects may not be moved directly by hand, they may, where necessary, be moved indirectly, or in an unusual way, such as with the back of one's hand.[14] Thus, for example, one may kick aside money dropped on the sidewalk on Shabbat in order to retrieve it after Shabbat.[15] It is also permitted on Shabbat to have a Muktseh object removed by a non-Jew.[16]

BENEFITING FROM THE WORK OF A NON-JEW ON SHABBAT
אמירה לנכרי

If you, yourself, may not perform a Melachah, you may not ask a non-Jew to perform it for you.[1] This is true both for Biblically prohibited acts, Melachot De'oraita, and Rabinically prohibited acts, Melachot Derabanan. This applies even if the non-Jew was instructed before Shabbat to perform the Melachah on Shabbat. This prohibition, known as אמירה לנכרי - Amirah Lenochri, was established by the Rabbis for three reasons. Firstly, they were concerned that by permitting the non-Jew to perform the Melachah, the Jew might come to perform the Melachah himself, or herself.[2] Secondly, appointing a non-Jew as an agent to perform the Melachah renders the Jew liable as principal.[3] Lastly, the prophet Isaiah[4] warns Israel to refrain from discussing Melachot on Shabbat. Amirah Lenochri involves such prohibited discussion.

If the Jew did not request it, but the non-Jew performed the Melachah of his or her own accord, may the Jew benefit from the outcome? The answer is that if the non-solicited Melachah provides direct benefit to the Jew, one may not benefit from it, unless the Melachah was performed primarily for the benefit of the non-Jew. Accordingly, a Jew may not benefit from a light turned on by a non-Jew on Shabbat, thereby enabling the Jew to read, unless the non-Jew turned it on to read himself.[5] The Jew, however, may benefit from a non-Jew turning the light off, thereby making it easier for the Jew to sleep. This is because it is possible, though not desirable, to sleep with the light on and the benefit is therefore considered an indirect benefit. Furthermore, a Jew may benefit from the unsolicited Melachah of a non-Jew where such Melachah merely provides additional benefit to an already existing benefit, such as turning on additional lights in an already lit room.[6] Whenever benefit is forbidden, the prohibition lasts the entire Shabbat and continues after Shabbat ends, for the duration of time it took for the non-Jew to perform the Melachah on Shabbat. Accordingly, a car delivered for repair to a non-Jewish mechanic just before Shabbat with instructions to have it ready immediately after Shabbat and on which the mechanic worked all day Shabbat, may not be used until Sunday.[7]

Hinting to a non-Jew to perform a Melachah is permitted when such a Melachah causes indirect benefit or additional benefit, but not when it causes direct benefit. Hinting, in such circumstances, is permissible on condition that the language used includes no command and no mention of the Melachah involved. Accordingly, one may not say to a non-Jew, "Please help me, I cannot turn off the lights on Shabbat." One may say, however, "It is difficult for me to sleep with the lights on."[8]

Because the prohibition of Amirah Lenochri is of Rabbinic origin, there is considerable flexibility in its application. This is particularly the case when the act performed by means of Amirah Lenochri is in itself only a Melachah Derabanan. Accordingly, the prohibition of Amirah Lenochri is relaxed in order to prevent substantial financial loss,[9] to enable the performance of a Mitzvah, in cases of sickness,[10] or in cases of "Psik Reishe."[11] Thus, one may ask a non-Jew to perform the following acts on one's behalf, on Shabbat: to reconnect a freezer-stocked with expensive food which became disconnected from electricity on Shabbat, the case of financial loss;[12] to reheat previously cooked food essential for a Shabbat meal by placing it directly on the flame;[13] to turn the lights on in the Synagogue to enable the congregants to pray, both cases of performance of a Mitzvah, i.e. participating in the Shabbat meal and prayer; to cook previously uncooked food for a sick person;[14] to turn up the heat for persons suffering from cold; to turn on a light for a child who is frightened of the dark,[15] because, for the purpose of Amirah Lenochri, persons suffering from cold and children who suffer are deemed to be "sick"; or to open the refrigerator door, even if this will be sure to activate a light which one forgot to deactivate before Shabbat, the case of Psik Reishe.[16]

KIDDUSH WINE, WHISKY, BEER, COFFEE, TEA, MILK, SODA, WATER
חמר מדינה

J ust because God has given us a weekly, lifetime subscription to paradise, that does not mean that we may take the Shabbat for granted. No gift should go unacknowledged and no giver should go forgotten. - זכור את יום השבת לקדשו - Zachor Et Yom Hashabat Lekadsho, "Remember the Shabbat and bless it."[1] We bless the Giver by reciting Kiddush and Havdalah, and we remember the Shabbat by drinking wine, which, in Scripture, is the beverage of fond memories.[2] Like us, the Shabbat guest wants to be welcomed when she arrives and missed when she leaves.

But you are vacationing in Cape Cod and the local liquor store does not carry "Kosher" wine! And the next Shabbat morning, back in town, you hover over the Synagogue Bar Mitzvah Kiddush table, and are about to recite Kiddush. And you wonder. "The whisky, or the wine?"

In determining whether there is any acceptable alternative to wine, the Rabbis differentiate between Kiddush on Friday night, Havdalah on Motzaei Shabbat and Kiddush on Shabbat morning. In view of the fact that Friday night Kiddush is a Biblical requirement,[3] the only alternative to Kiddush wine on Friday night is to recite Kiddush over bread.[4] The connection between the Shabbat and the Mishkan, the Sanctuary, which defines the 39 prohibited Melachot on Shabbat, may also explain why only wine and bread are acceptable. Both wine and bread were used in the Temple sacrifices. When reciting Kiddush over bread in the absence of wine on Friday night, the following procedure is followed. One washes one's hands, covers two loaves of bread with a cloth, places one's hand's on the cloth and recites ויכלו. One then removes the cloth, places one's hands on the Challot and recites the blessing for bread, "Hamotzi," instead of the blessing for wine. The blessing for wine, which would otherwise precede the Kiddush blessing, is replaced by the blessing for bread.[5]

Havdalah is, according to most opinions, of Rabbinic origin,[6] and accordingly, the Rabbis have a more flexible approach. The preferred beverage for Havdalah is still wine.[7] Nevertheless, if one finds oneself without wine, one may use other beverages which qualify as - חמר מדינה - Chamar Medinah, which, loosely translated, means, the "popular beverage of the location."[8] The precise meaning of Chamar Medinah, which beverages qualify as Chamar Medinah and under what circumstances they may be used instead of wine, is the subject of an animated Halachic debate.

According to the Shulchan Aruch,[9] all drinks, except water, qualify as Chamar Medinah. According to Rabbi Moshe Feinstein,[10] what sets Chamar Medinah apart from other beverages is that it is principally a social drink, rather than a thirst-quenching drink. Accordingly, soda and water, which people do not drink as a rule unless they are thirsty, do not qualify as Chamar Medinah and cannot be used for Havdalah. Conversely, whisky, beer, tea, coffee and perhaps even milk, do qualify as Chamar Medinah, in as much as people might drink them for social reasons, even when they are not thirsty. These drinks may, therefore, be used for Havdalah. Rav Ovadiah Yosef, however, vehemently disagrees.[11] A drink is not considered Chamar Medinah, he claims, unless it is both bitter in taste and intoxicating. The only reason, he argues, that one is allowed to drink non-alcoholic beverages before Kiddush on Shabbat morning is precisely because they are not considered "drinks" for the purpose of Kiddush. It follows, therefore, that they do not qualify for Kiddush or Havdalah. And the debate continues regarding the circumstances which justify using Chamar Medinah for Havdalah. According to most opinions, Chamar Medinah may only be used if wine is totally unavailable, at any price, in town or a distance of one day's journey from town.[12] According to the Rambam,[13] however, once a drink qualifies as Chamar Medinah, it may be used for Havdalah, even if wine is available in town.

The situation with Shabbat morning is the most lenient of the three. This is because it is of Rabbinic origin[14] and the Kiddush that welcomed Shabbat has already been made on Friday night. Accordingly, the accepted practice is to allow Chamar Medinah for Shabbat morning Kiddush, where wine, although available, is either not easily accessible, or too expensive. And on Shabbat morning, whisky is in a category all of its own. Unlike other beverages that qualify as Chamar Medinah, whisky can be chosen over wine, even where the two bottles are standing side by side.[15] According to the Mishnah Berurah, however, one would have to use a wine-size Kiddush cup which holds between 3-6 ounces and drink most of it in one shot. According to other authorities, a small whisky glass is sufficient.[16]

MAYONNAISE, HERRING AND KIDDUSH
סדר קדוש ונטילת ידים

If you eat mayonnaise with everything, or you attended Breuers, or you wash your hands before Kiddush, you are probably of German Jewish descent. The first two inferences are understandable. Where does the third one come from?

The Talmud[1] quotes the following ruling of Rav Bruna in the name of Rav: "One who washes his hands for bread, before reciting Kiddush on Friday night, should not recite Kiddush himself, but should rather fulfill his Kiddush obligation by having someone else recite Kiddush for him." The reason for Rav Bruna's ruling, as explained by the Rashbam,[2] is that there should be no interruption between washing one's hands - נטילת ידים - Netilat Yadayim, and eating bread. Reciting Kiddush between the two acts, would, according to Rav Bruna, constitute an interruption. Accordingly, if one did wash one's hands and then recite Kiddush, according to Rav Bruna as explained by Rashbam, one would have to wash one's hands again before eating bread. This passage in the Talmud is the source upon which the Poskim of the "Kiddush before Netilat Yadayim" camp rely. These Poskim include the Rambam, (Spain, Morocco, Egypt), the Shulchan Aruch, (Spain, Turkey) and the Vilna Gaon, (Lithuania). According to both the Rambam[3] and the Shulchan Aruch,[4] the consequence of inadvertently performing Netilat Yadayim before Kiddush on Friday night is that one would have to recite Kiddush over bread instead of wine. That way, Kiddush would not be considered an interruption.

Leading the "wash before Kiddush" camp are Rabbeinu Tam and the Ri[5] (both of France), the Rosh,[6] (German origin) and the Rema.[7] Based upon a remark of Rabbi Yitzchak, who observed Rav wash his hands before reciting Kiddush over bread, they point out that the recital of Kiddush after Netilat Yadayim and before eating bread does not constitute an interruption. This is because the Halachah rules in favor of Shmuel, who maintains that Kiddush must be recited over food - אין קדוש אלא במקום סעודה - Ein Kiddush Ela Bemakom Seudah, and against Rav, who maintains that Kiddush can be recited in the absence of food.[8] Accordingly, Shmuel considers both the bread and the wine an integral part of the Kiddush, and the recital of Kiddush between Netilat Yadayim and eating bread is not considered an interruption. Even the "wash before Kiddush" camp agrees, however, that the wine should be poured prior to Netilat Yadayim, since the mental concentration required for measuring out the correct quantity of wine for Kiddush would be considered an interruption.[9]

It appears that customs can differ even in the same family. Indeed, the Tur expresses reservations about the Rosh, his father, whose Minhag seemed to ignore the position of Rav described above.[10] There is also an 'in between' position taken by the Chafetz Chaim. He suggests that all those hearing Kiddush may perform Netilat Yadayim before Kiddush, whereas the person reciting Kiddush should wash after Kiddush.[11] My father, Dayan Grunfeld, Zt''l, seemed to follow an inconsistent approach. He would recite Kiddush before Netilat Yadayim on Friday night, and perform Netilat Yadayim before reciting Kiddush on Shabbat morning. I always attributed this to dual loyalties. Though born in Germany, he learned with Polish and Sephardi Rabbis. Only much later, did I discover that there was more to it. He was, in fact, following the opinion of the Tur. According to the Tur, the longer Kiddush of Friday night constitutes an interruption between Netilat Yadayim and eating bread. The shorter Kiddush of Shabbat morning, however, which requires only the recital of - בורא פרי הגפן - Boreh Pri Hagafen, does not.[12]

FEAR OF FLYING
עובדא דחול

If you took a bus to Synagogue on a rainy Shabbat or Yom Tov day, with umbrella in hand, would that be OK? There is no Melachah involved because you are not driving. There is no "Amirah Lenochri," (asking a non-Jew to perform a Melachah on your behalf) involved because you are not asking the non-Jew to drive for you. He is driving of his own accord for non-Jews. There is no violation of Techum Shabbat (the prohibition on Shabbat or Yom Tov not to travel more than 2,000 Amot beyond one's residence), because the bus travels only in the city. It is also difficult to find anything wrong with the umbrella. Presumably, there is an Eruv enclosure so there is no carrying violation involved. And according to the many authorities, including Rashi, who are of the opinion that building a provisional tent is permitted on Shabbat or Yom Tov, there is no Melachah involved in opening the umbrella. Similarly, if you walk to your office in the city on Shabbat to assist a client in connection with an important transaction, taking care not to write or touch anything Muktzeh yourself, what would be wrong with that? There is no Melachah involved in buying or selling on Shabbat.

But merely abstaining from the 39 Melachot is not what Shabbat and Yom Tov is all about. Abstaining from the 39 Melachot turns the weekday off, but it does not turn the Shabbat on.

"What would the Shabbat be like had the Torah merely prohibited the 39 Melachot?" asks the Ramban.[1] "A person could spend the entire Shabbat in physical labor. He could measure his grain and weigh his fruit, carry heavy furniture or barrels of wine from place to place. In a city enclosed with a valid Eruv, it would be possible for many to go about business as usual. Markets and stores would be open and people would go Shabbat shopping. Laborers would get up early and hire themselves out for work. And Yom Tov would vanish into a regular weekday. The Torah refers to Yom Tov and Shabbat as Shabbaton, which means a day of rest, not a day of exertion."

The liturgist in the Shabbat song "Ma Yeddidut" describes how the soul, once liberated from its weekday shackles, can soar on the wings of Shabbat, if we just let it. "Your steps should be leisurely; God made Shabbat for your pleasure, sleep is praiseworthy, it restores the spirit to the soul; my soul yearns to bask in Your affection." And the prophet[2] instructs us in the art of flying on Shabbat, as follows: אם תשיב משבת רגלך עשות חפציך ביום קדשי וקראת לשבת ענג לקדוש ה' מכובד וכבדתו מעשות דרכיך ממצוא חפצך ודבר דבר. אז תתענג על ה' והרכבתיך על במתי ארץ והאכלתיך נחלת יעקב אביך, כי פי ה' דבר.

"If you refrain from running errands and pursuing your ambitions on My Holy Day, and if you designate the Shabbat as a day of pleasure, dedicated to My honor, then you will rejoice with Me and you will soar on high." And so, anything that compromises the spirit of Shabbat and drags it down to weekday reality is prohibited, even if it is technically not a Melachah.

Certain activities by their very nature, spoil the atmosphere of Shabbat, such as walking to work, even if you do not write. Such activities are known as "Uvda Dechol,'' (weekday activities). Other activities demonstrate a disrespect for Shabbat - זלזול שבת - Zilzul Shabbat, such as keeping the television on. Yet other activities broadcast a workday atmosphere - אוושא מילתא - Avsha Milta, such as carrying an umbrella on Shabbat. Other activities simply confuse the onlooker - מראית עין - and make him question your motive when you step off the bus on Shabbat.

Even permitted activities, such as bringing gifts to friends, must be done in a way that does not take on a commercial air. Thus, for example, three or more people should not arrive on Shabbat or Yom Tov lugging groceries, because it looks as if they are returning from the market.[3] Rather, care should be taken to carry such items in a way that is different, Shinui, to the way they are carried on a weekday.

An illustrative example of what might and what might not constitute Uvda Dechol is given by the Chatam Sofer.[4] "Why," he asks, "is one permitted to travel by ship on Shabbat (boarded before Shabbat) but not by train?" Both are ten cubits off the ground and therefore the prohibition of Techum Shabbat does not apply. The Chatam Sofer answers that in a ship you can celebrate the Shabbat in the comfort you would at home. In a train, however, you are always aware that you are traveling. The countryside races past the windows and you are constantly shaken up and focused on reaching your weekday destination. That is Uvda Dechol.

MR. LIZZACK
בקור חולים בשבת ובחול

Most Shabbatot after Shul, Dad, Dayan Grunfeld זצ״ל would take me by the hand and together we would climb the steep stairs to the second floor of the tenement house in North London. There, in a large oak bed, lay Mr. Lizzack, the stockbroker, whom illness had confined to bed year after year. As Dad, in his finest black Rabbinic Shabbat clothes pulled up a chair, Mr. Lizzack would perk up, as they talked about stocks and shares, the Parshah and Mr. Lizzack's health.

Visiting the sick, Bikur Cholim, is one of the Mitzvot listed in the Hall of Fame prayer - אלו דברים שאין להם שעור - "These are the things that have no measure." According to our Sages, the Torah itself stresses the importance of Bikur Cholim in several places. When Yitro advises Moshe to educate the people of Israel by "showing them the way to go,"[1] he is referring to the duty to visit the sick.[2] "Walk behind God," Moshe advises the people of Israel.[3] "Is it possible for a human to walk behind God?" asks the Talmud.[4] Rather, says the Talmud, follow God by emulating his ways. Just as God visits the sick, so should you visit the sick. And how do we know that God visits the sick? Rabbi Chamma, the son of Chanina, said that God came to visit Abraham[5] on the third day following his circumcision.[6] And when Korach challenges the authenticity of Moshe's leadership, Moshe replies: "If Korach dies the death of all men and the visitation of all men is visited upon him, then it is proof that God has not appointed me." The death of all men, to which Moshe refers, is death following bedridden sickness. And the visitation of all men refers to visiting the sick, as they lie dying. From Moshe's reference to visiting the sick, the Talmud[7] rules that Bikur Cholim is referred to in the Torah.

According to the Ramban,[8] Bikur Cholim requires the one visiting the sick to do the following things: to make sure that the sick person is physically comfortable and is not in a state of anxiety concerning his immediate needs; to show him that he has friends who care; and most importantly, to beseech God that the sick person fully recover. Based on God's personal visit to Abraham, no person, however great, is absolved from the duty of Bikur Cholim and no task, however menial, may be overlooked. And so, when the great Rabbi Akiva noticed that one of his students was writhing with fever, alone, in his dormitory with nobody to take care of him, Rabbi Akiva himself took charge. He sat with him and swept and tidied and aired his room. "Rebbi, you have brought me back to life," the student said. Upon leaving his room Rabbi Akiva warned his students, "whoever does not visit the sick has blood on his hands."[9]

The leitmotif that emerges from various Halachot of Bikur Cholim is the call for identification. As Rabbi Avraham Weiss puts it: "The world is not divided between the sick and the healthy, but rather between the sick and the not yet sick." When a friend of the same age visits a sick person, he relieves the sick person of one sixtieth of his sickness.[10] Perhaps this is because the friend, being so close in age, keenly feels, "There, but by for the grace of God, go I." If the sick person is thrust into the situation where he is compelled to face his sickness head on, we, who are not yet sick, can encourage him by facing it with him. And so, even if the sick person is in too much pain to receive visitors, one must still stand outside his room, listen to his pain and pray on his behalf.[11] The other overriding principle of Bikur Cholim is to be careful not to tire the sick with one's presence. If the sick person is asleep during the visit one should quietly pray on his behalf and not wake him up. When he awakens, he will be soothed to hear that you were there. Persons suffering from certain types of sickness such as migraines, eye infections and stomach ailments are, according to Halachah, better off if they are not disturbed by a visit. Instead, one should enquire after their health, pray on their behalf and lend their families a hand. If there has been hatred between the sick and the one who wishes to visit him, caution should be exercised. The best course of action would be to ask for permission to visit in advance rather than unilaterally showing up. The primary concern is not your need to be there, but whether your presence will cheer up or upset the patient. Of course, in weighing these delicate considerations, the history and intensity of the hatred are important factors.[12] It is perfectly appropriate for a man to visit a sick woman and vice versa, in the company of others.[13]

Clearly, the three things that one should do for the sick, attending their needs, showing that their friends care and praying on their behalf, are best done through personal visits. Seeing your friend in pain motivates you to come to his assistance more than it would by just hearing about it. Sometimes, however, personal visits are not possible, either because of the nature of the sickness, or because of the inability of the visitor to get to the patient. In such cases, the next best thing is to call on the telephone,[14] or to visit by video hook-up.[15]

According to the Ran,[16] there are certain situations in which one may pray for mercy that the sick person should die. Such is the case when there is no medical possibility of survival and the pain of the continued struggle is unbearable. Of course, Halachah forbids any other action or omission to precipitate death. Such prayers for relief by death should not be offered by family members, or those tending to the sick, but rather by friends.[17]

When visiting the sick, one should dress with respect, as one would when entering a synagogue. This is because, according to the Talmud, the Divine Presence resides with and sustains the sick.[18] When taking leave of the sick, on a weekday, one should say - המקום ירחם עליך בתוך חולי ישראל - "God should have mercy on you together with other sick persons of Israel." And on Shabbat one should bid farewell with the words - שבת היא מלזעוק, ורפואה קרובה לבא - which means "Shabbat should afford you respite from crying out in pain and you shall soon be healed."[19]

At the end of the visit, Dad would bend over Mr. Lizzack and with deep concentration he would say "Good Shabbes, Mr. Lizzack," or so, for years, that is what I thought he said until I came across this passage in Talmud Shabbat. Now, I realize, that what Dad was, in fact, saying was "Shabbat He Milizzok."

CANDLE LIGHTING TIME
זמן הדלקת נרות
(שבת כ:)

1. Shulchan Aruch, Orach Chaim 261:1
2. Shabbat 34b.
3. Pesachim 94a.
4. Pesachim 94a; see Tosafot s.v. רבי יהודה אומר.
5. Rambam, Hilchot Shabbat 5:4; see also Magid Mishnah thereon s.v. משתשקע החמה.
6. See 1 above.
7. Biur Hagrah on Schulcan Aruch, Orach Chaim 261:1.
8. A "mil" is a distance of between 3000 and 4000 feet.
9. Biur Halacha to Shulchan Aruch, Orach Chaim 261:2, s.v. מתחילת השקיעה.
10. Responsa Igrot Moshe, Orach Chaim Chelek 1, Siman 96, p.157.
11. Simcha Rabinowitz, Piskei Teshuvot Chelek 5, p.307 to Shulchan Aruch, Orach Chaim 494:1.
12. Shemirat Shabbat volume 2, Chapter 44, paragraphs 2 and 3.

—∿—

THE DEATH OF REBBE
נרות שבת
(כתובות קג)

1. Samuel 1, 25:29.
2. Shabbat 152b.
3. Ketubot 104a.
4. Ketubot 103b.
5. Ketubot 103a.

—∿—

THE THIRTY NINE MELACHOT AND THEIR DERIVATIVES
ל"ט מלאכות
(שבת עג.)

1. Shabbat 73a.
2. For further discussion of this question, see Melachot, Permanence and Umbrellas, below.

MELACHOT AND INTENT
דבר שאין מתכוין
(ביצה כג:)

1. The prohibition against performing Melachot on Shabbat immediately precedes the Torah's description of the building of the Mishkan, Exodus 35:1-3.
2. Exodus 35:33.
3. Rambam, Hilchot Shegagot 7:4.
4. Rashi, Shabbat 72b s.v. נתכוון להגביה את התלוש.
5. Beitzah 23b.
6. Rambam, Hilchot Shabbat 1:5.
7. Shabbat 75a; Rashi, Succah 33b s.v. והא מודי; Rambam, Hilchot Shabbat 1:6.
8. Tosafot, Shabbat 103a s.v. לא צריכא דעביד בעראה דחבריה.
9. Shulchan Aruch, Orach Chaim 337:2 and Mishnah Berurah 14 thereon and Shaar Zion 10 thereon. The ערוך is a minority opinion which permits the performance of a Psik Reishe Delo Neecha Lei in the first place. See Tosafot, ibid.
10. Shulchan Aruch, Orach Chaim 646:2 and Mishnah Berurah 8 thereon; Shulchan Aruch, Orach Chaim 321:14, and Mishnah Berurah 57 thereon.
11. Responsa Igrot Moshe, Orach Chaim Chelek 4, Siman 74, subheading בישול, paragrah 28, p.138.

—ɷ—

THE PURPOSE OF THE MELACHAH
מלאכה שאינה צריכה לגופה
(שבת עג:)

1. "Melachot and Intent," above.
2. Shabbat 73b.
3. See Tosafot, Shabbat 94a s.v. רבי שמעון פוטר for definition and further examples of Melachah She'eina Tzericha Legufa.
4. Shulchan Aruch, Orach Chaim 316:9, and Mishnah Berurah 34 thereon. See also, Rambam, Hilchot Shabbat 1:7 who rules that a Melachah She'eina Tzericha Legufa is Biblically prohibited.
5. Rabbi Shimon D. Eider, Halochos of Shabbos volume 1, p.16.
6. Shulchan Aruch, Orach Chaim 342:1.
7. Shulchan Aruch, Orach Chaim 328:17 and Mishnah Berurah 50 thereon.
8. Thus one may, for example, spread a wet blanket over a piece of furniture in the path of a fire so that the fire would be extinguished upon reaching it. In such an instance of substantial financial loss, the Rabbinical prohibition of indirectly extinguishing a fire - גרם כיבוי - would be set aside. See Shulchan Aruch, Orach Chaim 334:22, and Biur Halachah s.v. גרם כיבוי there.

9. In case of sickness, dire need and for the sake of a Mitzvah, or to prevent substantial financial loss, see Shulchan Aruch, Orach Chaim 307:5, and Mishnah Berurah 20, 21 and 22 thereon.

10. Shabbat 11b; Beitzah 3a.

11. Tosafot, Succah 33b s.v. מודה רבי שמעון בפסיק רישא ולא ימות.

12, 13. Shulchan Aruch, Orach Chaim 342:1, and Mishnah Berurah 1 thereon.

14. Shulchan Aruch, Orach Chaim 328:17, and Mishnah Berurah 50 and Shaar Zion 27 thereon.

15. See Shulchan Aruch, Orach Chaim 328:25, and Mishnah Berurah 83 thereon.

16. Shaarim Metzuyanim Behalachah Chelek 2, p.82, note 6 to Kitzur Shulchan Aruch 80:2.

— ∞ —

MOUNTAINS HANGING FROM HAIRS
פסיק רישא דלא ניחא ליה
(שבת קג.)

1. For further discussion see "Melachot and Intent," above.

2. Tosafot, Shabbat 103a s.v. לא צריכא and Shulchan Aruch, Orach Chaim 320:18, and the Biur Halachah s.v. יש מי שמתיר thereon.

3. Tosafot, Shabbat 103a s.v. לא צריכא.

4. Shulchan Aruch, Orach Chaim 277:1, and Mishnah Berurah 10 thereon.

5. Shulchan Aruch, Orach Chaim 337:2, and Mishnah Berurah 14 and Shaar Zion 10 thereon; Shulchan Aruch, Orach Chaim 314:1 and Mishnah Berurah 11 thereon; and Chazon Ish, Orach Chaim, Hilchot Shabbat 50:41.

6. Shulchan Aruch, Orach Chaim 316:1, and Mishnah Berurah 5 thereon and also 321:14 and Mishnah Berurah 57 thereon.

7. Succah 33b; Tosafot, Shabbat 103a s.v. לא צריכא.

8. Tosafot, Shabbat 94a, s.v. רבי שמעון פוטר.

9. Responsa Tzitz Eliezer Chelek 1, Siman 20, Perek 6, p.111.

10. Ran to Rif on Shabbat 145 (in Rif, 61a) s.v. ובמקום.

11. Responsa Beer Yitzchak, Orach Chaim Siman 15, quoted in Responsa Ma'aseh Choshev Chelek 1, Siman 2 p.56.

12. Shulchan Aruch, Orach Chaim 277:3 and Mishnah Berurah 15 thereon.

— ∞ —

MELACHOT, PERMANENCE AND UMBRELLAS
דבר המתקיים
(שבת לא:)

1. Rambam, Hilchot Shabbat 9:13.

2. Rema on Shulchan Aruch, Orach Chaim 317:1, quoting the Tur and the Mordechai. There is

also a stricter opinion cited by the Rema that one may not tie a knot that will not be untied the same day. Regarding the Torah Scroll ribbon, see Yechiel Michel Stern, Sefer Melechet Shabbat, p.208.

3. Responsa Igrot Moshe, Orach Chaim Chelek 2, Siman 84 p. 274; Yechiel Michel Stern, Sefer Melechet Shabbat p.216 and 218.
4. Rambam, Hilchot Shabbat 11:15.
5. Rambam, Hilchot Shabbat 9:13.
6. Rashi, Shabbat 102b s.v. כל העושה מלאכה. See also discussion in Shaar Zion 68 to Mishnah Berurah 82 on Shulchan Aruch, Orach Chaim 303:26.
7. Jerusalem Talmud Shabbat 12:1.
8. Jerusalem Talmud 7:2.
9. Shabbat 31b.
10. Rif, Shabbat 138a and b (in Rif 56b) and Shiltei Giborim thereon who comments that the Rif considers this a Melachah De'oraita only where the top of the tent is one handsbreadth wide.
11. Rambam, Hilchot Shabbat 22:27.
12. Rashi, Shabbat 138b s.v. אלא טעמא לאו משום אוהל.
13. Rosh Shabbat 138a (in Rosh 179b) as explained by Shiltei Giborim, see note 10 above, only where the top is less than a Tefach.
14. Responsa Noda Beyehudah, Orach Chaim Siman 30.
15. Responsa Chatam Sofer, Orach Chaim Chelek 1 Siman 72.
16. Shulchan Aruch, Orach Chaim 315:8, and Biur Halachah s.v. טפח thereon.
17. Responsa Chazon Ish, Orach Chaim, Siman 52, Paragraph 6, p.154.
18. Responsa Yechaveh Daat Chelek 2, Siman 43, p. 162.

—∭—

MELACHAH, CREATIVE AND DESTRUCTIVE ACTS AND THE OPENING OF CANS AND LETTERS
כל המקלקלין פטורין
(שבת קה:)

1. Dayan Dr. I. Grunfeld, The Sabbath p.29.
2. Shabbat 106a: Rambam, Hilchot Shabbat 1:17.
3. Dayan Dr. I. Grunfeld, The Sabbath p. 28.
4. See, "The Purpose of the Melachah," above.
5. Responsa Igrot Moshe, Orach Chaim Chelek 1, Siman 122 Anaf 4, p.193; See also Shemirat Shabbat 9:1 recommending opening food containers before Shabbat.
6. Shabbat 105b; Shulchan Aruch, Yoreh Deah 340:28.
7. Pachad Yitchak quoted in Yechaveh Daat Chelek 6, Siman 24, p.131.
8. Shulchan Aruch, Orach Chaim 340:13, and Mishnah Berurah 41, and Biur Halachah s.v. הניר thereon.

9. Responsa Igrot Moshe, Orach Chaim Chelek 1, Siman 122 Anaf 8, p.200.

—〰—

INDIRECT MELACHAH AND SHABBAT CLOCKS
גרם מלאכה
(שבת קכ׃)

1. Exodus 20:10.
2. Shabbat 120b.
3. Shulchan Aruch, Orach Chaim 334:22.
4. Shemirat Shabbat 13:23 and authorities cited there, footnote 85.
5. Responsa Chazon Ish, Orach Chaim, Siman 38:2, p.56.
6. Responsa Igrot Moshe, Orach Chaim Chelek 4, Siman 60, p. 91.
7. Shemirat Shabbat 13:25, note 90 and Responsa Yabia Omer Chelek 3, Siman 18, p.52.
8. Shemirat Shabbat 13:26 and 28.

—〰—

BATHING, WASHING AND SWIMMING ON SHABBAT
רחיצה בשבת
(שבת מ׃)

1. Shulchan Aruch, Orach Chaim 326:1 and 2, and Mishnah Berurah 4+15 thereon.
2. Shabbat 40a.
3. Shulchan Aruch, Orach Chaim 326:1.
4. Igrot Moshe, Yoreh Deah Chelek 2, Siman 33, p. 44.
5. Magen Avraham to Shulchan Aruch, Orach Chaim 326:7.
6. Biur Halachah to Shulchan Aruch, Orach Chaim 326:1 s.v. במים שהוחמו מערב שבת.

—〰—

WARMING FOOD ON SHABBAT,
THE BLECH AND THE HOT PLATE
שהיה וחזרה
(שבת לו׃)

1. Shulchan Aruch, Orach Chaim 253:1, and Mishnah Berurah 9 thereon.
2. Shabbat 36b; Mishnah Berurah 4 to Shulchan Aruch, Orach Chaim 253:1
3. Kaf Hachaim, Orach Chaim 253:1:11.
4. Introduction of Mishnah Berurah to Shulchan Aruch, Orach Chaim 253:1.
5. Orach Chaim 253:1 and Mishnah Berurah 37; 253:2 and Mishnah Berurah 55 thereon.

6. Shulchan Aruch, Orach Chaim 253:2, and Remah and Mishnah Berurah 65 thereon.
7. Ibid.
8. Responsa Igrot Moshe, Orach Chaim Chelek 1, Siman 94, p. 154 and Chelek 4, Siman 74 Anaf Bishul, paragraph 32, p.138.
9. Responsa Igrot Moshe, Orach Chaim Chelek 4, Siman 74 Anaf Bishul, paragraph 3, p.134.
10. Responsa Yechave Daat Chelek 2, Siman 45, p.172.

—⁜—

MUKTSEH ON SHABBAT AND YOM TOV
מוקצה בשבת ויום טוב
(ביצה ב:)

1. Deutoronomy 5:14.
2. Dayan Dr. I. Grunfeld, The Sabbath p.73.
3. Mishnah Berurah, Introduction to Muksteh, Shulchan Aruch, Orach Chaim 308.
4. Shulchan Aruch, Orach Chaim 308:1; Shulchan Aruch Harav, Orach Chaim 308:4.
5. Shulchan Aruch, Orach Chaim 308:20, + 21; See also Mishnah Berurah Introduction to 308.
6. Shulchan Aruch, Orach Chaim 308:3.
7. Ibid. 310:7 and Mishnah Berurah 24 thereon.
8. Ibid. 310:8; See also response 31 of Rabbi Moshe Feinstein to questions posed by Rabbi Yisroel Pinchas Bodner, at end of Halochos of Muktzeh.
9. Simcha Rabinowitz, Piskei Teshuvot Chelek 1 p.60 paragraph 2 to Shulchan Aruch, Orach Chaim 276:2.
10. Responsa Tzitz Eliezer Chelek 12, Siman 30, p.76.
11. Beitzah 2b; Exodus 16:5.
12. Shulchan Aruch, Orach Chaim 495:4, and Mishnah Berurah 15 thereon.
13. Ibid., Mishnah Berurah 17 and Shaar Zion 25 thereon. See also Shulchan Aruch Harav 495:13.
14. Shulchan Aruch, Orach Chaim 276:4, and Mishnah Berurah 31 thereon.
15. Shulchan Aruch, Orach Chaim 311:8, and Mishnah Berurah 30 thereon.
16. Shemirat Shabbat 22:41.

—⁜—

BENEFITTING FROM THE WORK OF A NON-JEW ON SHABBAT
אמירה לנכרי

1. Rambam, Hilchot Shabbat 6:1.
2. Ibid.
3. Rashi Avoda Zarah 22a s.v. לא.
4. Isaiah 58:13.

5. Shulchan Aruch, Orach Chaim 276:2, and Mishnah Berurah 17 and Biur Halachah thereon.
6. Shulchan Aruch, Orach Chaim 307:22, and Mishnah Berurah 76 thereon.
7. Ibid., 325:6 and 325:8 and Mishnah Berurah 28 and 39 thereon.
8. Ibid., 307:22, and Mishnah Berurah 76 thereon.
9. Shulchan Aruch, Orach Chaim 307:5.
10. Ibid.
11. Rema, Shulchan Aruch, Orach Chaim 253:5. For an explanation of Psik Reishe see Melachot and Intent Chapter 1 above.
12. Responsa Minchat Yitzchak Chelek 3, Siman 23, p. 47; Shaarim Metzuyanim Behalachah Chelek 2, p.82, note 6 to Kitzur Shulchan Aruch 80:2
13. Shulchan Aruch, Orach Chaim 253:5, and Rema and Biur Halachah thereon, s.v. להחם הקדרה.
14. Ibid 328:17, and Mishnah Berurah 47 thereon.
15. Rema, to Shulchan Aruch, Orach Chaim 328:17.
16. Responsa Igrot Moshe, Orach Chaim Chelek 2, Siman 68, p. 262.

—∿—

KIDDUSH WINE, WHISKY, BEER, COFFEE, TEA, MILK, SODA, WATER
חמר מדינה
(פסחים קז·)

1. Exodus 20:8.
2. Hoshea 14:8; Songs of Songs 1:4.
3. Rambam, Hilchot Shabbat 29:1.
4. Shulchan Aruch, Orach Chaim 272:9; and Rema and Mishnah Berurah 27 thereon.
5. Ibid. 271 and Mishnah Berurah 41 thereon.
6. Rambam, Hilchot Shabbat 29:6.
7. Shulchan Aruch Harav, Orach Chaim 296:8 and Shulchan Aruch, Orach Chaim 182:2, and Mishnah Berurah 7 quoting the Bach thereon.
8. Shulchan Aruch, Orach Chaim 296:2 and Rambam, Hilchot Shabbat 29:17 ruling in accordance with the opinion of Ameimar brought in Pesachim 107a.
9. Orach Chaim 272:9.
10. Responsa Igrot Moshe, Orach Chaim Chelek 2, Siman 75, p.267.
11. Yehaveh Daat Chelek 2, Siman 38, p. 146.
12. Shulchan Aruch, Orach Chaim 272:9, Magen Avraham and Mishnah Berurah 24 thereon.
13. Biur Halacha ibid. s.v. שמקדשין על שכר.
14. Orach Chaim 272:9, and Mishnah Berurah 29 thereon.
15. For discusion see Tur, Orach Chaim 272, Bach s.v. ועל הפת.
16. Mishnah Berurah 30 on Shulchan Aruch, Orach Chaim 272:9.

MAYONNAISE, HERRING AND KIDDUSH
סדר קדוש ונטילת ידים
(פסחים קו:)

1. Pesachim 106b.
2. Rashbam, Pesachim 106b s.v. הנוטל ידיו לא יקדש.
3. Rambam, Hilchot Shabbat 29:10.
4. Shulchan Aruch, Orach Chaim 271:12.
5. Tur, Orach Chaim 271.
6. Rosh, Pesachim 106b (in Rosh 11a).
7. Shulchan Aruch, see note 4 above.
8. Beit Yosef on the Tur, Orach Chaim 271 s.v. כתב.
9. Mishnah Berurah 61 to Shulchan Aruch, Orach Chaim 271:12.
10. Tur, Orach Chaim 271.
11. Mishnah Berurah 58, to Shulchan Aruch, Orach Chaim 271:12.
12. Tur, Orach Chaim 289.

FEAR OF FLYING
עובדא דחול
(ביצה יד:)

1. Rambam to Parshat Emor 23:24.
2. Isaiah 58:13-14.
3. Beitzah 14b.
4. Responsa Chatam Sofer Chelek 6, Likutim, Chapter 97.

MR. LIZZACK
בקור חולים בשבת ובחול
(שבת יב:)

1. Exodus 18:20.
2. Bava Metzia 30b.
3. Deutoronomy 13:5.
4. Sotah 14a.
5. Genesis 18:1.
6. Bava Metzia 86b.
7. Nedarim 39b.
8. Torat Haadam as quoted by the Beit Yosef to Tur, Yoreh Deah 335 s.v. ומצווה גדולה.
9. Nedarim 40a.
10. Nedarim 39b

11. Shulchan Aruch, Yoreh Deah 335:8.
12. Maharil Chapter 197 quoted by Rema, Yoreh Deah 335:2 and the Rema there; Bach on the Tur, Yoreah Deah 335 and the Aruch Hashulchan, Yoreh Deah 335:6.
13. Aruch Hashulchan Yoreh Deah 335:11.
14. Igrot Moshe, Yoreh Deah Chelek I, Siman 223, p.450.
15. Minchat Yitzchak Chelek II, Chapter 84, p.169.
16. Nedarim 40 s.v. אין מבקש עליו רחמים
17. See Igrot Moshe, Choshen Mishpat Chelek 2 Siman 73, p.303 and Tzitz Eliezer, Ramat Rachel, Siman 5, p.6.
18. Shabbat 12b based on Psalms 41:4.
19. Shabbat 12b.

Chapter Two

Eruvin

CARRYING, ERUVIN AND MANHATTAN
תיקון עירובין

One of the thirty nine prohibited Melachot on Shabbat is carrying an object from a private domain - רשות היחיד - Reshut Hayachid, to a public domain - רשות הרבים - Reshut Harabim, or carrying an object a distance of four Amot, or cubits equal to between six to eight feet,[1] in a Reshut Harabim.[2] The Torah does permit however, carrying within the Reshut Hayachid itself.[3] The definition of a Reshut Hayachid and a Reshut Harabim is crucial, therefore, to the laws of carrying on Shabbat.

A Reshut Hayachid is an area of at least four Tefachim, or four handbreadths, (approximately 15 inches) square, enclosed by walls or other partitions that are at least ten Tefachim,[4] approximately 3 feet high.[5] The usual form of a Reshut Hayachid is a house or a garden, but the term also includes a depression or elevation of not less than the above dimensions in a public space, such as a ditch or a mound.[6] A Reshut Hayachid may extend for miles in each direction.[7] The partitions of Reshut Hayachid can be natural, such as the canals surrounding the Hague in Holland,[8] or even, as has been suggested, the cliffs surrounding all of the British Isle.[9] Private ownership is not a requirement for a Reshut Hayachid and therefore, as mentioned, even a ditch, of the described dimensions, in a Reshut Harabim, can constitute a Reshut Hayachid.

One of the more controversial aspects of the laws of Eruvin which has direct bearing upon how and if the construction of an Eruv, as we know it, is possible, lies in the definition of a Reshut Harabim. Although there is a wide spectrum of opinions amongst the Rishonim, the generally accepted definition is as follows: A Reshut Harabim is an unroofed, public area, or highway, open at both ends - מפולש - Mefulash, being at least sixteen Amot (between 24 feet to 32 feet) wide, through which at least 600,000 people (equivalent to the counted male adult population of the Jewish encampment in the desert) might pass in one day.[10]

Then too, there is an area which qualifies neither as a Reshut Hayachid nor as a Reshut Harabim because it lacks one of the necessary conditions. Such a betwixt and between area is known as a - כרמלית - Karmelit.[11]

In a typical city, most streets are not Mefulash, in that they do not cut through the entire city in one straight line, one end of the city to the other. Rather, they wind and curve so that they are always surrounded by walls and buildings on all three sides. Such streets which are partitioned off on all three sides are considered by the Torah to be a Reshut Hayachid, in which carrying would be Biblically permitted.[12] The Rabbis, however, fearing that people will not be able to distinguish between such streets and other streets that do qualify as Reshut Harabim, classify such streets as a Karmelit.[13] Accordingly, they prohibit carrying in streets, unless a Halachically valid enclosure is positioned at the open end and an Eruv ceremony is performed.[14] The purpose of the Eruv is to enclose the area in question, on all sides, so that it becomes a Reshut Hayachid, recognized as such by the Rabbis.

If the area in question qualifies as a Reshut Harabim, then it can only be converted into a Reshut Hayachid by installing real doors or gates at its perimeter, which, like the gates of Jerusalem of old, must be capable of being closed at night.[15] If, however, the area in question is not a Reshut Harabim but only a Karmelit, then it may be converted into a Reshut Hayachid by simply constructing a symbolic doorway known as a - צורת הפתח - Tzurat Hapetach, which usually takes the form of two poles with a wire across the top, or some similar construction. The Halachic license to carry in a street enclosed by a symbolic doorway, rather than by real doors which can be closed at night, is based on the theory that most streets, as we know them today, are not in the category of a Reshut Harabim.[16] If, however, there is a doubt whether a particular street is of such dimensions that it might qualify as a Reshut Harabim, then a potential Biblical violation of carrying is involved and a Tzurat Hapetach may not be acceptable. Most modern Tzurat Hapetach Eruvin utilize pre-existing structures, such as fences, walls, embankments, sides of buildings and long lines of overhead cables. Most gaps of up to ten Amot do not disqualify an Eruv, because they are considered entrances to the enclosure.[17] Gaps in excess of ten Amot do disqualify the Eruv, but can be fixed by bridging them with a Tzurat Hapetach, such as overhead cables or strategically placed wire.[18]

Whether the entire island of Manhattan can be enclosed by an Eruv remains a controversial question. The issues are whether the eighteen bridges around the island which can transport in excess of 600,000 people to and fro are considered directly connected to the highways running through Manhattan, so as to render them מפולש and, thereby, render the island a Reshut Harabim. If they, indeed, do, then traffic transporting in excess of 600,000 people in one day through Mefulash highways means the island cannot be enclosed by the unobtrusive device of Tzurat Hapetach, and the impractical device of gates capable of being locked at night would be required. Many Poskim, starting in 1949 with Rabbi Shimon Kalish of Amshinov, endorsed the enclosure of Manhattan by a Tzurat Hapetach Eruv.[19] Rabbi Moshe Feinstein, in a 1951 Teshuvah concerning Manhattan addressed to Rabbi Tzvi Hirsch Eisenstadt and in a 1981 Teshuvah concerning Brooklyn, questions the Halachic basis of such an Eruv.[20] Rabbi Feinstein's main concern is that the access to and from Manhattan of numbers of people far in access of 600,000, through bridges that connect to the highways, renders Manhattan a Reshut Harabim. Some Poskim of great stature, however, disagree.[21]

SEARCHING FOR A COMMUNAL HOME
עירובי חצרות ושיתופי מבואות

According to Biblical law, once an area has been converted into a Reshut Hayachid by enclosing it with a Halachically acceptable Eruv, one may carry inside the enclosed area.[1] But according to Rabbinical law, it is simply not enough to enclose an area in which one wants to carry, with an Eruv. This alone will not permit carrying from the home into the street, or vice versa. Neither will it alone permit carrying from a condominium apartment into the lobby or other common areas. The Rabbis were concerned that if they permit carrying from the private domain of the home to the public domain of the street even when enclosed by a properly constructed Eruv, people might come to carry from their homes into the street, even in the absence of an Eruv enclosure.[2]

In order to carry from one's home into the "street,"[3] the Rabbis require an additional procedure called the "Merging of Streets" or - שיתופי מבואות - Shitufei Mavo'ot.[4] In order to carry from one's apartment into the corridors or lobby of a condominium, an additional procedure called the "Merging of Courtyards" or - עירובי חצרות - Eruvei Chatzeirot, is required.[5] We shall refer to both Shitufei Mavo'ot and Eruvei Chatzeirot by the one name "Eruvin."

The purpose of Eruvin is to merge all homes, apartments and streets in the enclosed area, into a single Communal Entity. After the Eruvin ceremony has been performed, members of the Communal Entity are no longer considered to be carrying from private domains into public domains.[6]

The two ceremonies of Shitufei Mavo'ot and Eruvei Chatzeirot can be conducted simultaneously by depositing bread or Matzot in one designated home, or in a synagogue on behalf of all Sabbath observers in the enclosed area.[7] Because, according to Halachah, a person lives where he eats,[8] this symbolic gesture has the power to merge all residences in the enclosed area into one Communal Home.

When, one might ask, has one ever been invited to participate in this Eruvin ceremony? The answer is that it is performed on one's behalf, without one's participation, by a member of the community Eruv committee.[9] This agency is based on the Halachic principle that a benefit can be bestowed on one in one's absence זכין לאדם שלא בפניו[10] - Zachin Le'adam Shelo Befanav, and on the assumption that everybody benefits from the ability to carry on Shabbat.[11] The committee agent performs the ceremony once each year, on Erev Pesach, by placing a box of Matzot on behalf of all the Sabbath observers in the designated home or in a synagogue. When so doing, the committee agent recites the blessing, "Al Mitzvat Eruvin,"[12] and the Eruvin becomes effective for all the Sabbaths of that year.[13]

According to Halachah, in order for the Eruvin ceremony to be valid, it must be performed on behalf of ALL owners of streets and homes in the enclosed area.[14] This presents a problem, because non-Jews and others who do not observe Shabbat are not eligible to participate in the Eruvin ceremony.[15] The solution is for the committee agent to enter into a token lease by which the non-Sabbath observant owners lease their streets and homes to the Sabbath observers for the sole purpose of allowing them to carry from their homes to the streets.[16]

ERUVIN, DISSENTERS AND PROTESTERS
שכירת רשות

In order to carry from one's home into the street (even when enclosed by a properly constructed Eruv), the Eruvin ceremony must be performed. This ceremony involves the placing of food in one designated home on behalf of all Sabbath observers in the enclosed area.[1] In order for the Eruvin ceremony to be valid however, it must be performed on behalf of all owners of streets and homes in the enclosed area.[2] Because non-Jews and others who do not observe the Sabbath are not eligible to participate in the Eruvin ceremony, the Eruv Committee must enter into a nominal lease, by which the non-Sabbath observant owners lease their streets and homes to the Sabbath observers to enable the latter to conduct a valid Eruvin ceremony.[3] This rental procedure is known as - שכירת רשות - Sechirat Reshut. No written instrument and only token rent is required for Sechirat Reshut.[4]

Sechirat Reshut of streets and other public areas is entered into with those authorities and their agents that control them or exercise jurisdiction over them, such as mayors, borough presidents or even police officers.[5] It is, however, impractical to effect Sechirat Reshut with each non-Sabbath observant home owner in the enclosed area. The solution of the Chazon Ish and others is, once again, to rent such private homes from the governmental, municipal and police authorities that exercise jurisdiction over them.[6] This solution is based on the Halachic principle of Right of Entry or - תפיסת יד - Tefisat Yad. The Halachah recognizes the right of the authority to rent out the property over which it has a right of entry. The power of the government or the municipality to expropriate private property in times of war, or to build roads or the right of police, firemen or sanitation officials, under certain circumstances, to enter private homes without the owners' consent are a few examples of Right to Entry, upon which the Halachah relies for the purpose of Sechirat Reshut.[7]

What about those who refuse to participate in Sechirat Reshut or in the Eruvin ceremony and protest it in principle? For example, some Sabbath observers object to an Eruv, because they believe it to be invalid and wish to prevent others from mistakenly relying on it. Can the property of such protesters be included in the private domain brought about by the Eruvin ceremony? If it cannot, the Eruvin ceremony may be invalid and no carrying will be permitted by anybody from homes to streets, or vice versa, in the enclosed area.[8]

The late Rav Menachem Kasher,[9] in his treatise on the Manhattan Eruv, suggests that the Eruv protesters can be ignored and thus have no power to invalidate the Eruv for use by others who wish to rely on it. Rav Kasher cites several reasons for his opinion. Firstly, even if the protesters are correct in considering a particular Eruv invalid, this should not prevent others, who are unaware of the situation, from using the Eruv in good faith. "Better that they violate unintentionally, rather than deliberately" is a Halachic principle that applies to certain Rabbinic enactments, including the prohibition of carrying in a Karmelit. Accordingly, argues Rav Kasher, the protester bestows no benefit on others, but simply spoils for the sake of spoiling. Such conduct is called "Ethics of Sodom" and can be legally ignored. Moreover, Rav Kasher argues that once the authority has rented the area, it is irrelevant whether the individual resident condones the use to which it is put. In his treatise, Rav Kasher describes his visit to Rav Moshe Feinstein, a prominent dissenter of the Manhattan Eruv. After attentively listening with deference to Rav Kasher's arguments in favor of the Manhattan Eruv, Rav Moshe did not object to its use by those who wish to use it, but preferred not to use it himself.

THE RIVERDALE ERUV
גוד אסיק מחיצתא

The purpose of the Eruv is to enclose the area in which one wants to carry, on all sides, so that it becomes a private domain, a Reshut Hayachid. If the area in question is a Karmelit - an area that qualifies neither as a public domain nor as a private domain - gaps in the Eruv structure may be bridged by means of a constructive or symbolic doorway called - צורת הפתח - Tzurat Hapetach. A Tzurat Hapetach is made up of two posts, each called a - לחי - Lechi and a crossbeam or overhead wire called a - קורה - Korah.[1] Most streets today qualify as a Karmelit. Riverdale qualifies as a Karmelit and not as a Reshut Harabim because it does not meet all of the qualifications to classify as a Reshut Harabim. First, less then 600,000 people pass through the streets of Riverdale, including the Henry Hudson Parkway, in one day. Second, the streets of Riverdale are not - מפולש - open-ended on two sides, but are surrounded by walls and buildings on all three sides. Third, the Henry Hudson Parkway is covered with roofed bridges in several places. Even if the Henry Hudson Parkway were a Reshut Harabim, it has barriers which can be locked at night. This, in fact, occurred when tall ships passed through on the Bicentennial festivities. Many urban Eruvin utilize telephone poles and overhead cables as a Tzurat Hapetach, even though telephone poles are not meant to serve as doorways. The rationale for this is that the intent of the Jewish population to incorporate them in the Eruv as doorways, renders them doorways.

In order for the Tzurat Hapetach to be legally acceptable, the cable must run across the top of the telephone poles, the same way as a lintel runs across the top of door posts. If, as is often the case, the cable is attached to the side of the telephone pole, rather than to the top of the telephone pole, the Eruv is not valid. This problem can, however, be easily rectified by attaching a wooden plank to the telephone pole. By virtue of an Halachic principle known as - גוד אסיק מחיצתא - Gud Asek Mechitzatah,[2] the Halachah draws an imaginary line straight up from the top of the attached plank. If this imaginary line hits an overhead cable, then the wooden plank, rather than the telephone pole, is regarded as the doorpost, Lechi, thereby validating the Tzurat Hapetach and the Eruv. The application of this device can be witnessed in many neighborhoods.

As one can see from the map, on page 208, one of the boundaries of the Riverdale Eruv runs north-south, along Fieldston Road, between West 252 Street and West 254 Street. In that stretch of Eruv, the boundary of the Eruv is bridged by telephone poles, constituting a Tzurat Hapetach. As the attached photograph, on page 209, of a particular telephone pole situated in that stretch of Eruv shows, the cable passes alongside the telephone pole, rather than over it, thereby threatening to invalidate the Eruv. To overcome this problem, the Riverdale Eruv Committee has attached a wooden plank, Lechi, to the telephone pole. Were the plank to extend straight up, it would hit the overhead cable.

Accordingly, the attached plank together with the principle of Gud Asek Mechitzatah solves the problem and validates the Eruv. When carrying near the outside perimeters of the Eruv, care should be taken to walk inside the Eruv's boundary and not outside the Eruv's boundary. For example, when carrying between West 252 Street and West 254 Street, on Fieldston Road, in Riverdale, one should walk on the sidewalk opposite the Eruv's boundary and not on the sidewalk adjacent to the boundary. This will ensure that one does not, inadvertently, carry outside of the Eruv.

ERUVEI TECHUMIN, SHIPS, PLANES AND MOSCHIACH
תחום שבת וערובי תחומין

"On Shabbat, every person must remain in his residence," said Moshe to the people,[1] forbidding them to walk more than a certain distance beyond their desert encampment. This distance, which measures two thousand Amot, about 2/3 of a mile, is known as Techum Shabbat.[2] It is the same distance that stretched from the perimeters of the Levite cities to their outlying suburbs.[3] These are the Biblical sources on which the Rabbis rely when prohibiting one from walking beyond the Techum Shabbat. One may walk up to 2000 Amot in any direction from one's residence on Shabbat, but not beyond. The "Beyond the Techum" prohibition applies both on Shabbat and on Yom Tov, as well as on Yom Kippur.[4] It does not, however, apply in any area that can be legally defined as a Reshut Hayachid, a private domain, including an area which has been transformed into a Reshut Hayachid by means of an enclosure, an Eruv.[5]

What constitutes a person's residence from which the 2000 Amot is measured? That depends on where the person finds himself at the onset of Shabbat. If he finds himself in a walled or otherwise enclosed city, the 2000 Amot is measured from the city walls, irrespective of the size of the city.[6] Accordingly, a person can walk on Shabbat tens upon tens of miles to the city walls and then another 2000 Amot. If he finds himself at the onset of Shabbat in a city without walls, the 2000 Amot is measured from the end of the city.[7] For this purpose, a "city" is defined as any place that has at least three streets with at least two permanent houses in each street. The "end of the city" is that point at which one house is more than 70 Amot (between 105 feet and 140 feet) away from the next house. Accordingly, on Shabbat, a person can walk through country villages until he reaches the last house within 70 Amot of the previous one and then another 2000 Amot.[8]

What happens if one wants to attend a synagogue, visit a friend or just take a Shabbat stroll beyond the Techum Shabbat? One may do so by performing a ceremony called - עירובי תחומין - Eruvei Techumin. This ceremony allows one to walk a total of 4000 Amot in one chosen direction by symbolically moving one's point of residence at the onset of Shabbat 2000 Amot in the direction one wishes to walk on Shabbat. However, these additional 2000 Amot that one may now walk on Shabbat in one chosen direction are not free. One has traded them for the 2000 Amot one could have walked in the opposite direction had one not performed Eruvei Techumin.[9] There are two ways to conduct the Eruv ceremony. One method is to travel before Shabbat to a point not more than two thousand Amot from one's original residence, remain there until after twilight, Bein Hashmashot, and then walk home. This point then becomes one's new symbolic residence. The following day, Shabbat, one may walk back to one's symbolic residence, plus an additional 2000 Amot from there. The alternative, and most commonly used method, is for the person, or his agent, to place a sufficient amount of food for two meals at a point not more then 2000 Amot from one's original residence before Shabbat. At that point and time, one articulates one's intention to acquire that place as one's new symbolic residence. One then makes the Eruv Blessing and returns home, this time before Bein Hashmashot. This point then becomes one's new symbolic residence. This alternative method of Eruvei Techumin, once performed, is valid for all Sabbaths of the year, provided, however, that the food remains at the symbolic residence and remains edible. For this purpose, Matzot can be used.[10]

May a person who has boarded a ship before Shabbat sail beyond the Techum on Shabbat? This question is left unresolved in Tractate Eruvin.[11] It depends on whether the law, which provides that a public domain ends at the height of ten Tefachim above the ground for the purpose of carrying on Shabbat, also applies for the purpose of walking beyond the Techum on Shabbat. If it does, then one may sail beyond the Techum, because the hull of a ship is typically more than ten Tefachim above the bed of the sea, so that one is not deemed to be traveling in a Reshut Harabim. The Talmud comments that if, indeed, the Reshut Harabim extends beyond the height of ten Tefachim for the purpose of Techum Shabbat, then Eliyahu the prophet, Eliyahu Hanavi (who, according to tradition, will announce the arrival of the Messiah) and the Messiah himself, will not be able to arrive on Shabbat, because their descent from heaven would violate the Beyond the Techum prohibition.[12] Some Rishonim suggest that this passage in the Talmud is the reason why we welcome Eliyahu Hanavi after Havdalah because only then will he be able to arrive without violating the Beyond the Techum prohibition. Based on the majority opinion, that the Beyond the Techum prohibition is of Rabbinical origin, and, therefore, there is more room for leniency, the Rema concludes that sailing beyond the Techum Shabbat is permitted even when in doubt as to whether the hull is ten Tefachim above the bed of the sea.[13] For the same reason, Rabbi Blau, in his treatise on Eruvin, suggests that under certain circumstances, one may disembark from a plane that arrived after the onset of Shabbat because the distance of Techum Shabbat would be measured from the point of landing.[14]

CARRYING, ERUVIN AND MANHATTAN
תיקון עירובין
(עירובין נט.)

1. One Amah is a distance ranging from 18.9 inches to 22.8 inches. According to Rabbi Avraham Chaim Naeh, one Amah is 18.9 inches, according to the Igrot Moshe, it is 21.5 inches and according to the Chazon Ish it is 22.8 inches.

2. For the scriptual source of the Melachah of carrying, see Exodus 16:25, Exodus 36:6 and Shabbat 96b.

3. Rambam, Hilchot Shabbat 14:11.

4. A tefach, handbreadth, is a distance ranging from 3.1 inches to 3.8 inches (3.1 inches according to Avraham Chaim Naeh, 3.58 inches according to Igrot Moshe and 3.8 inches according to the Chazon Ish).

5. Shulchan Aruch, Orach Chaim 345:2.

6. Shulchan Aruch, Orach Chaim 345:2 and Dayan Dr. I. Grunfeld, The Sabbath, p.58.

7. Rambam, see note 3 above.

8. Responsa Chacham Tzvi, Siman 5.

9. Responsa Chacham Tzvi, Siman 5, but see Sheelat Yaavetz who explains that his father, the Chacham Tzvi, disqualified natural cliffs as opposed to man made trenches. This explains why all of England is not considered one big Reshut Hayachid.

10. Shulchan Aruch, Orach Chaim 345:7, based on Rashi, Eruvin 59a s.v. עיר של יחיד, and accepted as the Halachic definition by the Magen Avraham s.v. ויש אומרים. See also Mishnah Berurah 23 and 24 who quotes many Rishonim, including the Rambam, who are of the opinion that a street of the foregoing dimensions qualifies as a Reshut Harabim even if it is not frequented by 600,000 people. The Mishnah Berurah also questions the basis for limiting this traffic to one day.

11. Rambam, Hilchot Shabbat 14:4.

12. Magid Mishnah to Rambam Hilchot Shabbat 17:1. See also Shulchan Aruch, Orach Chaim 363:1 and Biur Halachah thereon s.v. אסרו חכמים.

13. Shulchan Aruch, Orach Chaim 303:18 "והשתא דלית לן רשות הרבים גמור הוה כל רשות הרבים שלנו כרמלית ודיינו כחצר שאינו מעורבת"

14. This Eruv ceremony, which involves depositing food on behalf of all Sabbath observers in the enclosed area in one designated place is known as "Eruvei Chatzeirot" or "Shitufei Mavo'ot" and is further explained in "Searching for a Communal Home," below.

15. Shulchan Aruch, Orach Chaim 364:2.

16. Tosafot, Shabbat 64b s.v. רבי ענני, and Note 13 above.

17. Shulchan Aruch, Orach Chaim 362:9, and Mishnah Berurah 52 thereon.

18. Shulchan Aruch, Orach Chaim 362:10.

19. Rabbi Yehoshua Siegel published a pamphlet in 1907 called "Eruv V'hotza'a," permitting residents of the Lower East Side to carry on Shabbat. He relied upon the three walls that border along the East River and the Third Avenue elevated train line for the fourth wall.

20. Responsa Igrot Moshe, Orach Chaim Chelek 1, Siman 139, p.232 and Siman 140, p.242 and Chelek 5, Siman 28, Anaf 2, paragraphs 6 and 7, p.96.

21. Responsa Rav Menachem Kasher, Divrei Menachem, Orach Chaim, Tikun Eruvin Be Manhattan.

—〰—

SEARCHING FOR A COMMUNAL HOME
עירובי חצרות שיתופי מבואות

1. Rambam, Hilchot Eiruvin 1:1.

2. Ibid. 1:4. See also Shulchan Aruch Harav, Orach Chaim 366:1.

3. When using the term "street," we assume that the street in question does not qualify as a Reshut Harabim but rather as a "Karmelit." A Karmelit may be enclosed for Eruv purposes by a symbolic doorway, known as a Tzurat Hapetach rather than by real doors capable of being locked at night. Most streets as we know them are classified as Karmelit because they do not meet the requirements of a Reshut Harabim. See Shulchan Aruch, Orach Chaim 303:18. See also Rabbi Yosef Gavriel Bechhofer, The Contemporary Eruv, page 2 Note 2. For a very broad definition of a public street that qualifies as a Karmelit, see Rambam, Hilchot Shabbat 17:3 and the Magid Mishnah thereon.

4. Rambam, Hilchot Eruvin 1:7; See Joseph Shechter, A Lexicon of the Talmud who trans lates the term "מבוי" as "רחוב." See also Rabbi Yosef Gavriel Bechhofer, The Contemporary Eruv, Introduction, p.1 - "Mavoi = alley or street"; Shulchan Aruch, Orach Chaim 386:1.

5. Rambam, Hilchot Eruvin 1:2 and Shulchan Aruch 366:1, and Mishnah Berurah 2 thereon.

6. See notes 4 and 5.

7. Shulchan Aruch, Orach Chaim 366:3 and Rema 387:1; Rambam, Hilchot Eruvin 1:19; See Shulchan Aruch Harav, Orach Chaim 387:1 "אין נהגים עכשיו לעשות עירובי חצרות לפי שסומכין על השיתוף שבבית הכנסת הנעשה מפת שמועיל גם לחצרות"
See also Jacob Yeshayahu Blau, Netivot Shabbat 30:4.

8. Mishnah Berurah 3 to Shulchan Aruch, Orach Chaim 366:1.

9. Shulchan Aruch, Orach Chaim 366:9.

10. Kiddushin 42a.

11. Jacob Yeshayahu Blau, Netivot Shabbat 31:35 Note 86.

12. Shulchan Aruch, Orach Chaim 366:14, and Mishnah Berurah 79 thereon, אם מניח ערובי תבשילין
וערובי חצרות בזמן אחד מברך ברכה אחת על שתיהן דהיינו על מצות ערובין.

13. Shulchan Aruch, Orach Chaim 368:5, and Rema thereon. But see also Mishnah Berurah 21.

14. Ibid. 380:1.

15. Ibid. 385:1 and Mishnah Berurah 1 thereon.

16. Ibid. 382:1. How and with whom these transactions are effected, see, "Eruvin, Dissenters and Protesters," below.

ERUVIN, DISSENTERS AND PROTESTERS
שכירת רשות

1. For further explanation, see "Searching for a Communal Home," above.
2. Shulchan Aruch, Orach Chaim 366:3.
3. Ibid. 382:1.
4. Ibid. 382:4.
5. Ibid. 391:1.
6. Responsa Chazon Ish, Orach Chaim Siman 82:9. See also Yaacov Yeshayahu Blau, Netivot Shabbat 37:26.
7. Rabbi Yosef Gabriel Bechhofer, The Contemporary Eruv, Chapter V.
8. Shulchan Aruch, Orach Chaim 380:1.
9. Responsa Rav Menachem Kasher, Tikun Eruvin Be-Manhattan, Divrei Menachem Al Shulchan Aruch, Orach Chaim, Siman 19, p.97.

THE RIVERDALE ERUV
גוד אסיק מחיצתא

1. Carrying, Eruvin and Manhattan, above.
2. Succah 4b.

ERUVEI TECHUMIM, SHIPS, PLANES AND MOSCHIACH
תחום שבת וערובי תחומין
(ערובין מג·)

1. Exodus 16:29.
2. Rambam, Hilchot Shabbat 27:1.
3. Numbers 35:4.
4. Rambam, Hilchot Eruvin 8:4.
5. Jacob Yeshayahu Blau, Sefer Netivot Shabbat 41:3.
6. Shulchan Aruch, Orach Chaim 398:11, and Mishnah Berurah 55 thereon.
7. Ibid. 398:10.
8. Ibid. 398:5.
9. Tur, Hilchot Shabbat 408.
10. Shulchan Aruch, Orach Chaim 409:7.
11. Eruvin 43a.
12. Eruvin 43b.
13. Shulchan Aruch, Orach Chaim 404, Rema.
14. Yaacov Yeshayahu Blau, Netivot Shabbat 45:15, Note 50.

Chapter Three

Pesach

SEARCHING FOR CHAMETZ ON EREV PESACH
WITH CANDLES, FLASHLIGHTS AND BREAD
בדיקת חמץ ובטולו

The Torah commands us to remove leavened bread - חמץ - Chametz, on Erev Pesach[1] in order to ensure that Chametz will neither be seen[2] nor found[3] on our premises during Pesach. The removal of Chametz is achieved either by renouncing one's ownership over it, - ביטול - Bitul, or by physically destroying it, - ביעור - Biyur.[4] The Rabbis established a procedure which combines both Bitul and Biyur.

Bitul Chametz is performed on the evening of the fourteenth day of Nissan.[5] The ceremony of Bitul Chametz commences with the searching for Chametz known as - בדיקת חמץ - Bedikat Chametz.[6] This is done by the head of the family upon his or her return from work[7] by means of a candle which can reach dark recesses of the house.[8] Before searching, the Blessing - על ביעור חמץ - "Al Biur Chametz" is recited.[9] After searching, the - כל חמירא - Kol Chamira declaration is recited, the effect of which is to nullify any Chametz which one may have missed.[10] During the fifth Halachic hour, on the morning of the fourteenth of Nissan,[11] Biur Chametz is performed by burning all Chametz in one's possession that one does not intend to sell to a non-Jew, including the Chametz recovered in the search the night before.

Because Pesach cleaning will probably have removed all Chametz before Bedikat Chametz begins, the Rabbis were concerned that the reciting of the blessing על ביעור חמץ might be a wasted blessing, a Beracha Levatalah, were no Chametz to be found in the search. Therefore, some Rabbis, including the Rema,[12] recommend strategically placing ten pieces of Chametz in various corners of the house before commencing the search. Others criticize this practice because one may forget where one placed them, or one may focus on retrieving them rather than looking for genuinely misplaced Chametz.[13] The practice has, however, survived the criticism and is generally accepted.[14] If one forgets where one has placed a piece of Chametz, it is not of grave concern, since the recital of Kol Chamira has a nullifying effect.[15]

The Acharonim discuss whether a flashlight, instead of a candle flame, may be used for Bedikat Chametz. According to some authorities,[16] a flashlight is prohibited because its broad light beam resembles a flaming torch - אבוקה - Avukah which, like the Havdalah candle, was made of several parallel wicks. The Talmud in Pesachim[17] expressly prohibits the use of the Avukah for Bedikat Chametz. Furthermore, such authorities argue that the light from the bulb streaming through the glass of the flashlight is like sunlight streaming through a window pane, the light of which may not be used for Bedikat Chametz.[18] Additionally, they contend that a flame is required for Bedikat Chametz and an electric light or a battery produced light is not a flame.[19]

Others, such as Rabbi Ovadia Yosef[20] and the Shaarim Hametzuyanim Behalachah,[21] quote authorities that permit the use of an electric light or a flashlight not only for Bedikat Chametz, but also for the lighting of Shabbat candles. These authorities argue that an electric light and a flashlight do not resemble the Avukah and that turning them on and off on Shabbat is Biblically prohibited under the Av Melachah of kindling and extinguishing fire. That being so, such sources of light can also be used for the above described purposes, including Bedikat Chametz. Indeed, it is told that Rav Chaim Soloveitchik would make Havdalah with an electric light.

CATCH 22: WHEN EREV PESACH
IS ON SHABBAT
ערב פסח שחל להיות בשבת

On Shabbat one should eat three meals. The Friday night and the Shabbat morning meals require Kiddush with wine and two Challot, Lechem Mishneh, and the third meal, the Se'udah Shlishit, requires Lechem Mishneh.[1] The correct time for Seudah Shlishit is the afternoon.[2] But it is Shabbat Erev Pesach and no Chametz may be eaten after the fourth Halachic hour of the day. No problem. Let's use Matzah for Seudah Shlishit. But that cannot be done either, because one may not eat Kosher LePesach Matzah on Erev Pesach[3] and, though it is Shabbat, it is also Erev Pesach. So if you cannot use Challot or Matzah for Seudah Shlishit, what should you do?

It depends. If you are Ashkenazi, you have the following options. You may eat the Seudah Shlishit meal in the morning before the fourth Halachic hour of the day with Challot for Lechem Mishnah. And this is the way some Poskim[4] recommend it should be done. First you make Kiddush and Netilat Yadayim for the Shabbat morning meal and eat a Kezayit amount of Challah. Then you immediately recite Birkat Hamazon, Grace after meals. After a short break of about a quarter of an hour (if you are pressed for time, right after Birkat Hamazon) you wash your hands again for Seudah Shlishit, finish all of the bread and recite Birkat Hamazon again. Alternatively, Seudah Shlishit can be made in the afternoon with no bread and a small amount of cooked food or fruit. According to Rabbi Avigdor Nebenzahl of Jerusalem,[5] one should do both, in order to satisfy the opinions of the authorities, (Sefer Yereim) who maintain that Seudah Shlishit with Lechem Mishnah is a Torah requirement, and the authorities (Shulchan Aruch) who maintain that Seudah Shlishit must be eaten in the afternoon. In either case, the following procedures are recommended. The Shabbat meals, except for the Challot, and all utensils with which they are prepared, should be Kosher LePesach. Small Challot rolls or pita bread should be used for Lechem Mishneh because they can be entirely consumed. The Challot should be kept under wraps, separate from the rest of the Kosher LePesach surroundings. At the Shabbat morning meal(s), a separate disposable tablecloth should be used together with disposable plates and tableware for the Challah. As soon as Kiddush and Lechem Mishneh for the Shabbat morning meal(s) are completed as described, the disposable tablecloth and plates should be discarded, one should remove the crumbs from one's clothes, rinse one's mouth and sweep the floor. Then, one spreads a new Pesach tablecloth, sets the table with Kosher LePesach tableware and continues with the Kosher LePesach meal. If one wishes to eat other Chametz food with the Challot, such food should be treated the same way as the Challot. Rabbi Nebenzahl[6] suggests that, in public places, such as hotels or hospitals, where there is a danger that people who are unaware of the Halachot may inadvertently violate the laws of Pesach, the following procedure may be adopted. Instead of Challot, Kosher LePesach Matzot may be used for all three meals, in the following way. On Friday night, one may wash and say Birkat Hamazon three times, in the way described above, thereby fulfilling the Mitzvah of the three meals all on Friday night.

If you are Sephardi and follow the ruling of the Mechaber, which requires Seudah Shlishit to be eaten on Shabbat afternoon, the following alternatives are available. Egg Matzah may be used for Lechem Mishneh, provided that this is done before 2:30 p.m, so that Kosher LePesach Matzah will be eaten with appetite at the Seder. Alternatively, one may cook Kosher LePesach Matzah in Kosher LePesach soup before Shabbat and when it has cooled off on Shabbat, one lifts it out of the pot and uses it for Lechem Mishneh.[7]

Shacharit is recited early and expeditiously, so that all Chametz can be eaten by the fourth Halachic hour of the day. Other differences to keep in mind when Erev Pesach is on Shabbat are as follows. Bedikat Chametz, searching for the Chametz, and Bitul Chametz, nullifying the Chametz by reciting Kol Chamirah, are preformed on the night preceding the thirteenth day of Nissan. Biyur Chametz, burning the Chametz, is performed without reciting Kol Chamirah on Friday, the thirteenth day of Nissan, before noon. Any Chametz to be used for Shabbat should be kept separate, and, if possible, Rabbi Nebenzahl suggests it be kept together with the Chametz sold for Pesach. After the Shabbat morning meal(s) are eaten and the remnants of the Chametz are discarded, but not later than the fifth Halachic hour of the day, the Chametz is again nullified by the recital of Kol Chamirah.[8] Seder preparations should be completed before Shabbat. These include roasting the Shank Bone and egg, mixing the salt water, making the Charoset, grating the horseradish and checking the lettuce for insects (Rav Dovid Feinstein). In view of the fact that one may not prepare on Shabbat for Yom Tov, the Seder table should be set after Shabbat ends. Because of the differing opinions in many of these matters, please consult a Rabbi.

KORBAN PESACH
קרבן פסח

We popularly refer to the eight day period from the fifteenth through the twenty second of Nissan as the festival of - פסח - Pesach. The Torah, however,[1] calls this period - חג המצות - Chag Hamatzot, during which time we eat Matzot and abstain from eating Chametz.

Pesach is an entirely different festival celebrated on a different day. Pesach, according to the Torah, is celebrated on the fourteenth of Nissan, the day we call Erev Pesach, and lasts until midnight of that day. Pesach is the day when all of Israel was busy sacrificing the Paschal Lamb.[2] So crucial was the requirement to sacrifice the Paschal Lamb on Pesach that the penalty for anyone failing to do so was premature death at the hand of God - Karet.[3] The Paschal Lamb was expensive to purchase and difficult to find. It had to be a male goat or sheep, not more than one year old.[4] Several days before Pesach, the Jews formed themselves into groups.[5] Each group purchased a Paschal Lamb. The number of people constituting a group was the same number it would take to consume the Lamb, with each person eating a portion no larger than the size of an olive.[6] The group then appointed one of its members to walk the lamb, on the fourteenth of Nissan, to the Temple Courtyard, in Jerusalem.[7] On the way, the member would meet up with a multitude of other group members, all walking their lambs to Jerusalem. According to one eye witness, the hills of Jerusalem were covered that day with a white, moving, woollen blanket. Because the Temple Courtyard was too small to accommodate all the group members and their Paschal lambs at the same time, the sacrificial service was conducted in three shifts.[8] The Paschal Lamb could not be slaughtered until after midday[9] and not before all Chametz was cleared away.[10] All Paschal Lambs had to be sacrificed before nightfall. The slaughtering of the lambs, but not the rest of the sacrificial service, could be performed by the group members themselves, even if not - כהנים - Kohanim, priests.[11] The Kohanim, holding silver and golden vessels, stood in neat rows, stretching all the way from the animals to the Altar. These vessels, which were used to capture the animals' blood, were handed from Kohen to Kohen, conveyer belt style, until they reached the Altar, on which they were then poured.[12] The sacrificial parts of the animal were then burnt on the Altar.[13] During the entire sacrificial service, trumpets were sounded and Hallel was recited.[14] Those parts of the animal that were not burnt on the Altar, that is, the vast majority of the animal, were then carried back home to the group, now seated around the Seder table.[15] The Torah sets forth explicit instructions as to when and how the Paschal lamb must be eaten.[16] "Eat the [sacrificial] meat during the [Seder] night, roasted over fire. Eat it with Matzah and bitter herbs... Do not leave any of it over until morning." In addition, the Paschal Lamb could only be eaten after the group members had first satisfied their hunger with the meat of the regular festival offering, the Korban Chagigah.[17] The

Paschal Lamb could not, according to most opinions, be eaten after midnight.

According to the Ramban, sacrificing the Paschal Lamb was an act of defiance against the Egyptians, who deified sheep. Rabbi Samson Raphael Hirsch[18] views the Paschal Lamb sacrifice as an antidote to the scene of the Brit Bein Habetarim. In that scene, the bull, the goat and the ram, symbolizing Jewish sovereignty, wealth and resistance, respectively, were torn asunder, presaging three generations of slavery in Egypt. After the liberation, human dignity, family and social life were restored to the liberated slaves through the Paschal Lamb. The Paschal Lamb of each Jew, as an individual, in his own right, was accepted by God and was enjoyed in the setting of family and friends.

Since the destruction of the Temple, Korbanot exist only in the prayer book. This does not apply to the Korban Pesach. It provides the structure for and is the centerpiece of the Seder night. Chametz must be cleared out by midday, the time the Korban Pesach would have been brought. We are required to place a bone on the Seder plate and to eat the Afikoman in lieu of the Korban Pesach. Like the Korban Pesach, the Afikoman has to be eaten after the meal, before midnight. Finally, the Maror sandwich, eaten between two Matzot, replaces the Korban Pesach which was eaten with Matzah and Maror. Seder night, then, is the meeting point of Chag HaPesach and Chag Hamatzot.

KASHERING
הכשר כלים - עקרונות

Taste is everything - טעם כעיקר - Ta'am Ke'ikar. The taste of forbidden food is treated in Halachah as the forbidden food itself and is equally forbidden.[1] If the taste of Chametz has been absorbed into a cooking vessel, such a vessel may not be used on Pesach, unless it undergoes a process called - הכשר - or - הגעלת כלים - Hagalat Kelim - popularly referred to as Kashering. Kashering is the Halachically prescribed way of expelling the flavor of forbidden food, such as non-Kosher foods, meat and milk mixtures, or Chametz on Pesach from utensils and restoring them for use.[2] The manner in which the utensil absorbs the forbidden flavor is the manner in which it must be Kashered - כבולעו כך פולטו - Kebolo Kach Polto[3] or in the words of the Torah, "Whatever was used over fire must be passed through fire and purged, however, that which was not used in fire need only be immersed in water."[4] Accordingly, utensils that have absorbed forbidden flavors while in direct contact with fire, such as spits, barbecue grills and baking tins, must be Kashered by direct contact with fire, until they become red hot. This process, which is the most powerful form of Kashering, is known as - ליבון - Libun. If such heat would ruin the utensil, then, if certain conditions are fulfilled, it can be heated to a temperature hot enough to ignite straw if it were placed on the heated utensil.[5] This process is known as ליבון קל - Libun Kal.

Utensils that have absorbed forbidden flavors through water in which forbidden foods were cooked must be Kashered by immersing them in a larger vessel, such as a cauldron containing boiling water.[6] Before immersing them in the cauldron, all surface dirt, or dirt residing in folds, dents or crevices must be removed.[7] They must remain immersed in the cauldron until the hot water bubbles over them,[8] then taken out and rinsed with cold water.[9] This process of Kashering is known as - הגעלה - Hagalah. In order to prevent the utensil, which is placed in the boiling cauldron, from reabsorbing the forbidden flavor from the boiling water into which it is immersed, it is advisable to either Kasher only such utensils that have not been used for 24 hours, or to immerse them into an amount of water equal to sixty times their own volume.[10] Of course, the cauldron containing boiling water, into which the utensils are immersed, must itself have been Kashered. Since utensils used to cook non-Kosher food within the last 24 hours are prohibited for use by the Torah, the custom is to Kasher, by means of Hagalah, only vessels which have not been used for the past 24 hours. Utensils which are too large to fit into the cauldron may be Kashered by filling them to the brim with water, heating them to boiling point and then casting in a red hot stone or piece of metal, so that the boiling water flows over the rim.[11] Handles of utensils must be included in the Kashering process.[12] Plastic handles, which would be ruined if immersed in seething water, or by direct contact with fire, (unless they had originally absorbed their forbidden flavor through immersion in boiling water) can be Kashered by pouring boiling water over them,[13] a process known as עירוי -"Irui," described below. Detachable handles should be removed and cleaned before Kashering.[14] Lids of utensils should be included in the Hagalah process.[15]

A vessel into which Chametz was poured from a pot on the fire, but was never directly on the flame itself, such as a cereal bowl, or a spoon used to stir the cereal in such bowl, is known as a - כלי שני - Keli Sheni. A Keli Sheni can be Kashered by pouring boiling water over it, from the vessel which was directly on the fire, the כלי ראשון, without actually immersing it in the boiling cauldron.[16] This process is - עירוי - Irui.

Vessels that were used for cold foods or liquids are Kashered by simply cleaning them out and washing them,[17] a process known as - שטיפה - Shetifah.

The Kashering method can always be stepped up but can never be stepped down.[18] Accordingly, as an alternative method to Hagalah, one could Kasher silverware or pots and pans through the process of Libun Kal, by heating them with a blowtorch to a temperature hot enough to ignite straw if it were placed on the heated surface.

Similarly, as an alternative to Irui, one could Kasher a Keli Sheni by means of Hagalah. One may not, however, substitute Libun with Hagalah. Accordingly, one cannot Kasher a spit or barbecue grill, or anything else that absorbed the forbidden flavor directly through fire, by the process of Hagalah. Neither is it effective to substitute Hagalah with Irui. Therefore, the process of Irui cannot be used to Kasher a vessel that absorbed the forbidden flavor through water, in which the forbidden food was cooked. In practice, Hagalah is also used for a Keli Sheni, unless the utensil would be destroyed or damaged by the heat.

KASHER MY KITCHEN
הכשר כלים - היבטים מעשיים

With the principles of Kashering as explained in the previous chapter in mind, what can we Kasher in the kitchen?

Utensils made of metal, stone,[1] wood, marble,[2] gold, silver, copper, lead,[3] aluminum, steel, stainless steel[4] and leather[5] can all be Kashered in the manner in which they absorbed the forbidden flavor.

Earthenware, china, porcelain or enamel utensils used hot cannot be Kashered at all.[6]

Glass is controversial. According to one opinion,[7] glass does not have to be Kashered at all, because its surface is so smooth that it cannot absorb any flavor. Another opinion maintains exactly the opposite.[8] Glass cannot be Kashered or used at all on Pesach because it is made of sand and is Halachically considered earthenware.[9] There is also a third opinion[10] that maintains that glass has the Halachic status of metal and can be Kashered. According to this third opinion, how does one Kasher glass without breaking it? If the glass never contained hot liquids, it can be Kashered by simply cleaning and rinsing it - שטיפה - Shetifah.[11] If it was only occasionally used for hot liquids, there is a Halachic debate as to whether it can be Kashered. According to the Shulchan Aruch, if it was mostly used for cold liquids, it can be Kashered with Shetifah.[12] According to the Remah, however, if it was occasionally used for hot liquids, it must undergo Hagalah and if Hagalah would destroy it, it cannot be Kashered at all.[13] Accordingly, many Ashkenazi families buy new glassware for Pesach. Others have the custom to Kasher glass by the process known as - מילוי ועירוי - Milui Ve'irui.[14] This process requires the glassware to be entirely immersed in cold water for 72 hours, provided that the water is changed every 24 hours.[15]

Plastic and nylon materials are the subjects of Halachic debate. According to Rav Moshe Feinstein,[16] synthetic materials made of chemical mixtures, such as plastic and nylon, cannot be Kashered for Pesach. According to other opinions,[17] plastic or nylon vessels may be Kashered. This can be done either by the process of Hagalah, or, if this will damage the vessel, it can be done by the dual process of immersing them in a cauldron of hot water that has been removed from the fire followed by the procedure of Milui Veirui.

Pyrex, Duralex and Corningware cannot be Kashered, according to Rav Moshe Feinstein.[18] Others permit the Kashering of pyrex and other heat-resistant glass utensils by the process of Hagalah if used for hot food and by the process of Milui Veirui if used for cold food.[19]

Tables and other wooden surfaces on which fobidden food may have been placed are Kashered as follows. First, the surfaces are thoroughly cleaned, paying special attention to cracks and crevices, left for 24 hours, and then boiling water is poured over them. Veneer or polished wooden surfaces, which would be ruined by boiling water, can only be used if cleaned and then covered. Dishwashers that are lined with plastic walls cannot be Kashered, according to Rav Moshe Feinstein.[20] According to other opinions,[21] a plastic lined dishwasher can be Kashered in the following way. First it must be thoroughly scrubbed. Then it should not be used for 24 hours. Then, the dishwasher should be turned on to allow boiling water to spray inside. Dishwashers lined with porcelain or enamel cannot be Kashered.[22]

Gas or electric ovens can be Kashered with a blow torch using the process of Libun and, according to some Poskim, even by Libun Kal.[23] Another way to Kasher a gas oven is first to thoroughly clean it, leave it for 24 hours, and then turn it on to maximum temperature for an hour. According to Rav Moshe, such ovens can be Kashered by running them through the self-cleaning cycle.[24] The tops of ovens should likewise be thoroughly cleaned, the burners should be turned on and boiling water should be poured on the surface top.

Microwave ovens can be Kashered. They should be thoroughly cleaned and not used for 24 hours. Then a bowl of water should be placed inside. The microwave oven should then be turned on until the inside is filled with steam.[25]

Mixers used for mixing dough or other Chametz can generally not be Kashered, because it is almost impossible to remove the Chametz particles trapped in the machine.[26] Blenders that can be dismantled should be thoroughly cleaned, their metal parts immersed in boiling water, and their bowls should be Kashered through Milui Ve'irui.[27] Coffee perculators, to the extent that they can be thoroughly cleaned of all Chametz particles, can be Kashered by boiling water inside them.[28] Rabbi Shimon Eider, however, writes that they should not be Kashered, because it is impossible to clean out all Chametz particles.[29] According to most opinions,[30] whisky glasses cannot be Kashered because they retain the smell and flavor of whisky. The Aruch Hashulchan, however,[31] rules that they can be Kashered by Milui Ve'irui.

In view of the fact that there are so many conflicting opinions in this area of Halachah, in case of doubt, a Rabbi should be consulted.

TOVELING
טבילת כלים

"You must sanctify yourselves and be holy," the Torah tells us, "for I, the Lord your God, am holy."[1] The service of God in our lives should simulate the service of God in the Temple. Just as the - Kohen - Priest, was required to enter God's Temple in a state of Taharah, - spiritual cleanliness - we are required to enter God's world in a state of Taharah. Natural water gathered in a Mikveh is our spiritual purifying agent. That is why the Torah asks of the woman, God's partner in the creation of the human being, to spiritually purify herself before conceiving a child. The convert, who has not been born to a Jewish mother, must be purified in a Mikveh before becoming Jewish. Following the destruction of the Temple, the Jewish table replaced the altar. Not only the food offered on the table, but the serving utensils, as well, must be pure. Accordingly, utensils owned by a non-Jew, like the non -Jew himself, must be consecrated by immersion in the Mikveh before entering the Jewish world.[2] The process of consecration of utensils owned by non-Jews is known as - טבילת כלים - Tevilat Keilim, and is colloquially referred to as "Toveling." The Scriptural source for Tevilat Keilim is the prohibition for the Israelite soldiers, upon returning from war carrying the spoils of Midian, against using Midianite eating utensils without first Kashering and Toveling them.[3]

Eating and drinking utensils, and utensils used in the preparation of food that are made of metal or glass, which come into direct contact with food, such as cups, plates, silverware, pots and pans, (but not coasters, knife sharpeners or other utensils, which have only indirect contact with food) and which were manufactured by, or acquired from a non-Jew, require Tevilah before they can be used by a Jew.[4] Wooden,[5] earthen[6] (if unglazed), bone, and paper utensils,[7] as well as disposable eating utensils,[8] including aluminium foil and baking tins,[9] are exempt from Tevilah. The Blessing - על טבילת כלי/כלים - Al Tevilat Keli/Keilim, is recited immediately before Toveling utensils made of metal or glass.[10] All Jewish persons, men, women and children, may Tovel with a Blessing.[11] Utensils with which food is prepared, or utensils in which food is stored but not eaten, such as a meat grinder, a potato peeler, a slaughterer's knife, or a sugar container, are immersed without the Blessing, unless immersed together with other utensils which require the Blessing.[12] Whether plastic or nylon utensils require Tevilah is debatable. Some authorities[13] suggest that they require Tevilah without a Blessing, while others rule that they require no Tevilah at all.[14] Eating utensils, which would require Tevilah if acquired from a non-Jew, are exempt from Tevilah, if the non-Jew retains ownership over them, such as, where the Jew rents or borrows them.[15] Accordingly, if one finds oneself in a place with no Toveling facilities, one may, as a temporary solution, use utensils, even without Tevilah, by employing the following device. One may give the utensils to a non-Jew as a gift, thereby transferring ownership to him, and then borrow them back. If no other eating utensils are available, this device may also be employed on Shabbat or Yom Tov, on which days it is forbidden to Tovel utensils.[16]

All dirt and adhesive labels (other than brand name labels, that would ordinarily be considered part of the utensil[17]) must be removed before Tevilah, so as to ensure 100% water contact on all inner and outer surfaces.[18] For the same reason, the utensil should be lowered into the water in a perforated container or, if hand-dipped, should be held with a loose grip.[19] An electric appliance, such as a coffee percolator or an electric toaster, acquired from or manufactured by a non-Jew, which would be damaged by Tevilah, can be dealt with as follows. One may ask a Jewish electrician to dismantle the appliance into its separate parts to the point where it loses its original identity and then to reassemble it. The appliance is then considered to be manufactured by a Jew and no longer requires Tevilah.[20] Alternatively, one can give it as a gift and borrow it back from a non-Jew in the way already described.[21] Tevilat Keilim may also be performed in the sea or in a river so long as the river contains the minimum amount of water required for a Kosher Mikveh.[22] In the absence of other facilities, glass utensils (but not metal utensils) may be Toveled in snow.[23]

Although Kashering and Toveling are sometimes required for the same utensil, they are fundamentally different procedures, serving different purposes. Kashering is the process required to expel the flavor of forbidden foods from the utensil's surfaces and is, therefore, inapplicable to a utensil which has never been used.[24] Toveling is required for a utensil (even unused) if manufactured by, or acquired from, a non-Jew. A utensil manufactured and used by a non-Jew, or used by a non-Jew and purchased by a Jew, requires both Kashering and Toveling.

PESACH MEDICATION AND ALCOHOL
חמץ, הגדרתו וסוגיו השונים

What is - חמץ - Chametz? What are the various categories of Chametz? Does the prohibition of Chametz on Pesach apply also to non-food products? Can medication containing Chametz be taken on Pesach? Can vitamins produced with no Pesach supervision be used? What about liquid medicine such as cough mixture? Can non-supervised body soap or liquid detergent be used? What about toothpaste? May one use rubbing alcohol? May one eat egg Matzah?

There are five types of grain which can become Chametz. They are wheat, spelt, barley, oats and rye.[1] They are prohibited on Pesach if they have come into contact with water for a prescribed period of time after they have been cut off from the ground. Matzah is made of flour and water mixed together for a period of time not long enough to permit the fermentation process to begin. There are three opinions as to how long it takes for such fermentation to begin. According to the Shulchan Aruch, fermentation sets in after 18 minutes;[2] according to Rashi,[3] after 22.5 minutes; and according to the Rambam,[4] after 24 minutes. All agree however, that if the mixture of flour and water become heated, fermentation may happen sooner, even immediately.[5] Accordingly, in order to avoid fermentation, the Matzah baking process must be rapid.

The prohibition of Chametz on Pesach means that Chametz may not be eaten[6] or enjoyed, may not be owned or possessed[7] and must be removed from one's premises.[8] The Biblical prohibition applies to pure Chametz - חמץ בעיין - Chametz Beayin,[9] as well as to mixtures which contain pure Chametz. There is another type of Chametz which the Rabbis forbid one to eat or possess on Pesach called - חמץ נוקשה - Chametz Nuksheh. Chametz Nuksheh includes spoiled or decomposed Chametz, which can only be eaten with difficulty and is not normally eaten at all.[10] An example would be bookbinder's paste, made of flour and water. Chametz Nuksheh also includes mixtures of five grains and moisture, where the fermentation process began but was not completed. An example of this type of Chametz Nuksheh is flour mixed with fruit juice and water, because it will never completely ferment. Included also in the category of Chametz Nuksheh is egg Matzah. That is why the Rema[11] prohibits, except in extenuating circumstances, such as sickness or old age, the consumption of egg Matzah on Pesach, because it is baked from dough made from flour, fruit juice and water.

There is yet another type of Chametz to which the Chametz prohibition does not apply, namely, Chametz that was unsuitable for human consumption before Pesach. Examples would include Chametz that was so burned or became so moldy before Pesach that even a dog would not eat it - נפסל מאכילת כלב - Nifsal Me'achilat Kelev.[12] May a person who wants to eat Chametz which everybody else finds inedible do so? According to the Rosh, he may not, because by eating it, he demonstrates - אחשביה - Achshevei, that it is, indeed, edible and, therefore, it is prohibited Chametz.[13]

According to many Poskim, including Rabbi Moshe Feinstein[14] and Rabbi Ovadia Yosef,[15] one may take medicine on Pesach to alleviate pain suffered by the whole body, even if it contains Chametz, because it is Nifsal Me'achilat Kelev. The principal of Achshevei does not apply here, because a person does not take medicine for food, but rather, for relief. Coated tablets need to be analyzed before they can be taken. If the coating is made of legumes, - קטניות - Kitniyot, as is often the case with dextrose and certain types of starch, they may be used. Many Poskin permit the sick to take medication in gelatin capsules.[16] For the same reason, unsweetened vitamin tablets can be eaten without having been supervised for Pesach.[17] Liquid medicine, such as cough medicine, is more problematic, because it may contain grain alcohol which is pure Chametz.[18] Isopropyl alcohol, such as rubbing alcohol, may be used on Pesach, because it is derived from petroleum and not from grain.[19] Ethyl alcohol is more problematic, because it is derived from the fermentation of starch and carbohydrates and may be made from the five grains.[20] Many Poskim rule that there is no problem using creams and ointments which contain grain alcohol. Of course, in life-threatening situations, all medicines may be used and, in any event, a Rabbi should always be consulted.[21] According to Rabbi Feinstein, although toothpaste is Nifsal Me'achilat Kelev and is, therefore, not prohibited on Pesach, nevertheless, one should use Kosher LePesach toothpaste, if available.[22] Similarly, body soap may be used, even if it contains Chametz.[23] Liquid dishwashing soap should, however, be approved for Pesach use.[24]

KOSHER LEPESACH LIGHT BULBS
תערובת חמץ

You are standing in front of the Kosher LePesach shelves in Pathmark, looking for the Kosher LePesach stamp of approval on the Coca Cola bottle. Your friend is frowning at the cap on the seltzer bottle, trying to decipher the Kosher LePesach stamp. The Glatt shop is closed and the Maxwell House coffee in the supermarket has no Kosher LePesach stamp. Your son, who is back from Yeshiva, in Israel, refuses to take home table salt without a Kosher LePesach stamp, and somebody told you that paper plates have starch. Short of hiring an escort Mashgiach, what do you do?

A few background principles regarding the prohibitions of Chametz mixtures on Pesach might provide some shopping guidance.

During the rest of the year, when forbidden food gets mixed up with permitted food, the mixture may be eaten if the ratio of the permitted food to the forbidden food is a certain prescribed amount and certain other conditions are met. Thus, if a piece of cold non-Kosher meat got mixed up with two cold pieces of Kosher meat, all three pieces may be eaten, provided they are not cooked together.[1] This permission is based on the Halachic principal, according to which the majority nullifies the minority - ביטול ברוב - Bitul Berov. Accordingly, it may be presumed that each piece of meat consumed belonged to the Kosher majority. If the non-Kosher piece of meat were cooked in a pot containing Kosher meat, and the ratio of the Kosher meat to the non-Kosher meat were 60:1 - בטל בשישים - Batel Beshishim, the whole mixture, including the non-Kosher meat, may be eaten.[2]

These permitting ratios do not apply, however, to Chametz on Pesach. If Chametz became mixed with non-Chametz **on** Pesach, the mixture is prohibited on Pesach even if the ratio of the permitted non-Chametz to the forbidden Chametz is 1000 to 1.[3] This applies both to foods that blend together - לח בלח - Lach BeLach, such as Chametz flour and Pesach flour, and foods that do not blend together - יבש ביבש - Yavesh Beyavesh, such as a piece of Kosher LePesach Matzah with a piece of non-Kosher LePesach Matzah. According to Rashi,[4] the reason for this stringency on Pesach, as opposed to the rest of the year, is twofold. First, the punishment for eating Chametz on Pesach is premature death at the Hand of God - כרת - Karet. Second, since the prohibition of Chametz exists for only seven days a year, one might come to forget about it - לא בדילי מיניה - Lo Bedilay Minay. The combination of the severity of the punishment and the ease with which the prohibition may be forgotten require that the smallest amount of Chametz - חמץ במשהוא - Chametz Bemashehu, be prohibited. According to the Rambam,[5] the reason for the stringency on Pesach is that the Chametz prohibition is a temporary prohibition - דבר שיש לו מתירין - Davar She'yesh Lo Matirin - because it lasts for only seven days. So, why eat even the minutest amount of Chametz on Pesach, when one can wait until after Pesach and eat it without any concern? A temporary prohibition cannot be nullified, irrespective of how high the ratio of the permitted food is to the forbidden food. A practical difference between Rashi's explanation and the Rambam's explanation is the case of spoiled or decomposed Chametz - חמץ נוקשה - Chametz Nuksheh. Although prohibited on Pesach, Chametz Nuksheh does not incur the punishment of Karet. According to Rashi, therefore, it could be Batel Beshishim, but according to Rambam, it could not.[6]

Certain combinations of Chametz and non-Chametz mixed together **before** Pesach, however, could become Batel Beshishim. For example, according to most opinions,[7] beer mixed with wine **before** Pesach, or Pesach flour mixed with Chametz flour **before** Pesach, which are both cases of mixtures that blend together - לח בלח - Lach Belach, can be Batel Beshishim on Pesach. However, solids which do not blend together cannot be Batel Beshishim on Pesach, even if they were mixed before Pesach. The reason for this is that in the case of solids, which remain visibly identifiable on Pesach, the prohibition of Chametz in the smallest amount - חמץ במשהוא - is revived, חוזר וניעור - Chozer Veniur, on Pesach. In the case of liquids or foods that blend together, the Chametz part is neither visible nor identifiable in the mixture and, therefore, the prohibition of the smallest amount of Chametz - חמץ במשהוא - is not revived on Pesach.

With these principles in mind, let us go back to the supermarket. The following foods may be purchased **before** Pesach without the Kosher LePesach stamp. This is because the ratio of Chametz to non-Chametz found in them is likely to be less than 1:60. These foods are, among others, granulated sugar, non-iodized table salt, instant coffee, freeze dried coffee or percolator drip coffee, tea or tea bags, cocoa and milk. The following items require no Kosher LePesach stamp, even if purchased on Pesach: club soda, seltzer, fresh concentrated frozen juices, such as orange or grapefruit juice, fresh vegetables, plastic tablecloths, paper plates, aluminum foil, freezer paper, plastic spoons and forks, toothpicks, etc. The following items always require a Kosher LePesach stamp: canned and processed juices, fruit drinks, frozen fruits and frozen vegetables, brown sugar, sugar substitutes, spices and condiments, ketchup, mayonnaise, instant tea, cheese and rennet. This is because they either contain Chametz in unacceptable concentrations, or because they are processed with Chametz machinery. The Chametz they contain includes enzymes, alcohol, corn syrup, dextrose, vinegar, corn-starch, yeast, glycerin, vitamin D or microbial rennet. Fresh vegetables and fruit should be washed, because they may be sprayed with Chametz substances, such as oleic acid.[8]

CHAMETZ CREDIT CARD
מכירת חמץ

It's 1 p.m. on Wednesday afternoon, Erev Pesach. The Rabbi has already sold the Chametz at 11:19 a.m. But I forgot to sell mine. Now, the Synagogue office is closed and I cannot get hold of the form that the Rabbi uses to sell the Chametz. The Torah requires me to remove all Chametz from my house on Pesach. But I just cannot bring myself to throw out that Glenfiddich. Is there a way that the whisky may remain in my house during Pesach, and after Pesach I can drink it too?

The Torah prohibits the consumption and possession of Chametz by a Jew after the seventh hour on Erev Pesach, and the Rabbis prohibit the consumption after Pesach of Chametz possessed by a Jew during Pesach - חמץ שעבר עליו הפסח - Chametz Sheavar Alav Hapesach[1] In order to create a safety zone and avoid the inadvertent consumption of Chametz on Erev Pesach after noon, the Rabbis prohibit the eating of Chametz after the fourth Halachic[2] hour of the day.[3] Between the fourth and the fifth Halachic hour of the day, one may not eat Chametz, but one may still derive benefit from it or sell it to a non-Jew.[4] By the end of the fifth Halachic hour of the day,[5] the Chametz must be both burned - בעור חמץ - Biyur Chametz, and legally nullified - בטול חמץ - Bitul Chametz, by reciting the nullifying declaration known as Kol Chamirah.[6] At the same time, the sale of Chametz to a non-Jew takes effect.[7]

If the Chametz has already been legally nullified and physically burned so that it is neither owned nor possessed by a Jew, why is it necessary to sell it to a non-Jew? The answer is that the intent to nullify one's ownership may not have been sincere (that bottle of Glenfiddich) or one may have entertained the thought during the בטול - Bitul declaration to sell certain Chametz, rather than nullify it.[8] Futhermore, one may have neglected to destroy all one's Chametz, such as certain brands of deodorants and colognes etc.[9] So, if the Chametz is sold, why is it necessary to burn it? The answer is that there is a positive commandment to destroy Chametz - Hashbatah.[10] While it is unnecessary to incur severe financial loss by destroying all Chametz, a token amount of Chametz should be burned to fulfill the Mitzvah of Hashbatah.[11]

Are you kidding? You know that the non-Jew is not going to consume your Chametz. He is not really paying you for it and neither is he taking possession of it. He does not even know where it is. Even if he did, how is he going to gain access to your house on Pesach? And what happens if, after Pesach, he refuses to sell it back to you? If properly done, the sale of Chametz is, indeed, an effective sale.[12] Such a sale should cause as little skepticism on our part as other everyday, legal structures, such as the sale and lease back of machinery, where the equipment never leaves the premises of the purchaser and little money initially changes hands. The fact that the non-Jew chooses not to exercise his right of ownership does not mean that he does not have this right. Neither does it render the sale fictitious.

In fact, if the non-Jew paid the full value of the Chametz and refuses to transfer ownership of the Chametz back to the Jew after Pesach, there is no way, under Jewish law, that one can compel him to do so.[13] The sale is irrevocable, unless the non-Jew chooses to rescind it after Pesach. The origins of this sale can be found in the Tosefta.[14] A Jew and a non-Jew were traveling together on board a ship on a business trip. It was Erev Pesach and the Jew had Chametz in his possession. He did not want to throw it overboard, neither did he want to give it away. The Tosefta permits the Jew to sell it to the non-Jew with the intention in mind of buying it back after Pesach. As long as the transaction is not structured as a conditional sale, it works.[15] Later, the Rabbis of the Jewish whisky merchants of medieval Europe further refined the legal structure. Because the taking possession of the whisky by the non-Jew often resulted in damage, and because few non-Jews were able to afford the full purchase price, the Rabbis devised Halachic ways to leave the Chametz in the possession of the Jew during Pesach even after the sale and to effect the sale for a token up front payment.[16] "If you cannot remove the Chametz," said the Rabbis, "sell or rent the room or space in which the Chametz resides."[17] And based on the concept of a credit sale, already known to the Talmud sages,[18] they permitted a token payment to be made up front and the rest to be deferred as an IOU, to be repaid by the non-Jew after Pesach. Immediately after Havdalah on Motzaei Pesach, the Rabbi asks the non-Jew if he would agree to sell the Chametz back. If the non-Jew agrees, the deposit is returned to him and the loan becomes void. It is just the same as when you return the air conditioner to the store that you purchased it at, with minimum payment on your credit card.

Since the terms of the sale of Chametz are complicated, it is our practice to leave the transaction in the professional hands of the Rabbi by signing a power of attorney in his favor, just as one would authorize an attorney to sell one's house.[19] The power of attorney sets forth the basic details of the type, value and whereabouts of the Chametz and how it can be accessed during Pesach, and the Rabbi then sells the Chametz and the location in the house where the Chametz resides to the non-Jew, on your behalf. According to Rabbi Moshe Feinstein, if you cannot get to the Rabbi to sign, you can empower the Rabbi over the telephone.[20] Based on the principal of "Zachin Le'adam Shelo Befanav" (one Jew may perform a Mitzvah for another Jew, even without his consent), many Poskim rule that the power of attorney can cover all members of the community, even those who forgot to sign the power of attorney or to call the Rabbi before Pesach.[21]

If you are traveling to Israel for Pesach, and you did not sell your U.S.A. Chametz before you left, you should sell it in Israel before the fifth hour, Israeli time,[22] even though it is long before Pesach in the U.S.A. On Motzaei Pesach however, you should wait until Pesach is out, U.S.A. time, before buying it back.

PORK CHOPS AND SCHNITZEL
ריחא מילתא

Y ou are invited to a company outing in the country club on Labor Day. Your boss provides the Jewish staff with glatt Kosher schnitzels, sprinkled with onions. In the open kitchen, on the south lawn, there stands a large, ventilated, open, brick barbeque, topped with a roof and towering chimney. On the new, unused barbeque grate, the happy Chef tosses pork chops, sprinkled with parmesan cheese, for Chris, and schnitzel, sprinkled with onions, for Yankel. On the far side of the grate, some distance away from the meat, the Chef flips French toast for the vegetarians. And in New York melting pot style, the pork chops, schnitzel and French toast singe and sizzle on the same grate. They never touch each other and their juices never mix. But their aromas do. If you tell your boss that you don't eat meat, he'll point you to the French toast. You're stuck! What do you do?

Don't worry. It happened before. In the third century, at a party thrown at the estate of the Exilarch, the political leader of Babylonian Jewry. Bacon and Kosher brisket were barbequed in the same oven. Rav ruled, don't eat the brisket. Levi said "You may."[1] Their dispute comes down to the question of - ריחא מילתא - Reicha Milta. That is, whether or not the aroma of forbidden food lends taste to and contaminates permitted food.

The Halachah sides with Levi, who rules - ריחא לאו מילתא - Reicha Lav Milta.[2] That means, in general, aroma does not have the power to contaminate otherwise permitted food. And provided you do not intend to roast the permitted food with the forbidden food at the outset, but you are confronted with the situation, after the fact, you may eat the schnitzel, even though it smells of pork.[3] In fact, if the grill is sufficiently large[4] **and** entirely roofless,[5] or if the food items are covered over,[6] or if both pieces of meat are lean,[7] or if the items are cooked in utensils placed on the grate, rather than roasted directly on the grate,[8] one may, in each such case, prepare the permitted food in this way, even at the outset. But the onions? The onions ruin it! Even Levi admits that pungent foods absorb aromas so aggressively that they do have the power to become contaminated.[9] If, however, the schnitzel sprinkled with onions was placed in a pot with a lid, or wrapped around in aluminum foil, the schnitzel could be eaten even if the pot or foil was placed on the grill next to the pork chops.[10]

If, however, contrary to the case described above, the Chef roasted meat and baked plain bread, rather than French toast, on the same grate, one may eat the plain bread alone, even though it smells of pork and schnitzel. One may not, however, add butter to it. That is, because the addition of butter would be equivalent to initiating the mixture of aromas, which even Levi prohibits, rather than being confronted with it, after the fact.[11]

It should be noted, however, that the rule that aroma does not contaminate permitted food applies only when the aroma is conveyed through dry vapor. Where, however, aroma is conveyed through wet, hot steam, it does have the power to contaminate. Accordingly, one may not cook a dairy dish in a pot without the lid in the same closed oven as a meat dish, where the hot steam from the dairy dish rises and comes into contact with the meat dish.[12]

There is no intrinsic prohibition against eating meat and fish together. In the days of the Talmud, however, cooking fish and meat together was prohibited, on the grounds of being a health hazard, and this prohibition was later extended to eating.[13] In fact, due to the fact that the prohibition was rooted in health concerns, it had, in some respects, a stricter application than the mixing of Kosher and non-Kosher foods. Accordingly, some authorities maintain that meat and fish roasted together, in general, remain prohibited, even post-facto, after the fact,[14] whereas Kosher meat roasted together with non Kosher meat, in the circumstances described previously, would be permissible, after the fact. That is because the Rabbis, who are sometimes lenient in matters of Issur and Heter, (issues of forbidden or permitted food), are not prepared to take risks with matters of health, - חמירא סכנתא מאיסורא - Chamira Sakanta Me'issurah. The Magen Avraham, however, suggests that what was considered a health hazard there and then may not be relevant here and now.[15] Nevertheless, the practice of refraining from the simultaneous consumption, cooking or roasting of meat and fish together has prevailed and is accepted by many. Accordingly, the Rema requires that one eat something else, like a piece of bread, and drink after eating fish and before eating meat.[16]

MEAT AND MILK
בשר בחלב

If the Torah does not wish us to mix meat and milk, why not just say so? How, one may ask, are we to understand this from the thrice-repeated refrain of - לא תבשל גדי בחלב אמו - Lo Tevashel Gedi Bachalev Immo, "Thou shalt not boil a kid in its mother's milk."[1]

This question would not have been asked at the time the Torah was given, for it was usual, in ancient times, to boil young animals, especially young goats, in their mother's milk.[2] The Torah's carefully chosen words speak not only to cuisine of ancient time, but also to dietary laws for all time. First, the verse is repeated three times to tell us that it is forbidden (1) to boil meat and milk together - איסור בישול - Issur Bishul, (2) to eat such a mixture - איסור אכילה - Issur Achilah and (3) to derive any benefit from it - איסור הנאה - Issur Hana'ah.[3] The word "Gedi," (kid), which exemplifies the class of - בהמות טהרות - Behemot Taharot - "clean" domesticated animals, such as the ox, cow, sheep and goat and the word "Immo," the Gedi's mother, are chosen, because the Issur Bishul and the Issur Hana'ah apply only to the mixture of meat and milk of clean, domesticated animals. The Issur Bishul and the Issur Hana'ah, as opposed to the Issur Achilah, do not apply to the mixture of milk of a clean, domesticated animal with the meat of either an unclean animal, or an undomesticated animal, such as a stag or a roe.[4] The Torah's choice of words also tells us that as far as - דאורייתא - De'oraita, Torah law is concerned, the three prohibitions do not apply to the mixture of milk and meat of a - חיה - Chayah, a non-domesticated animal, such as a deer or a roe. Neither does the prohibition apply, as far as Torah law is concerned, to the mixture of milk and chicken or other fowl. The Rabbis, however, have extended the Issur Bishul and Issur Achilah, but not the Issur Hana'ah, to non-domesticated animals and to fowl as well.[5] The word "Tevashel," (thou shalt not cook) is chosen because the Torah only prohibits the cooking but not other forms of food preparation, such as soaking, salting or pickling meat with dairy,[6] although the Rabbis have extended the prohibition to the consumption of these mixtures too.[7] Whether or not a particular mixture of meat and milk is prohibited by the Torah or by the Rabbis is important, because, where the mixture is only Rabinically prohibited, the Issur Hana'ah will not apply and there may be more leniency in border-line cases.

The prohibition of meat and milk mixture is considered a - חדוש - Chidush - a novel idea, by the Talmud,[8] because the Torah does not refer to it in terms of an "abomination to the soul," as it does in connection with the violation of other dietary laws.[9] Moreover, in the forbidden combination of meat and milk, the meat, in itself, and the milk, in itself, are permitted for food. The reason for the prohibition of the mixture of meat and milk may be that it infringes upon the Law of Species, which forbids interference with the created order of the universe. Similar laws are those which forbid us to crossbreed animals, to sow our fields with mingled seed and to wear a garment of mingled wool and linen.[10]

Torah Law prohibits the simultaneous consumption of meat and milk, but not the consumption of milk after meat. Nevertheless, the Rabbis legislated a mandatory waiting period after eating meat, chicken or other fowl and before eating milk products.[11] Some explain that the need for this waiting period is that meat leaves a fatty residue on one's palate, which exudes the taste of meat for several hours. Eating milk products with the meat taste that lingers is considered tantamount to eating meat and milk together.[12] Others[13] explain that the concern is for meat particles trapped between teeth, which would mingle with milk products, if these were eaten too soon after meat. There are various practices as to the length of the waiting period. The source of the waiting period is the statement of Mar Ukba who said, "I am as vinegar to wine (inferior) compared with my father. For, whereas my father used to wait 24 hours between meat and milk, I [Mar Ukba] do not eat (cheese) in the same meal, but I do eat it in the next meal."[14] The difference of opinions regarding the waiting period arise from different waiting periods between meals, prevalent among the communities of the Poskim. The Rambam and other Poskim require a six hour waiting period, because this was the usual interval between meals in their time.[15] Others,[16] including the Rema, require waiting only one hour. This is based on the opinion of the Tosafists,[17] who say that it is sufficient to terminate the meat meal, recite grace after meals, and then commence the milk meal.

HALACHIC PHYSICS
הלכות תערובת

Whereas eating milk after meat requires a waiting period, eating meat after milk, generally, does not.[1] This is because most milk products, unlike meat, do not leave a fatty residue on one's palate, nor are they likely to remain trapped between the teeth.[2] Accordingly, the prevailing view is that one may eat meat or fowl immediately after most milk products during the same meal, provided that one first rinses one's mouth and washes one's hands.[3] Other Poskim abide by a minority and stricter opinion that requires one to wait and recite grace after meals after eating milk products and before eating meat.[4] Perhaps this is the source of the custom some have to wait about one half hour between milk and meat.[5] Yet others, while permitting the consumption of meat after milk in the same meal with no waiting period in between, require, in addition to rinsing one's mouth and washing one's hands, that the table cloth be changed.[6] All, however, recommend[7] that after eating **hard** cheese (defined, for this purpose, as cheese more than six months old[8]), and before eating meat or fowl, one wait the same period of time (six hours, three hours or one hour, according to one's custom) as one waits between meat and milk. This is because hard cheese leaves a fatty residue on the palate and is more likely to get trapped between teeth.[9]

If a piece of cold, raw, unsalted and unroasted meat falls into a pot of cold milk, or if a piece of cold hard cheese falls into cold meat soup, then the milk can be drunk and the meat or the cheese that fell in can be eaten, as long as they are rinsed with water.[10] However, if the piece of meat which fell into the cold milk was either raw and hot, or cold and cooked, or roasted, or if it were salted to a degree that would make it inedible to some,[11] then, it is insufficient to simply rinse it in water. In such a case, although the milk may be drunk, the meat may be eaten only after its outer layer, which came into contact with the cold milk, is peeled off and the meat is thoroughly rinsed, provided that it has no cracks or crevices.[12] If however, the piece of raw and hot, or cold and cooked or roasted meat, which fell into the cold milk, had cracks and crevices, or if it was spiced, even if it had no cracks or crevices, then the meat is no longer salvageable and cannot be eaten.[13] This is because the cracks or spices allow the milk to penetrate the meat beyond its outer surface.

Food or liquid is considered hot in Jewish law when the degree of heat is high enough to scald one's hand.[14] According to Halachah, heat, when applied to a mixture of meat and milk, has the power to cause the taste of one to invade the other. Accordingly, if a piece of hot meat falls into a pot of hot milk, both the milk and the meat are prohibited.[15] Similarly, if a piece of cold meat falls into a pot of hot milk, or if cold milk falls into a pot of hot meat, both the meat and the milk are prohibited.[16] This is because the Halachah, based upon the principle that the food or the liquid which lies below has the decisive effect - תתאה גבר - Tatai Gavar - deems the hot milk or the hot meat lying below in the pot to have heated up the cold meat or cold milk that fell in. It follows, therefore, that if a piece of hot meat, which is neither cracked, salted or spiced, falls into a pot of cold milk, or if hot milk falls into a pot of cold meat, both the meat and the milk are permitted.[17] This is because the Halachah, based on the principle of Tatai Gavar, deems the cold milk or cold meat lying below in the pot to have cooled off the hot meat or the hot milk that fell in. In fact, in such a situation, the milk, if sixty times the volume of the meat, would be entirely permitted.[18] The meat would be permitted too, provided, however, that the outer layer of the meat is peeled off and the meat is thoroughly rinsed. This is because, although the cold milk in the pot is deemed to have cooled off the hot meat that fell into it, nevertheless, it takes the hot meat some time to cool off and during that time, the milk would have penetrated the outer layer of the meat. Several explanations are offered for the principle of Tatai Gavar. According to some, it is because the Halachah recognizes that heat rises and has the power to dominate the cold food or liquid above it. The Rashba explains that the decisive power of the food, or liquid lying below, derives from the fact that it is stationary and in its place and, as such, over-powers the mobile food or liquid falling into it.[19] Because of the complexity of these matters, it is always advisable to consult a Rabbi.

SEDER NIGHT AND BACK SEAT DRIVERS
ליל הסדר

There are lots of back seat drivers at the Seder. Your - כזית - Keza'it (portion) of Matzah, is not big enough, they chide. Red wine only; Shmurah Matzah or nothing; don't start the Seder before nightfall; you must finish the meal before midnight; don't drink wine between the four cups; the Seder plate is set in the wrong order. This article is intended as a defensible guide for the brave volunteer who leads the Seder ("Ba'al Haseder").

Let's start with the Seder Plate. According to the Ari and the Aruch Hasculchan, the following items are placed on top of the Seder Plate, in the following order. At the bottom of the top level, facing nearest to the Ba'al Haseder, lies - חזרת - lettuce or horseradish. Above the lettuce lies - חרוסת - Charoseth - on the right, and the - כרפס - Karpas, parsley, alongside it on the left. In the middle of the top level, facing the Ba'al Haseder, lies the Maror. Above the Maror, on the top level, facing the Ba'al Haseder, lies the Shank Bone on the right and the egg alongside, it on the left. Below the top level of the Seder plate lie the three Matzot.[1] The Haroseth is made of fruits, wine and spices to form a thick mixture, reminiscent of the mortar used by the Jews in their slave labor.[2] Karpas, which is mostly parsley, celery, or radish, may be any vegetable over which the blessing - בורא פרי האדמה - "Boreh Peri Ha'adama," is recited, except vegetables such as lettuce, which qualify for Maror.[3] The purpose of Karpas, not usually eaten before a meal, is to trigger the curiosity of the child, to whom the story of the Exodus should be principally addressed.[4] The word Karpas consists of the Hebrew letters which, when reversed, spell out ס' פרך, which means 600,000 Jews in slavery.[5] For Maror, horseradish is most frequently used, even though the Mishnah enumerates five species of eligible Maror.[6] The horseradish should not be eaten whole but should be grated after returning home from Synagogue and kept covered until used, in order to preserve its strength.[7] The purpose of the Maror is to remind us of the bitter times endured by the Jewish slaves.[8] The Torah requires the Maror to be eaten together with Matzah and the Korban Pesach (Paschal lamb).[9] Since this is no longer possible today, Maror is a Rabbinical and not a Biblical requirement.[10] Accordingly, there is more room for leniency and a sick person, or one who would become sick from ground horseradish, may instead eat the horseradish leaves, provided that they are fresh enough to be eaten.[11] The minimum amount of Maror required to be eaten is a Keza'it, approximately 1 fluid ounce, and it should be consumed within 9 minutes.[12] The Shank Bone, like the Paschal Lamb it signifies,[13] should be roasted before Pesach but, in the absence of the Temple, it should not be eaten on Seder night.[14] The roasted egg, which represents the Korban Chagigah, the regular Festival offering, was chosen for this purpose, because it symbolizes national mourning for the destruction of the Temple, which has rendered both the Korban

Pesach and the Korban Chagiga inapplicable.[15] Eating Matzah on the first Seder night is a Biblical requirement, independent of the Korban Pesach and, accordingly, there is less leniency in its application.[16] The minimum amount of Matzah that the Torah requires a person to eat on the first Seder night is a Keza'it which, according to the Chazon Ish, is approximately one half of a machine-made Matzah.[17] The additional Rabbinical requirements of eating Matzah with Maror and eating the Afikoman require the consumption of, at least, an additional whole machine-made Matzah, being a total of one and a half Matzot in all. All who are required to abstain from eating Chametz on Pesach are required, by the Torah, to eat Matzah on the first Seder night.[18] This includes men, women and children, even as young as five or six, who understand the Exodus story. Matzah may only be made from flour and water, the same ingredients that, if left together for more than 18 minutes, would become Chametz.[19] Shmurah Matzah is required for both Seder nights.[20] According to some Halachic opinions,[21] in order for Maztah to qualify as Shmurah, it is sufficient that it be guarded from becoming wet from the time the grain is ground into flour. According to this opinion, today's machine-made Matzot qualify as Shmurah. According to a stricter opinion of the Rif,[22] in order to qualify as Shmurah, the wheat must be guarded from becoming wet from the time it is harvested. The Matzot we refer to as Shmurah Matzah are those which comply with the stricter requirements of the Rif.

The Seder commences with - קדש - **Kiddush** recited over the first cup of wine. Whereas Kiddush may be recited before nightfall on Shabbat,[23] it must be recited after nightfall on Seder night.[24] Unlike Shabbat and Yom Tov,[25] on Seder night, there is a requirement that each participant drink from his own cup.[26] When reciting the Kiddush, one should remember that the same cup of wine is serving a dual function of Yom Tov Kiddush and the first cup for Seder night.[27] **Shehecheyanu**, the blessing for sanctified time, is recited on both Seder nights.[28] The minimum amount of wine in the cup should be a Revi'it which, according to Rabbi Moshe Feinstein, is between 3.3 and 4.42 fluid ounces.[29] In case of difficulty, the last three cups may each contain a minimum of 3 ounces.[30] The wine may be diluted with water, but the mixture should not exceed the ratio of 3.5 cups of water to one cup of wine.[31] A person who would become sick from wine may, instead, choose any of the following beverages in the following descending order of Halachic preference: wine mixed with grape juice, wine mixed with water, grape juice or raisin wine.[32] Following Kiddush, - רחץ - Rachatz, the Ba'al Haseder's hands are washed without reciting the blessing of Al Netilat Yadayim and the כרפס - **Karpas**, dipped in salt water, is eaten.[33] יחץ - **Yachatz** follows, with the breaking of the middle Matzah into two pieces, signifying poverty, the larger of which is put aside for the Afikoman,[34] and the smaller piece is used later for the eating of Matzah and Maror. מגיד - **Magid**, the Hagaddah is then recited, until one arrives at - רחצה

- **Rachtzah**[35] and - מוציא מצה - **Motze Matzah**. At this point, hands are washed with the Blessing and the Ba'al Haseder lifts up the two and a half Matzot and recites - המוציא לחם - Hamotze Lechem blessing. The bottom Matzah is then let go and the blessing of - מצה על אכילת - Al Achilat Matzah is recited and the כזית of Matzah is eaten in silence, before midnight.[36] After the Matzah, the - מרור - **Maror**, dipped in - חרוסת - Charoset - is eaten, first separately, without Matzah, in accordance with the opinion of the Sages, and then together with Matzah, - כורך - **Korech**, in sandwich form, in accordance with the opinion of Hillel.[37] Then שולחן עורך - **Shulchan Orech**, the meal should be eaten in reclining position and finished before midnight, so that - צפון - **Ztafun**, the Afikoman, like the Korban Pesach it signifies, may be eaten before midnight.[38] Nothing should be eaten after the Afikoman.[39] The third cup is drunk with a blessing after - ברך - **Barech**, Grace after Meals.[40] The fourth cup is filled and Hallel is then recited without a Blessing. The fourth cup is drunk with the conclusion of Hallel.[41] נרצה - **Nirtza**, reminiscing about Exodus, concludes the Seder.[42] Because Seder night is called - ליל שמורים - Lel Shimurim, the night in which God guards over us, no bedtime prayers are recited.[43]

THE FORTY NINERS
ספירת העומר

The Forty-Niners never drop the ball. But how many of us make it through forty nine nights, from the second night of Pesach all the way to Shavuot, without losing count. Sometimes, we never even make it on to the field. We are so busy preparing for second night Seder that we miss evening prayers in Synagogue and forget to count day one.

ספירת העומר - Sefirat Ha'omer, the counting of the forty nine days, connects the festival of - פסח - Pesach, which celebrates the Exodus, to the Festival of - שבועות - Shavuot, which celebrates the giving of the Torah. While still enslaved in Egypt, the Jews were told that following the Exodus - תעבדון את האלוקים על ההר הזה - Ta'avdun Et HaElokim Al Hahar Hazeh,[1] they would receive the Torah at Mount Sinai. The extra Hebrew letter "Nun" appended to the word "Ta'avdun" was a message to the enslaved Jews that fifty days after the Exodus their status would be changed at Sinai from servants of Pharaoh to servants of God.[2] In anticipation of the Revelation, the Jews began to count fifty days toward Shavuot.

Sefirat Ha'omer is linked to three concepts: (i) the - קרבן עומר - Omer Sacrifice, (ii) חדש - Chadash or new grain and (iii) שתי הלחם - the two loaves of bread brought on Shavuot as a first harvest offering to God, Bikurim LaHashem.

The Omer Sacrifice: On the evening preceding the 16th day of Nissan, the Jews of Temple times would go out into the fields and cut sheaves of barley.[3] The barley would then be brought to the Temple and ground into flour on the 16th day.[4] One tenth of the quantity of the ground barley was taken and mixed with oil and incense and waved in all directions before the altar and then burnt on the altar, together with a male lamb in its first year.[5]

Chadash: Until the Omer Sacrifice was brought on the day of the sixteenth of Nissan of the current year as described, it was prohibited to eat anything made of barley, wheat, oats, rye or spelt crops, which had been planted or had taken root after the sixteenth of Nissan of the previous year.[6] Such forbidden crops were called **Chadash** and could be eaten only after the completion of the Omer sacrifice.

Bikurim: On the Festival of Shavuot, the first harvest wheat offering was brought, consisting of two loaves of baked bread, together with seven lambs, one bullock and two rams.[7]

The Torah[8] asks us to begin counting seven complete weeks, starting on the evening preceding the sixteenth day of Nissan, which is the night of the second Seder. The Rambam explains that seven weeks were required to raise the Jewish nation out of the depths of despondency to which they had sunk during their slavery. Whereas one week is sufficient to restore an individual to his natural state of divine purity, the entire nation required seven weeks. The Omer Sacrifice of loose barley flour was more fitting for animal consumption than human consumption[9] and symbolizes the depths to which the Jewish slaves had sunk. The Bikurim sacrifice of baked wheat bread[10] symbolizes the refined spiritual heights they reached by Shavuot. After the destruction of the Temple, the Omer Sacrifice became inapplicable.[11] What about Chadash? Is one permitted to harvest or eat Chadash prior to the day the Omer Sacrifice would have been offered had the Temple not been destroyed? And what about Sefirat Ha'omer? If it is linked to the Omer Sacrifice, why has it survived the destruction of the Temple? Whether or not Chadash applies outside Israel depends on the interpretation of the words - בכל משבתיכם - Bechol Moshvoteichem, in the verse (Leviticus 23:14) which prohibits Chadash "in all your dwellings." According to the Rabbis,[12] the words "in all your dwellings" do not apply outside the land of Israel, but rather to the land of Israel, after the first fifteen years of its conquest and division by Joshua. According to Rabbi Eliezer,[13] however, the words "Bechol Moshvoteichem" give Chadash a worldwide application even today. Rabbi Eliezer's view is adopted by most of the Rishonim.[14] The Shulchan Aruch rules that Chadash applies inside and outside Israel and to Jewish and non-Jewish owned lands.[15] Nevertheless, based on the Rema, as clarified by the Shach,[16] one may eat Chadash outside of Israel on the strength of the Halachic rule of double doubt and the Halachic rule of the majority. The double doubt is as follows: (a) perhaps the grain took root in the previous year, and (b) even if not, it can be assumed that the grain took root at least in time before the 16th of Nissan. The rule of the majority is that most grain has been stored for a long time and comes from previous years' crops. As for Sefirat Ha'omer, the majority opinion[17] (with which the Rambam disagrees[18]) is that it has no Biblical application today and was instituted by the Rabbis - זכר למקדש - Zecher Lemikdash, in memory of the Temple.

The Torah[19] requires one to count both the days and the weeks of the Omer. On the first day one counts "Yom Echad La'omer" and not "Yom Rishon La'omer," so as to make it perfectly clear that the first day of the Omer is the day following the first day of Pesach and not the day following Shabbat. In so doing, we reject the opinion of the Saducees, who interpreted the words - ממחרת השבת - Mimochorat Hashabat, (Leviticus 23:16) to mean Sunday. Because the Torah requires one to count - שבע שבתות תמימת - seven complete weeks, one should count at the beginning of the day, which, in Jewish Law, begins on the preceding night.[20] The optimum time to recite Sefirat Ha'omer is after Ma'ariv, immediately following the appearance of three stars.[21] If, however, it is difficult to find a Minyan (quorum of ten men) at that late hour, one should recite Sefirat Ha'omer with an earlier Ma'ariv Minyan without a Blessing, rather than wait and count alone.[22] On Friday night and Yom Tov night, Sefirat Ha'omer is recited in the Synagogue after Kiddush[23] and at home before Kiddush.[24] On Motza'ei Shabbat, Sefirat Ha'omer is recited after Kaddish Titkabal and before Havdalah.[25] Based on the verse referring to "standing grain,"[26] one should count standing.[27] One must count the Omer for oneself - וספרתם לכם. One cannot rely on someone else to count on one's behalf.[28] Women are not obliged to count[29] but may volunteer to count the

Omer with a Blessing.[30] The verse that requires one to count "seven complete weeks" means that if one missed a whole day and did not remember to count until the following night, one can no longer recite the blessing before counting on the following days. If, however, one remembered one's omission during the same day, including at twilight, before nightfall, one may count that day, without the Blessing, and on the following days, one may count with a Blessing.[31] If one is not sure whether or not one counted the previous day, one may continue to count the following days with a Blessing.[32] If one is asked at twilight what day of the Omer it will be tonight, one should reply with yesterday's count.[33] But if asked before twilight, one may reply with tonight's count. According to some opinions, a Rabbi or a Chazan who leads the counting of the Omer may recite the Blessing, even if he knows that he omitted a previous day's count.[34] A person who crosses the dateline and gains or loses a day may, according to certain Halachic opinions, disregard the local count and continue counting as he would back home.[35] Although originally a time of anticipated joy, certain tragedies that occurred during the Sefirah time have lent it a more ominous mood.[36]

SEFIRAT HA'OMER AS A PERIOD OF MOURNING
אבילות בתקופת העומר

In the movie "The Paper Chase," the Harvard student rips out a page of the law report so that his fellow students will be unable to read it and will come to the lecture unprepared. About 2000 years earlier, a student lay feverishly ill in the Academy of Rabbi Akiva, in Bnei Berak. So caught up were the other students in the competitiveness of their learning that they found no time to visit him or take care of him. And, as the student lay dying, Rabbi Akiva, himself, entered the sick room, fed him, gave him to drink, made him comfortable and swept the dust from the floor.[1] The sick student survived. His peers did not. Between Pesach and Shavuot, 24,000 of them died from diphtheria because they acted inconsiderately to one another.[2] According to other sources,[3] the students of Rabbi Akiva were massacred by the Romans after the murder of Rabbi Akiva, himself. This was because they taught Torah in public, a violation of the Roman decree which forbade the study of all sacred texts. The behavior of Rabbi Akiva's students left them particularly vulnerable between Pesach and Shavuot, since this period is a time of celestial judgment.[4] Furthermore, as Rabbi Goren points out,[5] the Oral Torah, like the written Torah, could only be given when the Jews lived together in harmony.[6] Accordingly, Rabbi Akiva's students were not worthy of being the teachers of the Oral Law. The death of so many of Rabbi Akiva's disciples threatened the very survival of the Oral Law. Only a few students survived to become the standard bearers of tradition. They were Rabbi Meir, Rabbi Yehuda, Rabbi Yose, Rabbi Shimon Bar Yochai and Rabbi Elazar Ben Shamua.

To commemorate this sad event, it has long been the custom to adopt certain forms of mourning on the days on which the students died. There is, however, a difference of opinion as to when the deaths occurred. According to the opinion of the Shulchan Aruch, they died during the 34 days immediately following Pesach, including the day of and the day following Lag Ba'omer. Accordingly, one mourns for them from Pesach until daybreak following the day of Lag Ba'omer. Thereafter, the mourning stops.[7] The Rema[8] points out that because of the festivities of Lag Ba'omer, all forms of mourning cease on Lag Ba'omer itself. As is usually the case, people of Sephardi origin follow the ruling of the Shulchan Aruch and do not shave or arrange weddings on Lag Ba'omer. People of Ashkenazi origin do shave and arrange weddings on Lag Ba'omer. Rav Ovadia Yosef rules that the authorities in Israel must determine the Sephardi or Ashkenazi origin of a couple before registering them for marriage on Lag Ba'omer. In cases where the groom is Askenazi and the bride is Sephardi, or vice versa, the custom of the groom is followed.[9]

The second opinion is that of Tosafot. According to this opinion, no deaths occurred on the 16 days between Pesach and Shavuot, when Tachanun is not recited. Accordingly, there should be no mourning on the seven days of Pesach, the six days of Shabbat, the two days of Rosh Chodesh Iyar and on the day of Rosh Chodesh Sivan. According to the opinion of Tosafot, the thirty three days of mourning commence only after Pesach and, because there is no mourning on the sixteen days indicated, the mourning ends on Erev Shavuot.[10] Rabbi Moshe Feinstein points out that there are an additional three variations on the first opinion and one variation on the opinion of Tosafot, namely, that of the Ari, who mourned for the students from Pesach through to Shavuot, without any break. The period of mourning that one observes depends on the custom of the community to which one belongs.[11]

The forms of mourning that are observed are not shaving, not taking a haircut, not attending weddings and not listening to music, including the radio and tape recorder. According to one opinion, one may listen to tapes or to the radio when Jewish music with words from the scriptures is being played.[12] In former times, people would also cease all work after nightfall, in commemoration of the funerals of the students which took place at night. Engagements and engagement parties are permitted during the Sefirah period. The Mohel, the father of the child and the Sandek may shave in honor of a Brit ceremony during the Sefirah period. The playing of musical instruments at an engagement party, Brit, Bar Mitzva, Siyum or Pidyon Haben ceremony during the Sefirah period is prohibited by the Mishnah Berurah[13] but is permitted by Rabbi Ovadiah Yosef.[14] A musician who earns his living playing musical instruments may do so during the Sefirah period in the house of a non-Jew.[15] There is a view that a person learning to play a musical instrument may practice during the Sefirah period.[16] One may recite the blessing of Schehecheyanu over a new fruit or a new garment during the Sefirah period.[17] Rav Ovadiah Yosef[18] recommends, however, that a new garment be worn for the first time during the Sefirah period only on Shabbat.

According to Rabbi Moshe Feinstein,[19] business and professional people who may suffer financial loss if they attend meetings unshaven may shave during the Sefirah period. A person who observes the Sefirah period through Shavuot, in accordance with the second opinion described above, may attend a wedding of a person who observes the Sefirah period through Lag Ba'omer in accordance with the first opinion, described above. He may even shave for the occasion.[20]

Lag Ba'omer is a day of celebration for two reasons. First, none of the students of Rabbi Akiva died on that day. Second, it is the Yahrtzeit of Rabbi Shimon Bar Yochai, one of the surviving students. According to Kabbalistic tradition, on the day Rabbi Shimon Bar Yochai lay dying, he transmitted the secrets of the Kabbalah to his students, who wrote them down in the book of the Zohar.[21] On that day, the world was filled with Zohar, with light, like the sky in Israel that glows with the flames of bonfires on the night of Lag Ba'omer.

SEARCHING FOR CHAMETZ ON EREV PESACH
WITH CANDLES, FLASHLIGHTS AND BREAD
בדיקת חמץ ובטולו
(פסחים ב - ז:)

1. Exodus 12:15; Pesachim 4b.
2. Exodus 13:7.
3. Exodus 12:19.
4. Shulchan Aruch, Orach Chaim 431:1 and 434:2, Mishnah Berurah 6; Pesachim 4b.
5. Ibid.; Pesachim 2a.
6. Shulchan Aruch Harav, Orach Chaim 431:5 and 432:8.
7. Shulchan Aruch, Orach Chaim 433:1, and Mishnah Berurah 1 thereon.
8. Shulchan Aruch, Orach Chaim 433:1.
9. Ibid. 432:1.
10. Shulchan Aruch, Orach Chaim 434:2, and Mishnah Berurah 6 thereon.
11. Rema, Shulchan Aruch, Orach Chaim 434:2.
12. Rema, Shulchan Aruch, Orach Chaim 432:2.
13. Shulchan Aruch, Orach Chaim, 432:2 s.v. ומיהו אם לא נתן; Responsa of the Raavad in Tamim Deim paragraph 29.
14. Shulchan Aruch, Orach Chaim 432:2, and Mishnah Berurah 13, quoting Chok Yaacov and the Ari.
15. Shaarei Teshuvah on Shulchan Aruch, Orach Chaim 432:2 s.v. ונוהגים.
16. Responsa Ttitz Eliezer Chelek 1, Siman 20, Perek 11, p.132.
17. Pesachim 7b.
18. Magen Avraham to Shulchan Aruch, Orach Chaim 433:1 s.v. כנגד ארובה. See discussion in Responsa Yechaveh Daat Chelek 1, Siman 4, p.12
19. Responsa Yechaveh Daat Chelek 1, Siman 4, p.14 in the name of Rabbi Shimon Grunfeld, Responsa Maharshag volume 2, Siman 107.
20. Yechaveh Daat Chelek 1, Siman 4, p.12
21. Shaarim Metzuyanim Behalachah Chelek 3, p.30, note 4 to Kitzur Shulchan Aruch 111:2.

—⚶—

CATCH 22: WHEN EREV PESACH
IS ON SHABBAT
ערב פסח שחל להיות בשבת

1. Shulchan Aruch, Orach Chaim 274 and Mishnah Berurah 4 thereon and Shulchan Aruch, Orach Chaim 291:4.
2. Schulchan Aruch, Orach Chaim 291:2.
3. Shulchan Aruch, Orach Chaim 471:2, Rema.

4. Mishnah Berurah 8 to Shulchan Aruch, Orach Chaim 444:1.
5. Quoted by Rav Moshe Harari in Hilchot Lel Haseder, p. 53, Chapter 1, paragraph 44, note 65.
6. Quoted by Rav Moshe Harari in Hilchot Lel Haseder, p.57.
7. Responsa Yechaveh Daat Chelek 1, Siman 91, p.273
8. Shulchan Aruch, Orach Chaim 444:6.

—ɷ—

KORBAN PESACH
קרבן פסח

(פסחים ה·)

1. Leviticus 23:5-6.
2. Yosef Tabori, Moadei Yisrael, Chapter 1.
3. Rambam, Hilchot Korban Pesach 1:2.
4. Ibid. 1:1.
5. Exodus 12:3.
6. Rambam, Hilchot Korban Pesach 2:14.
7. Ibid. 3:1.
8. Ibid. 1:9.
9. Exodus 12:6; Leviticus 23:5; Numbers 9:3.
10. Exodus 34:25; Pesachim 5a.
11. Exodus 12:6; Rambam, Hilchot Korban Pesach 1:14.
12. Rambam, Ibid.
13. Ibid.
14. Rambam, Hilchot Korban Pesach 1:11.
15. Ibid. 1:17.
16. Exodus 12:8-10.
17. Toseftah, Pesachim 5:3.
18. The Hirsch Haggadah, p.8.

—ɷ—

KASHERING
הכשר כלים - עקרונות

(פסחים ל· + מד:)

1. Nazir 37a; Pesachim 44b; Chulin 108a.
2. The word הגעלה is derived from the root געל which means to expel; Rashi, Pesachim 44b s.v. גיעולי נכרים and Rema, Shulchan Aruch, Orach Chaim 451:3.
3. Avodah Zarah 76b; Pesachim 74a.
4. Numbers 31:21-23.

5. Avodah Zarah 75b. Shulchan Aruch, Orach Chaim 451:4. Rema and Mishnah Berurah 32 thereon.

6. Schulchan Aruch, Orach Chaim 451:5.

7. Schulchan Aruch Harav 451:3.

8. Schulchan Aruch, Orach Chaim 452:1, and Mishnah Berurah 8 thereon.

9. Ibid. 452:7.

10. Ibid. 452:1, and Mishnah Berurah, 1 thereon.

11. Ibid. 452:6.

12. Ibid. 451:12.

13. Rema, Shulchan Aruch, Orach Chaim 451:12 and Mishnah Berurah 68 thereon.

14. Shulchan Aruch, Orach Chaim 451:12 and Mishnah Berurah 68 thereon.

15. Shulchan Aruch, Orach Chaim 451:14.

16. Ibid. 451:5, and Mishnah Berurah 41 thereon.

17. Tur, Yoreh Deah 121.

18. Sefer Hagalat Kelim p.39, paragraph 43.

KASHER MY KITCHEN
הכשר כלים - היביטים מעשיים
(פסחים ל. + מד:)

1. Shulchan Aruch, Orach Chaim 451:8.

2. Hagalat Kelim 13:436.

3. Numbers 31:21-23.

4. Hagalat Kelim 13:293.

5. Shulchan Aruch, Yoreh Deah 135:10.

6. Leviticus 6:21; Pesachim 30b.

7. Rabeinu Tam, Avodah Zarah 33b, Tosafot s.v. קוניא; Tosafot Ketubot 107b s.v. הני; Mordechai, Pesachim 2:574 (in Mordechai p.31) in the name of Raviyah דכלי זכוכית שיעא ולא בלע, i.e. it is smooth and does not absorb; Pesachim 74b; Shulchan Aruch, Orach Chaim 451:26.

8. Responsa Terumat Hadeshen, Pesakim, Siman 151.

9. Shabbat 15b.

10. Or Zarua, cited in Hagalat Kelim 13:59:38; Avodah Zarah 75b.

11. Shulchan Aruch, Orach Chaim 451:25.

12. Ibid.

13. Rema, ibid.

14. Mishnah Berurah 150 to Shulchan Aruch, Orach Chaim 451:25.

15. Mishnah Berurah 118 to Shulchan Aruch, Orach Chaim 451:21.

16. Responsa Igrot Moshe, Orach Chaim Chelek 2, Siman 92, p.285.

17. Responsa Tzitz Eliezer Chelek 4, Siman 6, p.33 and the Minchat Yitzchak Chelek 3, Siman 67, p.112

18. Cited by Rabbi Shimon Eider in the name of Rav Moshe Feinstein, Halochos of Pesach XIII, A7, p. 140.

19. Shaarim Metzuyanim Behalachah Chelek 3, p.88, note 11 to Kitzur Shulchan Aruch 116:13; and Responsa Yechave Daat Chelek 1, Siman 6, p.19.

20. Responsa Igrot Moshe, Orach Chaim Chelek 3, Siman 58, p.366 and Yoreh Deah Volume 2, Siman 28+29, p.37-39.

21. Hagalat Kelim 13:225.

22. Hagalat Kelim 13:228.

23. Minchat Yitzchak Chelek 3, Siman 66 p. 110 and Dayan Rappoport, London Beth Din, cited in Hagalat Kelim 13:464:432.

24. Cited by Rabbi Shimon Eider, Halochos of Pesach XVI E4, p.181.

25. See Eider, ibid. XVI - E6 p.182 in the name of Rav Moshe Feinstein.

26. See Eider, ibid. XVI C9 p.176 based on Rema, Shulchan Aruch, Orach Chaim 451:18.

27. Hagalat Kelim 13:23. But see Eider Ibid XVI C10, p.177.

28. Hagalat Kelim 13:390.

29. Eider, ibid. XVI C8 p.176.

30. Shulchan Aruch, Orach Chaim 451:21, and Mishnah Berurah 120 thereon.

31. Aruch Hashulchan, Orach Chaim 451:50.

—ᴍ—

TOVELING
טבילת כלים
(עבודה זרה עה:)

1. Leviticus 11:44.

2. Ritva, Avodah Zarah, 75b.

3. Numbers 31:21-22.

4. Tur, Yoreh Deah 120.

5. Ibid.

6. Rambam, Ma'achaloth Asurot 17:6.

7. Responsa Yabia Omer, Yoreh Deah Chelek 4, Siman 8, p.241.

8. Responsa Tzitz Eliezer Chelek 7, Siman 37, p.161; Responsa Yabia Omer, Yoreh Deah Chelek 4, Siman 8, p.241.

9. Responsa Minchat Yitzchak Chelek 5, Siman 32, p.110.

10. Tur, Yoreh Deah 120.

11. Infered from Taz on Shulchan Aruch, Yoreh Deah 120:15 s.v. עלתה להם טבילה, who prohibits recital of blessing when Tevilah is performed by a non-Jew but does not prohibit recital of a blessing when performed by a Jewish person. See also Tevilat Kelim 8:2 note 6.

12. Shulchan Aruch, Yoreh Deah 120:5 and Rema; Tevilat Kelim 1:3:5.

13. Seems to the opinion of Shaarim Hametzuyanim Behalachah Chelek 1, p.220, note 4 to Kitzur

Shulchan Aruch 37:3; Rav Sternbruch, Sefer Taharat Hamishpachah, quoted in Tevilat Kelim 11:147, note 115, Responsa Minchat Yitzchak Chelek 3, Siman 76 - 78, p.126.

14. Responsa Tztitz Eliezer, and Responsa Yabia Omer Chelek 4, Siman 8, p.241, Rav Moshe Feinstein, quoted in Sefer Tevilat Kelim, 11:148.

15. Rambam, Hilchot Maachalot Asurot, 17:6. Tur Yoreh Deah 120.

16. Shulchan Aruch, Orach Chaim 323:7; Sefer Tevilat Kelim 3:5:10.

17. Responsa Minchat Yitzchak and Rav Wozner as quoted by Tevilat Kelim 5:2.

18. Rashba in his commentary to Avodah Zarah compares Tevilat Kelim to Tevilat Nidah where nothing is allowed to intercede between the person and the water.

19. Shulchan Aruch, Yoreh Deah 201:9 and Rema; Tur, Yoreh Deah 120.

20. Rabbi Shlomo Zalman Auerbach as quoted by Sefer Tevilat Kelim 4:16:24.

21. Chidushei Rabbi Akiva Eiger, Shulchan Aruch, Yoreh Deah 120:1 s.v. וכן נוהגים

22. Shulchan Aruch, Yoreh Deah 201:2.

23. Pitchei Teshuvah to Shulchan Aruch, Yoreh Deah 120:1 s.v. במקוה או במים in the name of Chochmat Adam.

24. Dayan Dr. I. Grunfeld, The Jewish Dietary Laws volume 1, P.196.

—∿∿—

PESACH MEDICATION AND ALCOHOL
חמץ, הגדרתו וסוגיו השונים
(פסחים מג.)

1. Rambam, Hilchot Chametz Umatzah 5:1; Shulchan Aruch, Orach Chaim 453:1.

2. Shulchan Aruch, Orach Chaim 459:2.

3. Rashi, Pesachim 94a.

4. Rambam, Commentary to the Mishnah, Pesachim 9:1.

5. See note 2 above.

6. Deuteronomy 16:3; Rambam, Hilchot Chametz Umatzah 1:8.

7. Exodus 12:19.

8. Exodus 12:15.

9. Rambam, Hilchot Chametz Umatzah 1:6.

10. Rashi, Pesachim 43a s.v. מאן תנא; Shulchan Aruch, Orach Chaim 442:2, Mishnah Berurah 9 thereon.

11. Rema, Shulchan Aruch, Orach Chaim 462:4; See also Aruch Hashulchan, Orach Chaim 462:4 and Kaf Hachayim, Orach Chaim 462:4:41 regarding the custom of Sephardim and egg matzot.

12. Shulchan Aruch, Orach Chaim 442:2, and Mishnah Berurah 9 thereon.

13. Rosh, Pesachim 21b (in Rosh 3b).

14. Responsa Igrot Moshe, Orach Chaim Chelek 2, Siman 92, p.285.

15. Responsa Yechaveh Daat Chelek 2, Siman 60, p.218

16. Responsa of Yitzchak Ben Shmuel Halevi (Maharia Halevy) 1:52 quoted by Rabbi Shimon Eider,

Halochos of Pesach II C 3, p.24.

17. Rabbi Shimon Eider, Halachos of Pesach, II C 3, p.24.
18. Ibid. C3, p.24.
19. Ibid. C6, p.25.
20. Ibid.
21. Shulchan Aruch, Yoreh Deah 155:3, and Igrot Moshe see note 14 above.
22. Rav Moshe Feinstein as quoted by Rabbi Shimon Eider, Halachos of Pesach, II C 12, p.27, note 108.
23. Responsa Igrot Moshe, Orach Chaim Chelek 3, Siman 62, p.368.
24. Responsa Igrot Moshe, Yoreh Deah Chelek 2, Siman 30, p.39.

—⚓—

KOSHER LEPESACH LIGHT BULBS
תערובת חמץ
(פסחים ל׃)

1. Shulchan Aruch, Yoreh Deah 98:2; Shulchan Aruch, Orach Chaim 447:9; Rashi, Beitzah 3b s.v. אפילו באלף לא בטיל.
2. Rashi, Chulin 97b s.v. ואמור רבנן בששים; Shulchan Aruch, Yoreh Deah 98:4.
3. Pesachim 30a; Shulchan Aruch, Orach Chaim 447:1 and 447:9 and Mishnah Berurah 92 thereon; Shulchan Aruch Harav, Orach Chaim 447:4; Aruch Hashulchan, Orach Chaim 447:7.
4. Pesachim 29b s.v. שלא במינו; Rosh, Pesachim 30a (in Rosh 4a).
5. Rambam, Hilchot Maachalot Assurot 15:9.
6. Aruch Hashulchan, Orach Chaim 447:3; Shulchan Aruch, Orach Chaim 447:3, and Mishnah Berurah 15 thereon.
7. Rosh, Pesachim 30a (in Rosh 4a); Shulchan Aruch, Orach Chaim 447:4, and Rema and Mishnah Berurah 32 thereon. See however opposing view of Rambam, in Magid Mishnah to Hilchot Chametz Umatzah 4:12.
8. Rabbi Shimon Eider, Halochos of Pesach III B, p.45.

—⚓—

CHAMETZ CREDIT CARD
מכירת חמץ
(פסחים כח.)

1. Pesachim 28a; Shulchan Aruch, Orach Chaim 448:3.
2. A "Halachic hour" is the unit of time derived by dividing the period of time between sunrise until sunset by 12. It can be more or less than 60 minutes depending on the time of the year.
3. Shulchan Aruch, Orach Chaim 443:1.
4. Ibid.

5. Shulchan Aruch, Orach Chaim 445:2, and Mishnah Berurah 11 thereon.
6. Shulchan Aruch, Orach Chaim 434:2, and Rema thereon.
7. Shulchan Aruch, Orach Chaim 445:2.
8. Shulchan Aruch Harav, Hilchot Mechirat Chametz; Magen Avraham to Shulchan Aruch, Orach Chaim 448:5 s.v. אע"פ שביטלו and Mishnah Berurah 25 thereon.
9. Rabbi Shimon Eider, Halochos of Pesach XI A 11, p.123.
10. Exodus 12:15.
11. Mishnah Berurah 10 to Shulchan Aruch, Orach Chaim 445:2.
12. Kitzur Shulchan Aruch 114:1.
13. Mishnah Berurah 13 to Shulchan Aruch, Orach Chaim 448:3.
14. Tosefta, Pesachim 2:6.
15. Shulchan Aruch, Orach Chaim 448:3, and Mishnah Berurah 16 thereon.
16. Tur, Orach Chaim 448, and Bach s.v. ואם.
17. Ibid. and Shulchan Aruch, Orach Chaim 448:3 and Mishnah Berurah 12 thereon.
18. Bava Metziah 77b.
19. Aruch Hashulchan, Orach Chaim 448:27.
20. Rabbi Shimon Eider, Halachos of Pesach XI A 8, p.122.
21. Rav Shlomo Yosef Zevin, HaMoadim Behalachah, p.304.
22. Kuntres Acharon in Shaarim Metzuyanim Behalachah Chelek 3, p.47, note 1; and Igrot Moshe Chelek 4, Siman 94, p.177.

—◆◆◆—

PORK CHOPS AND SCHNITZEL
ריחא מילתא
(פסחים עו:)

1. Pesachim 76b.
2. Shulchan Aruch, Yoreh Deah 108:1, and Beer Heitev s.v. מותר.
3. Tosafot, Pesachim 76b s.v. מאי לאו; Shulchan Aruch, ibid.
4. For definition of "large" for this purpose see Binat Adam 62:81; Shaar Issur Veheter 62 p.54.
5. Taz to Shulchan Aruch, Yoreah Deah 108:1 s.v. ואם התנור גדול
6. Shulchan Aruch, Yoreh Deah 108:1.
7. Taz to Shulchan Aruch 108:1 s.v. אין צולין בשר כשירה; Shach, ibid. s.v. אין צולין; however see dissenting opinion of Aruch Hashulchan, Yoreh Deah 108:9.
8. Shulchan Aruch, Yoreah Deah 108:2. According to the Mechaber this is permitted even if the utensils are uncovered and the oven is closed. According to the Rema it would only be permitted in an open oven.
9. Rema, ibid. 108:1; ibid. 96:2.
10. Rema, Shulchan Aruch, Yoreah Deah 108:1.

11. Rema, ibid.
12. Shulchan Aruch, Yoreah Deah 92:8 and Rema thereon.
13. Shulchan Aruch, Yoreh Deah 116:2.
14. Beer Sheva, quoted by Schach, ibid. s.v. וכן.
15. Magen Avraham to Shulchan Aruch, Orach Chaim 173:2 s.v. דקשה לד''א.
16. Rema, Shulchan Aruch, Yoreh Deah 116:3; See also Dayan Dr. I. Grunfeld, The Jewish Dietary Laws p.126.

—⚬⚬⚬—

MEAT AND MILK
בשר בחלב
(פסחים מד:)

1. Exodus 23:19, 34:26; Deut. 14:21.
2. Dayan Dr. I. Grunfeld, The Jewish Dietary Laws p.117,
3. Chullin 115b.
4. Chullin 113a; Rambam, Hilchot Ma'achalot Assurot 9, 1-3; Rashi, Exodus 23:19.
5. Shulchan Aruch, Yoreh Deah 87:3; Rema 87:4 and Shach thereon s.v. אבל בעוף דרבנן אין לחוש.
6. Beer Heitev 1 to Shulchan Aruch, Yoreh Deah 87:1 s.v בישול. According to some Halachic opinions, the frying or broiling of meat together with milk is not prohibited under Rabbinical law. Others, including the Beer Heitev, consider these forms of cooking forbidden under Torah Law.
7. Shulchan Aruch, ibid. 87:6, and Rema thereon
8. Nazir 37a and Pesachim 44b.
9. Leviticus 11:43, 20:25.
10. Dayan Dr. I. Grunfeld, The Jewish Dietary Laws p.118.
11. Shulchan Aruch, Yoreah Deah 89.
12. Rashi, Chullin 105a s.v. אסור לאכול גבינה
13. Rambam, Hilchot Ma'achalot Asurot 9:28.
14. Chullin 105a.
15. Rambam, Hilchot Ma'achalot Asurot 9:28; Shulchan Aruch, Yoreah Deah 89:1.
16. Rema, Shulchan Aruch, Yoreah Deah 89:1.
17. Tosafot, Chullin 105a s.v. לסועדתא.

—⚬⚬⚬—

HALACHIC PHYSICS
הלכות תערובת

1. Chullin 104b-105a; Shulchan Aruch, Yoreh Deah 89:2.

2. Badei Hashulchan note 40 to Shulchan Aruch, Yoreah Deah 89:2.

3. Mishnah Berurah 16 to Shulchan Aruch, Orach Chaim 494:3, and Magen Avraham s.v. חלב thereon.

4. Maharam of Rottenberg, cited by Beit Yosef, Tur, Orach Chaim 173 s.v. ויש מחמירים, This stringency is based upon the Zohar, Parshat Mishpatim p.125a+b. כל האוכל מאכלי בשר וחלב, בסעודה אחת, או בשעה אחת, גורם לעורר דינים בעולם, as translated by Rav Ovadiah Yosef, Responsa Yechaveh Daat, Chelek 3, Siman 58, p.185

5. Badei Hashulchan Note 65 to Shulchan Aruch, Yoreh Deah 89:2.

6. Mishnah Berurah, See Note 3, above.

7. Rema, Shulchan Aruch, Yoreh Deah 89:2.

8. Taz, Shulchan Aruch, ibid. s.v. ויש מחמירין

9. Badei Hashulchan 72 to Shulchan Aruch, Yoreah Deah 89:2.

10. Chullin 112a s.v. ההוא בר גוזלא דנפל לכדא דכמכא. This ruling follows the opinion of the Rosh. The Ran however rules that the same applies even if the meat is roasted, as long as it is cold. See Beit Yosef, Tur, Yoreh Deah 91. This ruling also follows the view of the Beit Yosef that even if the raw meat has cracks and crevises, it may be rinsed and eaten as long as it is cold. There is however, a stricter view of the Baal Trumot which rules that rinsing is sufficient only where the raw cold meat is smooth. See Beit Yosef, Tur Yoreh Deah 91 s.v. ודווקא בבשר חי.

11. Chullin 112a s.v. אינו נאכל מחמת מלחו.

12. Tur, Yoreh Deah 91, Beit Yosef s.v. בד''א thereon.

13. Tur and Beit Yosef, Yoreh Deah 91, Shulchan Aruch, Yoreh Deah 91:7 and Rema thereon. This follows the ruling of the Rema that this applies even if the meat was cold, except where serious financial loss is involved.

14. Yad Soledet Bo is between 110 to 160 degrees Fahrenheit.

15. Shulchan Aruch, Yoreah Deah 91:4.

16. Ibid.

17. Ibid.

18. Tur, Yoreah Deah 91 in name of the Raviah.

19. Badei Hashulchan 22 to Shulchan Aruch, Yoreah Deah 91:4.

—〰—

SEDER NIGHT AND BACK SEAT DRIVERS
ליל הסדר
(פסחים צט:)

1. Shulchan Aruch, Orach Chaim 473:4 and Beer Heitev s.v. ויסדר.

2. Rema, 473:5; Shulchan Aruch Harav, Orach Chaim 473:32-33; Tosafot, Pesachim 116a, s.v. צריך.

3. Shulchan Aruch, Orach Chaim 473:4, and Mishnah Berurah 20 and Beer Heitev 5 thereon.

4. Ibid., and Mishnah Berurah 21 thereon.
5. ibid., and Mishnah Berurah 19 thereon.
6. Ibid., and Mishnah Berurah 36 thereon.
7. Ibid.
8. Exodus 1:14; Pesachim 116b.
9. Numbers 9:11.
10. Pesachim 120a; Rambam, Hilchot Chametz Umatzah 7:12.
11. Mishnah Berurah 38, Shulchan Aruch, Orach Chaim 473:5.
12. Chazon Ish, Kuntrus Hashiurim 39:18.
13. Shulchan Aruch, Orach Chaim 473:4.
14. Ibid., and Mishnah Berurah 32 thereon.
15. Ibid., and Mishnah Berurah 23 thereon.
16. Exodus 12:18; Rambam, Hilchot Chametz Umatzah 6:1.
17. Chazon Ish, Sefer Shiurei Hamitzvot 26.
18. Pesachim 43b; Rambam, Hilchot Chametz Umatzah 6:10; Shulchan Aruch, Orach Chaim 472:14, and Mishnah Berurah 44 thereon.
19. Pesachim 35a; Rambam, ibid. 6:4.
20. Mishnah Berurah 21 to Shulchan Aruch, Orach Chaim 453:4; Shulchan Aruch Harav, Orach Chaim 453:14.
21. Rosh, Pesachim 40a (in Rosh 6b)
22. Rif, Pesachim 40 (in Rif 12), Rambam Hilchot Chametz Umatzah 5:2.
23. Shulchan Aruch Orach Chaim 271:1, and Beer Heitev s.v. מיד.
24. Shulchan Aruch,Orach Chaim 472:1, Mishnah Berurah 5 thereon.
25. Shulchan Aruch,Orach Chaim 271:14, and Mishnah Berurah 14 thereon.
26. Shulchan Aruch, Orach Chaim, 472:10.
27. Shulchan Aruch, Orach Chaim, 473:1, and Mishnah Berurah 1 thereon.
28. Ibid.
29. Rabbi Shimon Eider, Halochos of Pesach XX D5, p.225
30. Ibid.
31. Ibid., XX B6, p.224
32. Ibid. XX B8 p.225; Shulchan Aruch, Orach Chaim 472:10-12, and Beer Heitev 15 thereon.
33. Shulchan Aruch, Orach Chaim 473:6, and Mishnah Berurah 52 thereon; Pesachim 115.
34. Mishnah Berurah 58 to, Shulchan Aruch, Orach Chaim 473:6
35. Shulchan Aruch, Orach Chaim 475:1.
36. Ibid., Mishnah Berurah 2.
37. Pesachim 115a.
38. Shulchan Aruch, Orach Chaim 477:1, and Mishnah Berurah 6 thereon.
39. Ibid. 478:1.
40. Ibid. 479:1.
41. Ibid. 480:1, and Mishnah Berurah 1 thereon.

42. Ibid.

43. Ibid. 481:2, and Rema thereon.

—∿∿—

THE FORTY NINERS
ספירת העומר
(מנחות סה)

1. Exodus 3:12.
2. Rabbeinu Nisim, quoted by Eliahu KiTov in Sefer Hatodaah 2:368, p.458
3. Menachot 65a; Rambam, Hilchot Temidim Umusaphim 7:11.
4. Menachot 66a; Rambam, Hilchot Temidim Umusaphim 7:12.
5. Leviticus 23:12; Sefer Hachinuch Mitzvah 302.
6. Leviticus 23:14; Sefer Hachinuch Mitzvah 303; Rambam, Hilchot Temidim Umusaphim, 7:13 and Lechem Mishneh s.v. אסור thereon.
7. Leviticus 23:17-18; Sefer Hachinuch Mitzvah 307; Rambam, Hilchot Temidim Umusaphim 8:1.
8. Leviticus 23:15.
9. Sotah 14a; Menachot 68b; Rambam, Hilchot Temidim Umusaphim 7:11.
10. Exodus 34:22.
11. Sefer Hachinuch Mitzvah 302.
12. Kiddushim 37a.
13. Ibid.
14. Rambam, Maachalot Asuroth 10:4; Sefer Hachinuch Mitzvah 303. Many Achronim take a less stringent view. See Aruch Hashulchan, Yoreah Deah 293:5 and other authorities quoted there.
15. Shulchan Aruch, Yoreh Deah 293:1-2.
16. Rema, ibid. Schach s.v. מכוח ס''ס. See also Dayan Dr. I. Grunfeld, The Jewish Dietary Laws volume 2, p.42, footnote 5.
17. Sefer Hachinuch Mitzvah 306; Shulchan Aruch, Orach Chaim 489:1, and Biur Halachah s.v. לספר העומר.
18. Rambam, Hilchot Temidim Umusaphim 7:24.
19. Leviticus 23:15-16.
20. Menachot 66a; Rambam, Hilchot Temidim Umusaphim 7:22.
21. Shulchan Aruch, Orach Chaim 489:2.
22. Shulchan Aruch Harav, Orach Chaim 489:12.
23. Shulchan Aruch, Orach Chaim 489:9.
24. Ibid., and Mishnah Berurah 39 thereon.
25. Ibid.
26. Deutoronomy 16:9.
27. Shulchan Aruch, Orach Chaim 489:1 and Biur Halachah s.v. ומצוה על כל אחד.
28. Biur Halachah to Shulchan Aruch, Orach Chaim 489:1 s.v. ומצווה על כל אחד.

29. Rambam, Sefer Hamitzvot 161.
30. Birkei Yosef, quoted in Kaf Hachaim to Shulchan Aruch, Orach Chaim 489:1 note 9.
31. Shulchan Aruch, Orach Chaim 489:7, and Mishnah Berurah 34 and Shaar Zion 43 thereon.
32. Shulchan Aruch, Orach Chaim 489:8. See explanation of Mishnah Berurah 38 based on ספיק ספיקא.
33. Shulchan Aruch, Orach Chaim 489:4.
34. Piskei Teshuvot Chelek 5, p.283, note 20 to Shulchan Aruch, Orach Chaim 489:8.
35. Piskei Teshuvot Chelek 5, p.273, note 6 to Shulchan Aruch, Orach Chaim 489:1.
36. See "Sefirat Haomer as a Period of Mourning," below.

—ᴍ—

SEFIRAT HA'OMER AS A PERIOD OF MOURNING
אבילות בתקופת העומר
(נדרים מ.)

1. Nedarim 40a.
2. Yevamoth 62b.
3. Rabbi Sheriah Gaon, cited by Harav Goren in Mo'adei Yisrael 264.
4. Eduyot Mishnah 2:10.
5. Mo'adei Yisrael p.270.
6. Mechilta, Exodus 19:2.
7. Shulchan Aruch, Orach Chaim 493:2, and Biur Halachah s.v. יש נוהגים.
8. Rema, ibid.
9. Yechave Daat Chelek 3, Siman 31, p.94.
10. Biur Halachah to Shulchan Aruch, Orach Chaim 493:3 s.v. יש נוהגים
11. Responsa Igrot Moshe, Orach Chaim Chelek 1, Siman 159, p.279.
12. Kuntrus Achron, Sa'if Katan 2 in Shaarim Hametzuyanim Behalachah Chelek 3, p.140 to Kitzur Shulchan Aruch 122:2
13. Mishnah Berurah 3 to Shulchan Aruch, Orach Chaim 493:1.
14. Responsa Yechaveh Daat Chelek 6, Siman 34, p.176.
15. Rabbi Shimon Eider, Halachos of Pesach XXIX A4, p.328.
16. See note 12 above.
17. Mishnah Beurah 2 to Shulchan Aruch, Orach Chaim, 493:2 and Kaf Hachaim 4 to Shulchan Aruch, Orach Chaim 493:2
18. Responsa Yechave Daat Chelek 1, Siman 24, p.69.
19. Responsa Igrot Moshe, Orach Chaim Chelek 4, Siman102, p.189.
20. Responsa Igrot Moshe, Orach Chaim Chelek 1, Siman 159, p.279
21. Rabbi Lau, Yahadut, Halachah Lema'aseh p.294.

Chapter Four

Yom Tov

PRIME-TIME PRAYER
חודש אלול

Prayer is always an avenue to God. But in the month of Elul, the last month of the Jewish year, and during the ten days between Rosh Hashanah and Yom Kippur, God lends a particularly sympathetic ear. And so, when Moses trudged despondently up the mountain that first day of Elul, after dashing the tablets of the Law, and for forty days and forty nights begged God's forgiveness, the sin of the golden calf was forgiven. On that Yom Kippur, the shattered pieces of God's faith in the Jews was restored and the twin tablets of their eternal relationship renewed.[1] And ever since, these forty days between Rosh Chodesh Elul and Yom Kippur have been prime time for prayer.

The romance in this prayer date is picked up in Midrashic literature. The Midrash points out that the first letters of each word of the verse - אני לדודי ודודי לי - "Ani Ledodi Vedodi Li," "I am my beloved's and my beloved is mine,"[2] spell out the word אלול - Elul. So too the first letters of the verse - ואשר לא צדה ואלוקים אנה לידו ושמתי לך מקום - "Veasher Lo Tzada Velokim Ina Leyado Vesamti Lecha Makom," "if he did not plan to kill his victim, but God caused it to happen,"[3] referring to the cities of refuge for manslaughter, spell out אלול. For אלול too is a safe harbor in time, during which God protects us from the damaging consequences of our sins. Similarly, the first letter of each word of the verse - איש לרעהו ומתנות לאביונים - "Ish Lere'ehu Umatanot La'evionim," "sending choice portions to one another and gifts to the poor,"[4] which emphasize the role of charity in procuring God's forgiveness, also spell out אלול.

When Moses ascended the mountain that first, fateful day of Elul, the Shofar (ram's horn) was sounded daily in the Camp of Israel, heralding his expected return. This eliminated the possibility of the disastrous conclusion, previously drawn from his prolonged absence, which resulted in the sin of the Golden Calf. This is the source of the Rabbinical requirement that we sound the Shofar each day of Elul.[5] The Shofar awakens us and admonishes us not to slumber through this unique period of communication with God.

Commencing with the first day of Elul, through Rosh Hashanah and Yom Kippur and culminating on the last day of Succot, we recite Psalm 27 - לדוד ה' אורי וישעי - Ledavid Hashem Ori Veyishi, "The Lord is my light and salvation," after each morning and evening prayer service.[6] The focal point of reference therein is to the word "light," denoting the spotlight of judgment trained upon us on Rosh Hashanah, as well as to the word "salvation," denoting God's outstretched Hand of salvation on Yom Kippur. The Psalm also reminds us of God's protective roof on Succot.

If repentance is not to be used merely as a credit card to postpone payment at maturity date, then we must endeavor sincerely to honor our commitment and repent before the Day of Judgment. This concept is alluded to in the words - לא יחל דברו ככל - "Lo Yachel

Devaro Kechol, "if a man makes an oath to obligate himself, he must not break his word."[7] The last letters of each of these words spell out - אלול - Elul. But, just in case, despite our sincere endeavors, we fail to meet such commitment before Rosh Hashanah, God does grant us an extension. Accordingly, it is our custom to annul our vows on the last day of Elul.[8]

SELICHOT
ימי הסליחות

However remote the prospect of acquittal, a Jew must never give up. God commands us to challenge indictment with prayer. And the Rabbis urge us to confront sentencing with hunger strikes. And so, the Midrash tells us[1] when Moses stood before God, lost for words with which to defend the sin of the Golden Calf, God Himself donned a Tallit, a prayer shawl, took to the Bima - prayer stand - and showed Moses how to pray and what to say. - ויעבר ה' על פניו ויקרא ה' ה' אל רחום וחנון ארך אפים ורב חסד ואמת - "And God passed before [Moses] and proclaimed, [His Thirteen Attributes]: The Lord, The Lord, mighty, merciful and gracious, long suffering, and abundant in love and truth; He remembers deeds of love for thousands of generations, forgiving iniquity and transgression and sin; He does not forgive those who do not repent."[2] And the Midrash continues, "that day, God covenanted with Moses that, whenever and whatever their sin, Israel will always be forgiven if they recite The Thirteen Attributes."

Accordingly, in the past, religious leaders would combine the - עשרת ימי תשובה - the Ten Days of Repentance between - ראש השנה - Rosh Hashanah and - יום כפור - Yom Kippur with ten days of fasting and prayers for forgiveness - סליחות - Selichot. However, because fasting is prohibited on four out of the Ten Days of Repentance, namely, on the two days of Rosh Hashanah, on Shabbat Shuvah and on Erev Yom Kippur, they would begin to fast and to recite Selichot four days before Rosh Hashanah.[3] These four days of fasting and prayer are known as the - ימי הסליחות - Days of Selichot. When Rosh Hashanah occurs on a Wednesday or a Thursday, Selichot begin on the Sunday of the same week. When Rosh Hashanah occurs before Wednesday, Selichot begin on the Sunday of the week preceding the week of Rosh Hashanah.[4] Today, few people fast during the Days of Selichot, but the custom is to rise early to recite Selichot. Another reason for observing the Days of Selichot is that a person's status before Rosh Hashanah is compared to that of a sacrifice about to be offered up in the בית המקדש, the Temple. Four days prior to its offering, each sacrifice underwent close examination to ensure the absence of any blemishes that would disqualify it for sacrifice. We, too, should examine ourselves during the four Selichot days for any defects that would render us unacceptable to God on the Day of Judgment.[5]

In addition to The Thirteen Attributes, there are seven categories of Selichot prayers. These are: introductory prayers called- פתיחות - Petichot, prayers in the form of refrains called - פזמונים - Pizmonim, two stanza prayers called - שניות - Sheniyot, three stanza prayers called - שלישיות - Shelishiyot, four stanza prayers called - שלמוניות - Shalmoniyot, prayers recalling the binding of Isaac called עקידה - Akeida, and prayers for grace called - תחינות - Techinot. Many of the Selichot prayers contain verses or phrases culled from the following scriptures: Exodus 32:11 and 34:9; Numbers 14:13-19; Psalms 25:11;

1 Kings; 8:36; Amos 7:2; Daniel 9:4-9 and Nehemiah 9:31-37.

According to one opinion in the Talmud,[6] at midnight God rises from His seat of judgment and occupies the seat of mercy from which He sustains the world. Midnight, therefore, according to this opinion, is the best time for Selichot. According to another opinion, God rides His chariot through our world during the last three hours of the night.[7] According to this opinion, the best time for Selichot are the last three hours before dawn. If one rises before dawn, one should recite - ברכת התורה - Birkat Hatorah, the blessing of the Torah, before reciting Selichot,[8] and the Chazzan, the reader, should wear a Tallit, a prayer shawl, without reciting the Tallit blessing.[9] Selichot may be said after day break.[10] Selichot written in the Hebrew language may be recited by an individual in the absence of a Minyan, a quorum of ten men, but Selichot written in the Aramaic language may not.[11] The Thirteen Attributes may not be recited in the absence of a Minyan, but they may be read in the absence of a Minyan with the tune used by a Ba'al Koreh when reading the Torah in public.

The Tur[12] points out that a person undergoing trial for an offense carrying capital punishment would don dark clothes and be in a general state of mourning. We, on the other hand, are so confident of God's mercy, that we wear white and festive clothes, and celebrate the Day of Judgment.

HAPPY BIRTHDAY
מוסף של ראש השנה

Rosh Hashanah - ראש השנה - is the birthday of the human race. Adam, the first human being, was created on Rosh Hashanah.[1] Whereas individual birthdays are celebrated with parties and gifts, the birthday of mankind is a day of reckoning and taking stock. We take stock of the extent to which we have fulfilled our purpose to complete and perfect God's world. "On the seventh day, God rested from all the work which God created [for us] to do."[2] On Rosh Hashanah, God sat in judgment over Adam for the first sin and commuted his sentence from the prescribed death penalty to expulsion from the Garden of Eden. The Midrash guarantees that in judging us, God will apply the same measure of mercy.

On this Day of Judgment, God instructs us how to conduct our own defense. "Recite before Me on Rosh Hashanah verses of Kingship, Remembrance and Shofar: Verses of Kingship, so that you may accept My Sovereignty over you; verses of remembrance, so that I should remember you favorably; and with what shall these verses be recited - with a Shofar." This passage from the Talmud[3] lays out the structure of the Mussaf prayer on Rosh Hashanah. Accordingly, on Rosh Hashanah the blessings of - מלכויות - Malchuyot - Kingship, זכרונות - Zichronot - Remembrance and - שופרות - Shofarot are added to the regular Shabbat and Yom Tov Mussaf, afternoon prayer, blessings. The result is a total of nine blessings that are recited in the Rosh Hashanah Mussaf prayer.[4] The nine blessings correspond to the nine times that Chanah invoked the name of God in her request for a child, which was granted on Rosh Hashanah.[5]

As understood by the Maharsha,[6] מלכויות, זכרונות, ושופרות correspond to the following three principles of faith: recognition of the existence of God; acknowledgment of Divine Providence and accountability to God and acknowledgement of the Divine Revelation of the Torah.

Each of the מלכויות, זכרונות and שופרות blessings is made up of ten descriptive verses, four from the Torah, three from Psalms and three from the Prophets. The ten verses correspond to the Ten Commandments given at Sinai and the Ten Divine Utterances[7] with which God created the world.[8]

The מלכויות blessing commences with the - עלינו לשבח - Aleynu Leshabe'ach - prayer and ends with the blessing - מקדש ישראל ויום הזכרון - Mekadesh Yisrael Veyom Hazikaron. The ten verses included in the מלכויות blessing describe the Jewish belief in one God and the eventual universal acceptance of monotheism in the Messianic era.[9]

The זכרונות blessing commences with the words - אתה זוכר מעשה עולם - Ata Zocher Ma'aseh Olam - and ends with the words - ברוך אתה ה' זוכר הברית - Baruch Atah Hashem, Zocher Habrit. The ten verses included in the זכרונות blessing describe God's awesome knowledge and unfailing memory of all of mankind's thoughts and actions. Nothing escapes

Him. In arriving at His final Judgment, we ask God to take into account His covenant with Noah and the Patriarchs that the world will never again be destroyed by a flood and that the Jewish people will always survive. We remind God of the Jewish nation's blind faith following Him through the Sinai desert for forty years and of Abraham's ultimate sacrifice with the binding of Isaac. We ask God to return the faith in the Jewish people and extend our time on earth to perfect His world.[10]

The שופרות blessing commences with the words - אתה נגלית - Ata Nigleitah - and ends with the blessing - שומע קול תרועות עמו ישראל ברחמים - Shomea Kol Teruat Amo Yisrael Berachamim. The ten verses included in the Shofaroth blessing describe the sound of the Shofar blasted by God at the time of the Divine Revelation. They also describe the sound of the Shofar that will herald the coming of the Final Redemption, when all the nations of the world will embrace God and His Torah.[11]

The sound of the Shofar is the leitmotif that binds the three blessings of מלכיות, שופרות, זכרונות into one symphonic prayer. Ten blasts of the Shofar, echoing the ten verses, are sounded at the end of each blessing, followed by - היום הרת עולם - Hayom Harat Olam - "Today is the birthday of the world." Just as song invokes in us the love of God, so too does the Shofar invoke in God the love of the Jewish people. It brings back to Him fond memories of Divine Revelation and the Binding of Isaac. It signals to Him our acceptance of His Sovereignty and our yearning for the coming of the Messiah.

SHOFAR
שופר

The Torah[1] calls Rosh Hashanah, - יום תרועה - Yom Teruah, the day of the "sounding" of the Shofar. The Shofar is the central theme of the day. The Psalmist tells us that the sound of God's - שופר - Shofar announces the God of Judgment - עלה אלקים בתרועה - Ala Elokim Betruah.[2] But the sound of Israel's Shofar brings out the God of Mercy, - ה' בקול שופר - Hashem Bekol Shofar. This is because the Shofar reminds God both of - עקידת יצחק - the binding of Isaac and of - מעמד הר סיני - the Revelation at Mount Sinai. Both events demonstrate to the Judge Israel's absolute trust and faith in God. And so, when God promised Abraham children, but then commanded him to slay his only child, and then reversed Himself and commanded him to sacrifice a ram in Isaac's place, Abraham would only comply but would not ask why. And when Abraham's descendants were commanded, at the foot of Mount Sinai, to accept the Law, they chose, like Abraham, to comply and not ask why. The Shofar recalls both the Akeidah and Revelation and urges God to reciprocate and trust in Israel.

The Torah requires of us, on Rosh Hashanah, to listen to nine blasts of the Shofar.[3] These are, the sounds of three blasts of - תרועה - Teruah, each of which is immediately preceded and immediately followed by the sound of a - תקיעה - Tekiah, a level, uninterrupted sound. The - תרועה - Teruah, according to some opinions, resembles a short, staccato-like cry, similar to the shrieks of Sarah when she learned of the Binding of Isaac. According to others, the Teruah resembles a series of cries of longer duration, more like groans, emulated by the sound of the - שברים - Shevarim. In order to satisfy both opinions, the Rabbis require that both the staccato-like sounds, which we call Teruah, and the longer groaning like sounds, which we call Shevarim, be sounded between the level sounds of the Tekiot. As a result, the nine Biblically mandated Shofar sounds are increased to 30. These 30 blasts are sounded on Rosh Hashanah day (but not by night)[4] after the reading of the Law and before the prayer of Mussaf.[5] These תקיעות are referred to as מיושב - Meyushav, because one may sit while listening to them. In addition, the Rabbis added another 30 blasts during the repetition of Mussaf, 10 blasts after - מלכויות - Malchiot, the verses celebrating God's sovereignty, 10 blasts after - זכרונות-Zichronot, the verses urging God to recall our good deeds and be merciful, and 10 blasts after - שופרות-Shofarot, the verses recalling the role of the Shofar in Israel's history. These תקיעות are referred to as מעומד - Me'umad, because one should stand when listening to them.[6] In addition, the Rabbis require another 40 Shofar blasts after Mussaf, totaling 100 blasts in all.[7]

The blessings recited prior to sounding the Shofar focus on listening to the Shofar - לשמוע - Lishmoa, rather than sounding - לתקוע - Litkoa, the Shofar.[8] Although not free from debate,[9] it is concluded that the Mitzvah is to HEAR the Shofar and that sounding the

Shofar is merely the means through which the Mitzvah is fulfilled. This is similar to the Succah, the blessing for which is - לישב - Leishev, the dwelling in the Succah, rather than the building of the Succah.[10] In view of the fact that listening to the Shofar is a time-bound commandment, women are exempt.[11] Nevertheless, women are encouraged to listen to the Shofar and to recite the blessing. This is in accordance with the opinion of Rabbi Yossi and Rabbeinu Tam that women have the option, if not the obligation, to participate in time-bound commandments and recite the appropriate blessing when doing so.[12]

The Midrash relates that the right horn of the ram sacrificed in lieu of Isaac was the Shofar which was later sounded at the Revelation. The left horn of that ram will be sounded on the day of Redemption.[13] "And it shall come to pass on that day [of Redemption], that a great Shofar shall be blown."[14]

It is told that Rabbi Levi Yitzchak of Berditchev would open the ark of Torah scrolls on Rosh Hashanah, turn toward Heaven and plead, "God Almighty, You have asked the Jews to sound the Shofar once on Rosh Hashanah and they have done so hundreds of times for thousands of years. We have been asking You for thousands of years to sound the great Shofar just once, on the day of Redemption. We are still waiting."[15]

WHERE'S THE SHOFAR?
ראש השנה שחל להיות בשבת

osh Hashanah without the Shofar, Succot without the Lulav, or Purim without the Megillah, is like a play without the main character. Why is the sounding of the Shofar prohibited on Shabbat? According to the Talmud Yerushalmi,[1] the prohibition is of Biblical origin. It is inferred from the fact that the Torah gives Rosh Hashanah two different names, - יום תרועה - Yom Teruah,[2] which means "the day of sounding the Shofar" and - זכרון תרועה - Zicharon Teruah,[3] which means the day of "remembering the Shofar." On Shabbat/Rosh Hashanah, explains the Yerushalmi, the actual sounding of the Shofar is prohibited and is replaced by references to the Shofar in the Rosh Hashanah prayers. On a weekday Rosh Hashanah, the words "Yom Teruah" require the actual sounding of the Shofar. Another explanation for the prohibition of sounding the Shofar on Shabbat mentioned in the Yerushalmi is that only the members of the High Court, before whom witnesses testified to the sighting of the new moon on Shabbat, knew for sure that Shabbat was also the day of Rosh Hashanah. Everywhere else, the doubt still remained as to whether Shabbat or Sunday was Rosh Hashanah. And in the presence of such doubt, there was no justification to sound the Shofar on Shabbat.[4]

The Talmud Bavli[5] disagrees and mounts a four pronged attack on the Yerushalmi. First, argues the Bavli, the sounding of the Shofar is not included in the 39 Melachot employed in the construction of the Mishkan. Second, the sounding of the Shofar is not a - מלאכה - Melachah but rather a - חוכמה - Chochmah (skill). Third, when the Torah states - יום תרועה יהיה לכם - Yom Teruah Yiheye Lachem, it means that the Shofar should be sounded on whatever day Rosh Hashanah occurs, whether on a weekday or a Shabbat.[6] Otherwise, the Torah would have simply said - תרועה יהיה לכם - Teruah Yiheye Lachem. Lastly, if, in fact, the prohibition of sounding Shofar on Shabbat is Biblical, how could it be sounded in the Temple? Therefore, the Bavli maintains that the prohibition against sounding the Shofar on Shabbat is the product of Rabbinic legislation (a "Takanah"). Because all males are commanded, and women take it upon themselves, to adhere to the Mitzvah of Shofar, and because most people are untrained in the skill of sounding the Shofar, the Rabbis were concerned that people might carry the Shofar through the streets to a Ba'al Tokeah (a person skilled in the art of blowing) to sound the Shofar on their behalf. Out of a similar concern, the Rabbis prohibited picking up a Lulav on Shabbat/Succot, or reading the Megillah on Shabbat/Purim.[7]

The Shofar was always sounded in the Temple Sanhedrin (High Court) on Shabbat, because Rabbinical Shabbat legislation did not apply in the Temple - אין שבות במקדש - Ein Shevut Bemikdash.[8] When the Sanhedrin was exiled to Yavneh, the question arose whether the Shofar could be sounded in Yavneh on Shabbat. Rabbi Yochanan Ben Zakhai ruled that the Shofar could be sounded on Shabbat in the presence of a Beit Din (court of law), even outside the Temple. In Rabbi Yochanan Ben Zakhai's opinion, the presence of a Beit Din would deter the people from carrying on Shabbat.[9] The question is, what does the term Beit Din include? According to one opinion in the Talmud Bavli,[10] it means the Great Sanhedrin of 71 judges. According to a second opinion, the term Beit Din includes the district courts of 23 judges.[11] And according to the Rif, the term Beit Din refers to any court of three persons at any time, in any place. Indeed, the Rif sounded the Shofar in his Beit Din in Fez on Shabbat/Rosh Hashanah. However, his disciples did not follow his custom.[12]

The Rabbinical prohibition of sounding the Shofar on Shabbat has come under machine gun fire from Rishonim and Acharonim. First, if the sole concern is that of carrying on Shabbat, why can one not carry the Shofar in a location equipped with an Eruv? Perhaps it could be suggested that the sounding of the Shofar cannot be dependent upon the arbitrary question of whether or not an Eruv is in place. It is inconceivable that the Shofar be sounded in one neighborhood, where there happens to be an Eruv, but not in another, where there is no Eruv. On the other hand, that is precisely what happened in the days of the Temple. They sounded the Shofar in the Temple, but not outside the Temple, and later, in the Beit Din, but not outside of the Beit Din. In rebuttal of this argument, one might suggest that everybody knows when the Sanhedrin or the Beit Din is in session, but not everybody knows whether the Eruv is up. Furthermore, the crowds that gather in the Synagogue on Shabbat/Rosh Hashanah might be oblivious to the laws of Eruv and conclude that, because they saw the Shofar carried in one location, it may be carried in all locations.

Others ask, if one may perform a Brit Milah, circumcision, on Shabbat, why may one not sound the Shofar on Shabbat? In both cases, the Torah requires the Mitzvah to be performed on a particular day whenever that may occur, whether on a weekday, or on a Shabbat. If the Rabbis are concerned that the Shofar may be carried in the streets, why are they not concerned that the Milah knife or the baby be carried in the streets? Several answers are offered to distinguish Shofar from Milah. Whereas everybody is commanded to perform and is simultaneously preoccupied with the Mitzvah of Shofar, few individuals perform the Mitzvah of Milah at the same time. Accordingly, there will always be an uninvolved bystander, aware of the law, to remind the preoccupied parent of the prohibition of carrying.[13] Others answer that whereas almost anybody can quickly learn the art of sounding the Shofar or waving the Lulav, nobody would undertake to perform Milah unless fully trained and qualified. Accordingly, the Mohel, who is highly qualified in all the laws of Milah, will be conscious of the prohibition against carrying the Milah knife on Shabbat.[14] Others ask, why did the Rabbis single out carrying on Shabbat, when they should have been equally concerned with the prohibition of mending a musical instrument - שמא יתקן כלי - Shema Yetaken Kli?[15] They answer that, whereas the prohibition of carrying a Shofar in the street applies on Shabbat but not on Yom Tov (because of the principle of Mitoch), the prohibition of Shema Yetaken Kli applies both on Shabbat and on Yom Tov. Thus, if the Rabbis would prohibit the sounding of the Shofar because of the concern for Shema Yetaken Kli, the Shofar would never be sounded on Rosh Hashanah.

Some Halachic commentators, after winding their way through the tortuous paths of the Rabbinical prohibition against sounding the Shofar on Shabbat / Rosh Hashanah, throw up their hands in despair, declaring that it defies all logic. Rabbi Yitzchak Mirski, in Hegyonei Halachah, suggests that the logic is in the lack of logic. The Rabbis' request to refrain from sounding the Shofar on Shabbat Rosh Hashanah is as illogical as Abraham's request that Isaac become a human sacrifice. Despite the inability to make any sense of Abraham's request, Isaac was prepared to go along with it, only because his father and his teacher required it. Similarly, our willingness to go along with the seemingly illogical Rabbinic prohibition against sounding the Shofar on Shabbat reminds God in the most poignant way of the faith that the Jews have in their Rabbis who ultimately derive their inspiration from God.[16]

And then there are the conscientious objectors that just don't buy it. One such objector, Rabbi Yaakov Schlezinger, caused a religious riot in Jerusalem when he insisted on blowing the Shofar on Shabbat/Rosh Hashanah in the Rabbi Yochanan ben Zakhai Synagogue in the Old City in the presence of a Rabbinical court. Rumor has it that when he met with violent dissent, he locked himself up in his apartment and sounded the Shofar.[17]

Reb Levi Yitzchak of Berditchev suggests that the whole purpose of the Shofar is to arouse God's sympathy to inscribe us in the Book of Life and not in the Book of Death. However, on Shabbat, God, like us, is not allowed to write, unless it is a matter of Pikuach Nefesh, saving a life. Accordingly, God may not write on Shabbat in the Book of Death. Therefore, sounding the Shofar on Shabbat/Rosh Hashanah is unnecessary.

TWO DAYS ROSH HASHANAH, ERUVIN AND EGGS
ראש השנה. יומא אריכתא

W hy is - ראש השנה - Rosh Hashanah, the Jewish New Year, so different from other Jewish Holidays? On the face of it, it does not seem to follow any pattern. It is celebrated for two days, not only in the Diaspora, but also in Israel.[1] Yet, the Sages refer to the two days of Rosh Hashanah as one long day, - יומא אריכתא - Yoma Arichta.

On Pesach, Shavuot, and Succot we keep Yom Tov for two days because, during the time of the Second Temple, there was doubt whether the month preceding Yom Tov was a - חודש חסר - Chodesh Chaser of 29 days or was a - חודש מלא - Chodesh Maleh of 30 days.[2] But on Rosh Hashanah, the doubt was exacerbated for the following reason. In the case of other festivals, such as Pesach, the emissaries that the Beit Din dispatched to advise outlying districts of a Chodesh Chaser had 14 days to reach their destination. In the case of Rosh Hashanah, however, the emissaries had no time at all. In fact, as soon as the witnesses had testified on the 30th day of Elul that they had sighted the new moon, that very day was declared Rosh Hashanah. And on Rosh Hashanah, the emissaries could not travel more than the Techum Shabbat distance of 2/3 of a mile beyond Jerusalem. As a result, even people living inside Israel, but outside of Jerusalem, remained in doubt.

And even inside Jerusalem, confusion reigned. Nobody knew whether the witnesses who would testify to the sighting of the new moon would arrive on the day of the 30th, in which case Rosh Hashanah would be on the 30th day, or whether they would not arrive, in which case Rosh Hashanah would be on the 31st day. On the night immediately following the 29th day of Elul and on 30th day of Elul itself, people hedged their bets. They ceased work, went to the Synagogue, recited the Rosh Hashanah prayers and blew the Shofar, all in a tentative state of mind. Perhaps, they fretted, the witnesses will not come today, the 30th, and tomorrow, the 31st, will be Rosh Hashanah by default, and a day's work would have been wasted. But then again, perhaps the witnesses would come. So how could they risk working?

The Levites in the Temple fretted, too. If the witnesses would not arrive by Minchah time on the afternoon of the 30th, the Levites had to proceed to offer up the Tamid, the afternoon daily sacrifice. But they did not know which Psalm to sing when doing so. Should they sing the special Rosh Hashanah Psalm or the weekday Psalm? One year they bet on the weekday Psalm only to see the witnesses arrive after Minchah and prove them wrong.[3] In this situation, the Rabbis decided to dispel the doubt. They decreed that if witnesses would arrive after the afternoon sacrifice on the 30th day of Elul, their testimony would be ignored and the 31st day of Elul would be declared Rosh Hashanah. Furthermore, in order to provide certainty for the Levites and in order to prevent people from working on the 30th of Elul after Minchah time, the Rabbis merged the 30th day of Elul with the 31st day, declaring them both one long day or - יומא אריכתא - Yoma Arichta.[4]

From this decree on, the two days of Rosh Hashanah, unlike the two days of Pesach, Shavuot and Succot, were no longer celebrated out of doubt, but out of certainty. This distinction between the status of the two days of Rosh Hashanah and the two days of the other festivals has practical ramifications.[5] For example, on Rosh Hashanah, one may not extend the Techum Shabbat 4000 Amot in two directions, as one may on the two days of Pesach, Shavuot and Succoth. Because the two days of Rosh Hashanah are merged into one Yoma Arichta, only one Eruv Techumim could be placed for both days to walk 4000 Amot in only one chosen direction. Similarly, the argument that an egg laid on the first day of Pesach, Shavuot or Succoth could be eaten on the second day of these Festivals[6] would not apply. An egg laid on the first day Rosh Hashanah could not be eaten on the second.

Following the destruction of the Second Temple, the dilemma of the Levites was no longer a concern. Accordingly, Rabbi Yochanan Ben Zakkai decreed that the testimony of witnesses arriving after Minchah on the 30th of Elul would once again be accepted, thereby rendering Rosh Hashanah one day.[7] If witnesses did not arrive by nightfall of the 30th, Rosh Hashanah would be two days. Rabbi Yochanan Ben Zakkai's decree did not, however, apply to the Diaspora, where it could not be known, on the 30th day, whether the witnesses had arrived or not. Accordingly, in the Diaspora, Rosh Hashanah remained two days, by decree.[8] The Babylonian Rabbis who came to Israel applied the same decree to the land of Israel, even after the time of Rabbi Yochanan Ben Zakkai.[9] Although we now know which day is genuinely Rosh Hashanah, we continue to celebrate two days everywhere, out of respect for the tradition of our ancestors - מנהג אבותיכם בידיכם - Minhag Avoteichem Beyedeichem.[10]

YOM KIPPUR
יום כפור

Even Moses, who spoke with God one on One, was not allowed to see Him during his lifetime. "You cannot see My face, for no man shall see Me and live."[1] Ultimately, we shall all see God, one on One, and face not only Him, but also ourselves and the lives we led. Our desire to see Him will then be consummated, and His existence will be proven beyond all doubt. But our ability to repent and prepare ourselves for that Day of Judgment will have passed. And so, one day a year, God gives us the opportunity to come as close to Him as humanly possible and still repent. Yom Kippur is the dress rehearsal of our own Yahrzeit. We wear the shrouds in which we will ultimately face Him, and we discard the shoes that we will no longer need. We neither eat, drink, nor bathe as we stand alone before Him. We crowd the synagogue, just as the throngs of Israelites crowded the Temple,[2] praying, fasting and waiting with bated breath for the Sheliach Zibbur, - the High Priest - to successfully complete the Yom Kippur Temple Service. For if the High Priest does not survive the day, Israel might not survive the year.

And before the silent and anxious crowd, the High Priest walks the tight rope between life and death from dawn to dusk. One procedural slip in the Temple Service, and it will be all over,[3] just as it was for Aaron's sons, whose bodies had to be retrieved from the Holy of Holies.[4] The High Priest's task is not easy, and the stakes are high. Single-handedly, he has to juggle the performance of the daily Temple Service and the special Yom Kippur Service, darting, as he does so, back and forth between the Holy of Holies, the Temple Sanctuary and the Temple Courtyard. Fifteen sacrifices, (two lambs for the daily sacrifice, one bullock, one ram and seven lambs for the Mussaf sacrifice, one bullock for the priests' atonement, one ram for the people's burnt offering, one he-goat for the people's atonement and finally, the scapegoat, which is sent to die in the wilderness) have to be slaughtered, offered up or attended to by the High Priest on Yom Kippur.[5] The High Priest must, among other things, sprinkle the sacrificial blood on the altars, offer up the incense, prepare the Sanctuary lamps for lighting, burn the limbs of the animals on the altar, offer up the baked cakes of the High Priest, pour the drink offerings, confess his own, his family's and the priests' sins, cast lots for the two he-goats, tie a crimson ribbon on the head of the scapegoat, pray for the welfare of the people, confess their sins and read to them from the Torah. Each of the four times the High Priest enters the Holy of Holies to perform the Yom Kippur Service, he must change out of his routine, golden garments into his Yom Kippur, white garments, so as not to remind God of the sin of the Golden Calf. Each time the High Priest enters the Temple Sanctuary or Temple Courtyard to perform the daily Temple Service, he must change back into his golden garments. And between each change of garments, he must wash his hands and feet and then immerse himself in the cold waters of the Temple ritual bath.[6] The precision required and the time constraints imposed make the High Priest's task almost humanly impossible. Indeed, according to the Midrash's interpretation of Leviticus 16:17, when entering the Holy of Holies, the High Priest was temporarily transformed into a ministering angel. We are told that when the High Priest finally emerged from the Holy of Holies alive and well, having successfully completed his mission, he was swept up by the waiting crowds who celebrated with him deep into the night.[7]

The Midrash relates that during Moses' 40 day visit to the mountain of God, he overheard and memorized the angels' secret prayer - ברוך שם כבוד מלכותו לעולם ועד - Baruch Shem Kevod Malchuto Le'olam Va'ed, Blessed is the name of His Glorious Kingdom forever. When Moses returned to earth, he taught this prayer to the Jews but cautioned them to utter it under their breath, so that the angels would not detect the infringement. On Yom Kippur, however, when we most closely resemble angels, we are asked to recite this prayer out loud.[8]

יזכור - Yizkor, the prayer for the dead, is always recited on the last days of Yom Tov. Because Rosh Hashanah and Yom Kippur are, in a sense, considered one Festival, Yizkor is said on Yom Kippur,[9] but not on Rosh Hashanah. By reciting Yizkor, we pray for the atonement of those that can no longer acquit themselves.

As the Ne'ilah curtain falls, and we descend from the Seventh heaven where, we are told, God and the angels reside, we declare seven times, "The Lord, He is The God." And on returning from our brief visit to heaven, we recite the prayer uttered by those that leave this world for ever, - שמע ישראל ה' אלוקינו ה' אחד - Shema Yisrael, Hashem Elokeinu, Hashem Echad, Hear, O Israel: the Lord our God, the Lord is One.

SUCCOT
סוכות

The Torah[1] proclaims the 15th day of Tishrei the beginning of the seven day Festival of סוכות - Succot and requires that during this Festival, we dwell in Succot. Typically, the Torah gives no reason for its commandments, and we are left to fathom them for ourselves. But the Mitzvah of Succot has a stated reason, - למען ידעו דרתיכם כי בסכות הושבתי את בני ישראל בהוציאי אותם מארץ מצרים - "That your generations may know that I made the children of Israel dwell in booths when I brought them out of the land of Egypt." If the Festival of Succot commemorates the exodus from Egypt, which took place in the first month of Nissan, why are we asked to dwell in Succot in the seventh month of Tishrei? The answer may lie in the mystery the Torah invests in the number 7. On the seventh day of each week, we dedicate time, that precious and irretrievable asset, to God. And in return, God shelters us in His cloud, where the pressures of time are suspended for the day. Give and take is the kernel of every relationship, including God and man. But when we came out of Egypt, we did not understand that. The wealth we accumulated from the Egyptians on the way out, was invested in the Golden Calf. And so, God summoned back His cloud of protection and left us to the pressures of our own possessions. It was only on the seventh month of Tishrei, when Moses returned from the mountain of God with the gift of amnesty,[2] that we finally agreed to donate our cherished possessions to the building of God's house, rather than to building our own.[3] Between the 11th and the 15th day of Tishrei, the Jews busied themselves with the building of the Mishkan, God's residence.[4] When the Mishkan was completed on the eve of the 15th day of Tishrei, God and man each renounced their respective permanent residences. God descended from his lofty residence and resided in the House we built Him. And we leave behind the house we built ourselves and reside in the Succah He builds for us.[5]

What were the desert Succot made of? Some maintain they were God's clouds that protected us from the elements as we trudged through the desert.[6] Others maintain they were real booths we built ourselves.[7] And there are many commentaries which side with the one opinion or the other.[8] The Netziv,[9] however, suggests that both opinions are right. According to him, when the Jews encamped, they built their own Succot. And when they were on the move, God protected them with His Cloud of Glory. Indeed, the very construction of the Succah seems to incorporate both opinions. The - סכך - Sechach - roof, must be made of natural vegetation, unprocessed and unused by man, and like all Godly things, it must be of a substance that cannot be contaminated, - אינו מקבל טומאה - Eino Mekabel Tumah.[10] Without the Sechach, there is no Succah. But without the walls, there is no Sechach. In fact, the walls must be erected first, or else the Succah is disqualified.[11] Just as the Shabbat is a joint venture in time between God and man, so too is the Succah a joint venture in space between God and man. This, perhaps, explains why so many of the fundamental laws of - עירובין - Eruvin (- צורת הפתח - Tzurat Hapetach, - לבוד - Lavud, - גוד אסיק - Gud Asik, - קורה - Korah and - לחי - Lechi) are derived from the laws of Succot. When we are on the move in life, exiled from place to place, we turn to God, our Partner, for the protection of His cloud. When we are given the luxury of settling down, God turns to us, His partner, for the protection of our walls. Perhaps that is why the - אושפיזין - Ushpizin (the Guests), Abraham, Isaac, Jacob, Moses, Aharon, Joseph and David, who, according to the Kabalah, reside with us in our Succot, feel so at home there. For each of their lives was a nomadic existence in which they shared their fragile homes with God and God with them.

On the first two nights of Succot, eating in the Succah is a Torah requirement which must be fulfilled.[12] A person may not say, "I would rather skip dinner altogether and not eat in the Succah." One must, unless one is sick,[13] have dinner in the Succah. On the other days of Succot, there is no Torah requirement to eat in the Succah and one may decide (except on Shabbat and Yom Tov) to skip all meals and eat fruit or snacks outside the Succah. Regular meals, however, must be eaten in the Succah. If it rains on the first two nights, one should wait a while, some say up to two hours, until it stops and then enter the Succah, unless it is clear that it will not stop.[14] If one cannot wait, or if the rain will not stop, one enters the Succah, recites Kiddush and Shehecheyanu, does not recite the Succah blessing of Leshev Basuccah, washes ones hands, eats some bread and returns indoors to eat. If it stops raining before going to bed, one returns to the Succah, recites Leshev Basuccah, eats some bread and recites Birkat Hamazon, Grace after Meals.[15] Some see rain on Succot as Divine rejection.[16] Others see it as Divine acceptance. After all, on Succot, we pray for rain.

UNDER THE OAK TREE
תעשה ולא מן העשוי

The equivalent of the American Ⓤ Kashrut certification in England is the certification of the London Beit Din. There is also a competing Kashrut certification called "Kedassia." Those who eat Kedassia do not eat Beit Din. My father, being one of the principal Dayanim on the bench of the London Beit Din, who had invested much of his working life on matters of Kashrut, ate Beit Din. His good friend ate only Kedassia. My father didn't like that. One Erev Succot, shortly before Yom Tov, the friend invited my father to admire the Succah he had built with much care and enthusiasm. "Beautiful," remarked my father, "but unusable." "Look up," he said, "you have built your Succah under the branches of an oak tree." But, never mind," said Dad, "come and eat in our Succah." We do, of course, eat only Beit Din."

The - סוכה - Succah, which means "shade," must be originally built for the purpose of providing shade and must be outside under the open sky. There can be nothing interceding between the Succah and the sky. Accordingly, the Succah cannot be built in a house or under a tree, which already provides shade and which, therefore, renders the Succah redundant.[1] But why couldn't my father's friend's Succah be fixed by cutting away the overhanging branches? The answer is that the Succah must be valid when originally constructed. It cannot originally be built as invalid and then corrected and made valid.[2] Thus, for example, a Succah fashioned by hollowing out an existing haystack is invalid. This disqualification is known as - תעשה ולא מן העשוי - Ta'aseh Velo Min Haasui, which means you must create a valid Succah and not fix an invalid one. This principle is derived from the verse - חג הסכת תעשה לך - Chag Hasuccot Ta'aseh Lecha, "the festival of Succot you shall make for yourself."[3] The principle of Ta'aseh Velo Min Haasui is derived from the fact that the word "Succot" precedes the word - תעשה - "make."[4] The only way to save my father's friend's Succah would have been to cut away the overhanging oak tree branches and then pick up each piece of the existing - סכך - Sechach, and lay it down again on the roof of the Succah. That way, by laying the Sechach again, the Succah would be Kosher at inception, because it is the laying of the Sechach which is the essence of the Succah.[5] Being shortly before Yom Tov, however, there was no time. Another remedy would be to bend the branches of the tree over so that they merge with the existing Kosher Sechach, already on the roof of the Succah. Based on the Halachic rule of - ביטול ברוב - Bitul Be'rov, the majority nullifies the minority, and as long as the Kosher Sechach outnumbers the invalid tree branches, the Succah is Kosher.[6] In the same way as one may save the Succah by cutting down the branches and laying the Sechach again, one could also remove roof tiles from a roof and sit under the wooden beams.[7] The very act of removing the roof tiles is considered a sufficient act of "Ta'aseh" and renders the remaining construction a valid Succah. Because of the principle of Ta'aseh

Velo Min Haasui, a rain roof on a Succah should be open when the Sechach is laid down and the Sechach should not be inserted from the inside with the roof closed.[8]

Other examples of Ta'aseh Velo Min Haasui are Tzizit and Mezuzah. From the order of the words - גדלים תעשה לך - Gedilim Ta'aseh Lecha, "make yourself fringes on the four corners of your garments,"[9] the Rabbis derive that four separate fringes must be inserted into the garment and then doubled over into eight, which must then be tied and knotted in the prescribed way. One cannot, however, insert one long string, double it over twice, tie and knot it and then snip the ends to make eight.[10] Similarly, one may not fix a Mezuzah onto a detached door post and then build the door post with the Mezuzah on it into the house.[11]

THE BROKEN STEM
ארבע מינים

Lowenstein's Shtiebel (make shift Synagogue) on the second floor of the apartment house was packed tight, from wall to wall, that balmy Succot morning. Congregants jostled for space to place their spear-like Lulavim and cotton-cradled Etrogim. "Hold my Etrog while I go outside for a moment," said Dad, "and mind the Pitam. Don't drop it." Honored with the trust, I fondled the Etrog carefully, but alas, it rolled out of my hands and plunged head first onto the floor. Even before it hit the ground, I knew it. The worst had happened. The Pitam, the stem, had broken off. I recall being down on my knees among the swaying Tzizzit and flapping frock-coats trying to piece it back on. And then, my father's expression. Even more horrified than when I dropped and broke his cordless mechanical shaver.

The - ארבע מינים - Arba Minim, the four species of plants that we are required to take on the Festival of Succot, are mentioned in Leviticus.[1] - ולקחתם לכם ביום הראשון - "And you shall take for yourselves on the first day, פרי עץ הדר - Pri Etz Hadar," "the fruits of the Hadar tree, - כפת תמרים - Kapot Temarim, branches of palm trees, - ענף עץ עבות - Ve'anaf Etz Avot, boughs of thick leaved trees, - ערבי נחל - Ve'arvei Nachal, and willows of the brook." The Talmud interprets these words as referring to the following plants. Pri Etz Hadar means the - אתרוג - Etrog, that is both beautiful, הדר and - ה-דר - resides in trees all year round.[2] Kapot Temarim, which can also be read - כפות - bound together Temarim, means the לולב, shoots of date palms which, in their early stages, before they fan out into palm branches, are tightly bound and spear shaped. Anaf Etz Avot, boughs of covered trees, means the הדס, myrtle, because "Avot" means braided, and the myrtle leaves look as though they are braided around the branch.[3]

The Lulav is bound with three myrtle branches on its right and two willow branches on its left.[4] The Lulav is held in the right hand, and the Etrog is held in the left hand.[5] Although the Torah only commands us to pick up the Arba Minim - ולקחתם - Ulekachtem, the Rabbis require that we wave them in all four directions of the compass, as well as upwards and downwards.[6] Achievements are often flaunted in all directions. The Torah reminds us that all achievements are gifts from God. And so, on Succot, the rain festival, we wave the Arba Minim in all directions, acknowledging that God, the Rainmaker, brings the rains from the four corners of the earth. The Talmud in Succot tells us that waving the Arba Minim also wards off destructive winds that would otherwise drive harmful rain.[7] The Lulav also symbolizes the scepter of victory with which we emerge after vanquishing the Yom Kippur prosecutor. Although the Mitzvah of Arba Minim can be fulfilled at any time during the day,[8] there is a close connection between the Mitzvah of Arba Minim and the reciting of Hallel. "Is it possible," asks the Talmud,[9] "to perform the Mitzvah of Lulav without reciting Hallel?"

Accordingly, the Lulav is waved when reciting certain verses of Hallel which both thank God for His kindness - הודו לה׳ כי טוב - Hodu Lashem Ki Tov, and ask Him for further mercy - אנא ה׳ הושיעה נא - Ana Hashem Hoshea Na.[10] During the Temple era, the Lulav was taken inside the Temple on all of the seven days of Succot but outside the Temple on the first day only.[11] After the destruction of the Temple, Rabbi Yochanan Ben Zakkai ruled that the Arba Minim be taken on all seven days of Succot, everywhere. Accordingly, Lulav on the first day of Succot is Biblical and on the last six days Rabbinical.

The minimum requirements for a Kosher Etrog that apply to all seven days of Succot are as follows: (i) it must be at least the size of an egg (there is no maximum size limit),[12] (ii) it may not be round like a ball,[13] (ii) it must be Halachically edible as food and not subject to any Shemitah, Terumah or Orlah eating restrictions,[14] (iv) it must be free from certain types of blemishes that reduce its size,[15] (v) and it may not be the product of grafting with a lemon tree (Murkav).[16] Other features that add to the beauty of the Etrog, but are not essential, are that it have a Pitam, that the Pitam be in a straight line with the stem and that it have bumps and ridges. If the Pitam broke off, then, although it is preferable to use another Etrog, according to many authorities the broken Etrog may be used on the first day of Succot, as long as part of the Pitam remains intact. If the Pitam broke off entirely, the Etrog may not be used on the first day of Succot unless it is the only Etrog in town. It may, however, be used on the last six days of Succot. Of course, an Etrog that never had a Pitam is Kosher.[17]

The Lulav must measure 12.4 inches along its backbone,[18] and the central leaf - תיומת - Te'yomet, must be double-leafed, closed, intact and straight.[19] The Hadas must have small, triple leaves over a majority of the branch,[20] should be between 9.3 inches and 11.4 inches long,[21] and the tip should be intact.[22] The Aravot must have red stems,[23] their leaves must be narrow and lip-shaped, and they must be smooth-edged. Other requirements, common to all the Arba Minim, are as follows: (i) on the first day of Succot, the Arba Minim must belong to the person using them and not be stolen or borrowed, since this would defeat the - ולקחתם לכם - Ulekachtem Lachem requirement,[24] (ii) on the first day of Succot,[25] the Arba Minim may not be dried out and withered since this defeats the Hadar requirement which, according to some opinions, applies only on the first day, and (iii) they may not be subject at any time during Succot to condemnation for having been used in connection with idolatry.[26] In order to fulfill the Mitzvah with a borrowed Lulav on the first day, the owner should stipulate that he is giving the Lulav to the user as a gift to be returned after use.[27] According to some authorities, such a condition may be implied even if not expressed.[28] Out of the same concern, the Arba Minim should be fully paid up before Yom Tov.

When the Arba Minim are picked up for the first time each Succot day, the Blessing

על נטילת לולב - Al Netilat Lulav, is recited all seven days and Schehecheyanu is added the first day.[29] These blessings are recited with the Etrog in the left hand, the pitam facing down.[30]

When the blessing is completed, the Etrog is then turned the right way up. The reason for this is to allow for the Blessing to be recited before the Mitzvah is performed, in accordance with the rule of - עובר לעשייתן - Over Le'assiyatan. On Shabbat, no Arba Minim are taken because of the Rabbis' concern that this might lead to carrying the Arba Minim in the streets.[31]

The Arba Minim have been compared to the human being in prayer. The Lulav symbolizes the backbone; the Etrog the heart; the Hadas the eyes; and the Arava the lips, moving in the service of God.

WHOLE HALLEL, HALF HALLEL, NO HALLEL
הלל

Hallel is a "song," - שיר - Shir, sung by people and angels in praise of God. Whole Hallel is recited on Jewish festivals which, in the Temple era, were celebrated by the offering of special sacrifices and on which weekday work is prohibited. Hallel is also sung on days which commemorate national miracles, such as Chanukah.[1] There are 21 days on which Hallel is sung in its entirety - הלל שלם - Whole Hallel: 9 days of Sukkot, 8 days of Chanukah, the first 2 days of Passover (including Seder Night) and 2 days of Shavuot. The Biblical source for Whole Hallel is Isaiah - השיר יהיה לכם כליל התקדש חג - "You shall sing a "song" ('Shir') as on the night when the festival (Passover) is sanctified."[2] From here we derive that only that type of Hallel which is recited on the night of Passover, i.e. whole Hallel, is considered a "song." Except for Seder night, when it is recited without a blessing,[3] whole Hallel is always preceded by a - ברכה - blessing, God "Who has commanded us to recite Hallel."[4]

So why is Whole Hallel not recited on Rosh Hashanah, Yom Kippur and the last 6 days of Passover, all of which are Jewish festivals on which weekday work is prohibited? According to tradition, the angels asked God this question and were told that it is inappropriate to recite Hallel on days of judgment, when life and death are in abeyance.[5] Similarly, in the spirit of - בנפול אויבך אל תשמח - "when your enemy falls do not rejoice," it is inappropriate for us to recite Whole Hallel on the last 2 days of Passover, which recall the painful death of our Egyptian persecutors.[6] In view of the fact that Whole Hallel is not recited on the last 2 days of Passover, Whole Hallel is also not recited on the days of Chol Hamoed, so as not to make those days appear more significant than the last two days of Passover. Instead, Half Hallel is recited on the last six days of Pesach.[7]

Half Hallel means, Whole Hallel minus the paragraphs of - אהבתי - Ahavti and לא לנו - Lo Lanu.[8] By virtue of - מנהג - custom, Half Hallel is recited on days which, though worthy of celebration, do not qualify for Whole Hallel because they are neither Festivals nor do they commemorate national miracles. Accordingly, it is a מנהג to recite Half Hallel on ראש חודש - Rosh Chodesh, the first day of each Jewish calendar month.[9] Whether or not one may recite a blessing over Half Hallel depends upon whether one can say - וצוונו - "God has commanded us" in connection with a custom.[10] Rambam maintains one may not recite a blessing over a custom.[11] Rabbeinu Tam[12] maintains that one may, and cites as proof the fact that women who participate in the Mitzvah of Lulav may recite a blessing, even though they are not commanded to perform the Mitzvah of Lulav. Furthermore, the second day of Yom Tov is kept on account of מנהג אבותיכם - Minhag Avoteichem - the custom of your fathers - and yet we recite הלל with a ברכה.

Modern Poskim differ on whether and what type of Hallel should be recited on days of national celebration for recent miracles, such as - יום העצמאות - Yom Ha'atzmaut (Israel Independence Day). According to Rav Ovadiah Yosef,[13] a miracle only qualifies for Whole Hallel with a Blessing if the entire Jewish nation, not just a community, was saved thereby. According to Rav Ovadia Yosef, Yom Ha'azmaut would not qualify, because it was the Jewish community in Israel and not outside Israel whose lives were threatened by the Arab onslaught. In addition, writes Rav Ovadia Yosef, the Israeli War of Independence was won at the cost of many casualties and even today the enemy remains a life threatening presence. Furthermore, writes Rav Ovadia Yosef, Hallel with a ברכה should only be said for a super-natural miracle, "גלוי נס," and the miracle of Israel's victory in the War of Independence can be explained in natural terms. Accordingly, Rav Ovadia Yosef recommends Hallel without a blessing. Others,[14] however, rely on the precedent of Rosh Chodesh for the proposition that Hallel can be said with a blessing when there is a custom to do so. Rabbi Moshe Feinstein rules that in these matters, one should follow the custom of one's synagogue and if one is praying in a synagogue where Hallel is recited, one should join in for the sake of peace.[15]

SECOND DAY YOM TOV, ERUVIN AND EGGS
יום טוב שני של גלויות

W hy two days Yom Tov outside Israel and one day Yom Tov in Israel? The answer to this question depends on the answer to another basic question, namely, how many days constitute a month in the Jewish calendar ?

The rebirth of the moon, approximately every thirty days, determines the number of days in the Jewish month.[1] The precise duration of the Jewish month is 29 days, 12 hours and 793/1080 parts of one hour.[2] Because it is impractical to commence Rosh Chodesh in the middle of the day,[3] the most pragmatic thing to do is to alternate the months of the year between 29 days and 30 days, respectively. That is how it is done today. A 30 day month is called - מלא - Maleh and is born with two days Rosh Chodesh. A 29 day month is called - חסר - Chaser and is born with one day Rosh Chodesh.[4]

Whether a month is Chaser or Maleh makes a crucial difference to our Jewish lives. If, for example, one mistakenly believed that the month of Elul was Maleh when, in fact, it was Chaser, one might find oneself eating on Yom Kippur and fasting on a weekday. If one mistakenly believed that the month of Adar was Maleh when, in fact, it was Chaser, one might find oneself eating bread on Pesach.

So who decides which month is 29 days or 30 days? Today, it is decided by the Jewish calendar, instituted in 358 CE by Hillel II, the Nassi, leader, of Israel.

Prior to that, during the time of the Second Temple, a Chodesh Chaser was determined by the empirical evidence of two witnesses, who testified in the Jerusalem Court of law, the Beit Din, that they had seen the new moon on the 30th day.[5] Once their testimony was accepted, the thirtieth day, counted from the previous Rosh Chodesh was declared the Rosh Chodesh of the new month. If no witnesses came on the 30th day, Rosh Chodesh was declared by default on the 31st day, rendering the previous month a Chodesh Maleh.[6] At first, the news of a Chodesh Chaser was spread on מוצאי ראש חודש, the night of the thirtieth, by means of torching beacons on mountain peaks.[7] If no torches were lit, all understood that the month was Maleh. The Cutheans,[8] however, disrupted this system by torching beacons on days when the Jerusalem Beit Din had not declared a Chodesh Chaser. In this situation, the only alternative was to dispatch emissaries to outlying districts, in the hope that they would arrive with the news of the Chodesh Chaser before Yom Tov. In the case of Rosh Chodesh Nissan, for example, the emissaries would have 14 days to arrive before Pesach. Those communities too distant from Jerusalem for the emissaries to arrive before Yom Tov, such as communities in the Diaspora, were forced to hedge their bets and keep Yom Tov for two days. These two days are called יום טוב שני של גלויות, Yom Tov Sheni Shel Galuyot. One of those days would genuinely be Yom Tov and one would not. Because, at the time, they did not know which one was which, they kept both, out of doubt.

That was then. But now, we have Hillel's calendar. There is no doubt. We know which day is Yom Tov. So why are we celebrating "Yom Tov" again on a "weekday?" The comforting, yet chilling, answer is to be found in Tractate Beitzah.[9] - מנהג אבותיכם בידיכם - "Hold on to the customs of your ancestors," the Talmud advises, "for someday, an oppressive government may confiscate your Jewish calendar and forbid you to teach it. Then, having forgotten the methods of your ancestors, you will lose track of the days, and eat bread on Pesach." And so, in the darkness of Auschwitz and Soviet prisons, Jews, in our own day, have celebrated Yom Tov, based on the trustworthy tools of yesteryear.

Because the Second Day Yom Tov was kept out of doubt as to which day, in fact, was Yom Tov, the Rabbis permit one, under certain circumstances, to take advantage of the doubt. Thus, although Eruvei Techumim[10] for Shabbat can only extend the Techum Shabbat to a total of 4000 Amot, in one direction, on Yom Tov (but not on Rosh Hashanah) one may extend the Techum Shabbat to 4000 Amot in two directions in the following manner. One places one Eruv before the first day Yom Tov, thereby extending one's Techum Shabbat on the first day of Yom Tov to 4000 Amot in one chosen direction. The following day one places a second Eruv before the second day Yom Tov, extending one's Techum Shabbat on the second day Yom Tov to four thousand Amot in the opposite direction. Similarly, although an egg laid on a Shabbat preceding a Yom Tov may not be eaten on the next day of Yom Tov, because food cannot be prepared on Shabbat for Yom Tov, an egg laid on the first day of Yom Tov may be eaten on the second. This is because one of the two days is not truly Yom Tov. Accordingly, the following logic may be applied. If the first day is truly Yom Tov, then the second day is a weekday and the Yom Tov restrictions are inapplicable. If the second day is truly Yom Tov, then the first day was a weekday and one may, of course, prepare food on a weekday to eat on Yom Tov.[11]

ERUV TAVSHILIN
ערוב תבשילין

Although cooking food on Yom Tov for a Yom Tov meal is permitted,[1] cooking or preparing a meal today, on Yom Tov, for tomorrow is prohibited.[2] This prohibition applies equally whether tomorrow is a weekday, a Yom Tov or Shabbat. This is because one is not allowed to misuse the rest day in - הכנה - Hachanah, preparation for a another day. But what happens when Yom Tov is on Friday? May one cook on Friday-Yom Tov for Shabbat? Or is this also considered Hachanah and prohibited?

The answer is that, Biblically, it is permitted to cook during the day on a Friday-Yom Tov for Shabbat. The Talmud[3] gives two reasons why the Torah permits cooking on Yom Tov for the following Shabbat day. According to Rabbah, it is because you never know how much food you may need on Yom Tov. There is always the possibility that unexpected guests may arrive. And "since" you are allowed to cook on Yom Tov for possible guests, you may also cook for Shabbat. The logic of "since," on which Rabbah bases the permit, is referred to in Halachah as - הואיל - Ho'il. According to Rav Chisdah,[4] both Yom Tov and Shabbat are frequently referred to in the Torah as "Shabbat."[5] Accordingly, the permission given by the Torah to cook on Yom Tov applies not only to the Yom Tov meal, but also to the Shabbat meal prepared on Yom Tov for the following Shabbat day. As pointed out by Tosafot,[6] there is a practical difference between the two approaches. According to Rabbah, it would be Biblically prohibited to cook on Friday afternoon, shortly before sundown, because by that time any Yom Tov guests would have come and gone. According to Rav Chisdah, however, this would be permitted.

Despite the fact that the Torah permits cooking on Yom Tov for the following Shabbat day, both Rabbah and Rav Chisdah forbid it unless one performs, on Erev Yom Tov, a special ceremony called - ערוב תבשילין - Eruv Tavshilin. Eruv Tavshilin is a ceremony in which one makes minimum preparation for Shabbat on Erev Yom Tov by setting aside some bread and some cooked food for the Shabbat meal.[7] In this way, the Shabbat meal has already been prepared before Yom Tov and all that is required on Yom Tov is its completion. This bridge, spanning from Erev Yom Tov to Shabbat, makes Rabbah more comfortable relying on the Ho'il exemption described above. The Eruv Tavshilin ceremony honors both the Yom Tov and the Shabbat. It honors the Yom Tov, because people who see that there is a Rabbinic prohibition to cook on Yom Tov, even for Shabbat, without the Eruv, will never violate the Yom Tov by cooking for a weekday.[8] It honors the Shabbat by focusing one's mind already on Erev Yom Tov on the needs of Shabbat, which might otherwise lie unattended in the shadow of Yom Tov.[9] Based on the words of the Torah שבתון שבת - קודש לה' מחר את אשר תאפו "אפו ואת אשר תבשלו בשלו" - "Tomorrow is a day of rest... bake what you want to bake and cook what you want to cook, today,"[10] the cooked food, typically an egg or piece of meat, that one sets aside on Erev Yom Tov, as part of the Eruv, permits one to cook on Yom Tov for Shabbat, and the bread one sets aside permits one to bake.[11]

When Yom Tov begins on Wednesday night, the Eruv Tavshilin ceremony is performed on Wednesday and when Yom Tov begins on Thursday night, it is performed on Thursday, in each case by the head of the household.[12] The bread and the cooked food is lifted in one's right hand and the blessing - על מצות ערוב - Al Mitzvat Eruv is recited. The following text should be read: בהדין ערובא יהא שרא לנא לאפויי, ולבשולי ולאטמוני ולאדלוקי שרגא ולתקנא ולמעבד כל צרכנא מיומא טבא לשבתא - "With this Eruv, let it be permitted for us to bake, cook, insulate, light the Shabbat candles, prepare for and perform all our Shabbat needs on Yom Tov." Even those who eat out on Shabbat, and, therefore, have no need to cook on Yom Tov for Shabbat, are required to perform the Eruv Tavshilin ceremony without a ברכה to enable them to light the Shabbat candles on Yom Tov for Shabbat.[13] The Eruv ceremony should be performed before lighting the Shabbat candles.[14] When the first day of Yom Tov is Thursday, the Eruv permits cooking on Friday for Shabbat, but not on Thursday for Shabbat.[15] The Challah used for the Eruv should be used as the second loaf - לחם משנה - Lechem Mishneh, for the Shabbat meals and should be eaten at the third Shabbat meal.[16]

If, when reciting Minchah on Erev Yom Tov, in Synagogue, you realize that you forgot to perform Eruv Tavshilin, there is no need to run home. You can either call home and ask a family member to do it for you, or you can do it yourself, from Synagogue, by setting aside in your mind, food at home for the Eruv and actually setting the designated food aside when you arrive home.[17] In most communities, the Rabbi will perform the Eruv ceremony on Erev Yom Tov for all community members. This ceremony, conducted on your behalf, without your knowledge at the time, is based on the principle that a benefit can be bestowed on a person in his absence - זכין לאדם שלא בפניו - Zachin Le'adam Shelo Befanav.[18] As a last resort, this communal Eruv may be relied upon, but the Rabbis frown upon those that make a habit of it.[19] Because the Halachah is in accordance with Rabbah, who prohibits cooking on Yom Tov shortly berfore sundown, care should be taken to complete cooking for Shabbat well before sundown on Friday.[20] For this reason, Ma'ariv, the evening prayer, is usually set early on Yom Tov Friday to encourage people to finish cooking before the early Ma'ariv service. Based on Rav Chisda's position described above, however, the Chafetz Chaim permits one, in the case of an emergency, to finish cooking just before sundown.

WHAT YOU CAN DO ON YOM TOV
THAT YOU CAN'T ON SHABBAT
אוכל נפש

O f the thirty nine Melachot which are prohibited on Shabbat, some, which relate to the preparation of food and to other matters of physical and spiritual comfort, are permitted on Yom Tov. - אך אשר יאכל לכל נפש הוא לבדו יעשה לכם - "The only work you may perform [on Yom Tov] is that which is required for your nourishment (Ochel Nefesh)."[1] Accordingly, based on the Ochel Nefesh permit, one may, for the purpose of Yom Tov pleasure, carry food from domain to domain[2] and light a fire from an existing flame[3] in order to cook food, warm up the house,[4] kindle lights,[5] or heat water to wash the dishes[6] or parts of one's body.[7] Although one may not cook on Yom Tov for a weekday, or on the first day Yom Tov (which is of Biblical origin) for the second day Yom Tov (which is of Rabbinical origin),[8] one may add to the amount of food being cooked for the first day, so that it lasts for the second day Yom Tov, provided that this is done before the meal is eaten, and provided further that one does not explicitly state that one is cooking for the next day. The justification for this is that in the absence of such an explicit statement that one is adding more food today for tomorrow's meal, one may rely on the probability that the extra quantity can enhance the flavor of the food to be eaten today.[9]

If one is allowed to cook on Yom Tov, why, one may ask, is one not permitted to initiate, as opposed to transfer, fire on Yom Tov?[10] After all, you cannot cook without fire. The answer is that the Torah **does** permit one to initiate fire on Yom Tov,[11] but the Rabbis forbid it. This is because the Rabbis restrict the Ochel Nefesh permit to such activities which cannot reasonably be performed before Yom Tov. Thus, while they fully appreciate that freshly cooked food tastes better than frozen food and therefore permit cooking on Yom Tov, they do not permit one to kindle the source (or pilot) light on Yom Tov if one could just as well have lit it before Yom Tov.[12] Nevertheless, if one was unable or forgot to do so and finds oneself without any source of fire on Yom Tov, some authorities permit one to ask a non-Jew to initiate the fire on one's behalf.[13] If one accidentally lit a new fire on Yom Tov, there are Halachic opinions that permit one to eat food cooked on such fire.

Unlike Shabbat, on which extinguishing or reducing a flame is prohibited in all circumstances, on Yom Tov one may, under certain circumstances, in connection with cooking, extinguish or reduce a flame.[14] Accordingly, if one were to extinguish a piece of coal while grilling a damp piece of meat on top of a barbecue, one would not have violated any Yom Tov law. Similarly, one may lower the gas flame (but not an electric coil) in order to avoid burning food. According to Rav Moshe Feinstein, this may be done even when the alternative exists of lighting a new, but lower, flame from an existing pilot light and transfering the pot to it.[15] Whereas one may not turn off an electric light on Yom Tov, some authorities permit one to turn off an electric light that keeps one awake at night.[16]

One of the conditions for the application of the Ochel Nefesh permit is that the desired Melachah be one that generally appeals to everybody[17] - דבר השווה לכל נפש - Davar Hashave Lekol Nefesh, such as cooking, as opposed to individual tastes or needs, such as, perhaps, smoking. Accordingly, in view of the fact that today, unlike in the past, smoking is not generally appealing, there is much discussion among modern day Poskim whether smoking should continue to be permitted on Yom Tov.[18] The consensus is that, while those that suffer severe withdrawal symptoms can avail themselves of the Ochal Nefesh permit, occasional smokers may not.[19] In any event, those that smoke on Yom Tov should take care to light up only from an existing flame, to let the cigarette burn out rather than put it out and to let the ash drop rather than flick it off.

Based upon the opinion of Hillel,[20] the Ochal Nefesh permit may be extended to apply not only to physical enjoyment on Yom Tov, but to spiritual enjoyment as well. By virtue of this extension, referred to as Mitoch Shehutra Letzorech, Hutra Nami Shelo Letzorech, explained below, or just - מתוך - Mitoch, one may, on Yom Tov, even in the absence of an Eruv, carry a Machzor, Yom Tov prayer book, Tallit, Lulav or Etrog or push a baby carriage to synagogue.

On the first night of Yom Tov, except Shavuot,[21] candles can be lit either at the same time as on Erev Shabbat, or from an existing light after returning from the Ma'ariv evening prayer service. On the second night, however, as well as whenever Shabbat precedes Yom Tov, and on both days of Shavuot, they should be lit from an existing light, after nightfall.[22]

MITOCH. A YOM TOV DRIVING LICENSE?

מתוך שהותרה לצורך הותרה נמי שלא לצורך

The only work you may perform on Yom Tov is that which is required for your nourishment," - אוכל נפש - Ochal Nefesh.[1] The Ochal Nefesh permit allows the performance of certain Melachot required for the preparation of food, such as cooking, baking, carrying food from one domain to another, lighting a fire from an existing flame and slaughtering an animal for food.[2] If the Halachah were to prohibit these activities on Yom Tov and would require them to be performed before Yom Tov, food would not be fresh and would be less appetizing on Yom Tov. The Ochal Nefesh permit does not, however, permit the performance of Melachot for the preparation of food that could have been performed before Yom Tov without compromising the taste of such food.[3] Accordingly, on Yom Tov, one may not reap one's field, winnow corn, hunt or fish.[4] Such activities are prohibited for the additional reason that they consume many hours of the day and remove one from the atmosphere of Yom Tov, - עובדא דחול - Uvda Dechol, weekday pursuits.[5]

Based on the opinion of Hillel, the Ochal Nefesh permit may be extended to permit the performance of certain Melachot unrelated to the preparation of food. Thus, according to Hillel, one may heat water on Yom Tov to bathe oneself or light a bonfire to warm oneself, provided all this is done from an existing flame.[6] In the Temple era, one could slaughter an animal on Yom Tov for a voluntary sacrifice - עולת נדבה - even though it would have been entirely burnt on the altar and no part of it eaten.[7] Hillel's extension of the Ochal Nefesh permit is known as - מתוך שהותרה לצורך הותרה נמי שלא לצורך - Mitoch Shehutra Letzorech, Hutra Nami Shelo Letzorech, or just - מתוך - Mitoch. The Mitoch extension also permits one to carry a child, a prayer book, a Lulav or a Sefer Torah from one domain to another on Yom Tov, even in the absence of an Eruv.[8]

What is the justification for the Mitoch extension? How does Hillel arrive at the conclusion that a Melachah may be divorced from the realm of food preparation where it has been specifically permitted by the Torah and applied to non-food activities? Several theories are offered to explain this phenomenon. According to some,[9] Hillel's Mitoch extension is based on the principle of הואיל ואישתרי אשתרי - Ho'il Ve'ishtere, Ishtere, which means that once a specific action is permitted for one purpose, it can be permitted for other purposes.[10] According to others,[11] the basis for Hillel's Mitoch extension is that Melachot relating to the preparation of food on Yom Tov were never part of the 39 Melachot to begin with. They are intrinsically permitted on Yom Tov and, accordingly, can also be performed for purposes unrelated to food preparation. The Ramban[12] points out that, whereas in connection with Shabbat, the Torah prohibits all types of work - לא תעשה כל מלאכה - Lo Ta'aseh Kol Melachah,[13] in connection with Yom Tov, the Torah[14] prohibits only certain types of work, - כל מלאכת עבודה לא תעשו - Kol Melechet Avodah Lo Ta'asu. The Ramban explains that there are two types of work, - מלאכת עבודה - Melechet Avodah, which is work related to earning a living and - מלאכת הנאה - Melechet Hana'ah, which is work performed for one's own pleasure.[15] And on Yom Tov, explains the Ramban, Melechet Hana'ah, such as the preparation of food, is Biblically permitted. According to the Sefer Yerayim,[16] the principle of Mitoch is not a Rabbinical extension of the Ochal Nefesh permit at all, but rather it is part of the Biblical Ochal Nefesh permit itself. The word - אוכל - Ochal, explains the Sefer Yerayim, has two meanings, to eat and to derive physical or spiritual pleasure. Thus, the words - כל מחמצת לא תאכלו - Kol Machmetzet Lo Tocheilu, you shall eat nothing leavened,[17] prohibit one from both eating Chametz - איסור אכילה - Isur Achilah, and from deriving pleasure from Chametz, - איסור הנאה -Isur Hanaah, on Pesach.[18] Conversely, the permission to perform Melechet Hana'ah on Yom Tov permits one to perform work necessary for eating, as well as for other physical or spiritual pleasures. The expression - מתוך - Mitoch, explains the Yerayim, means "out of." "Out of" the very verse in the Torah that permits work for the preparation of food we derive the permission to work for spiritual pleasure.[19]

What activities other than the preparation of food does the Mitoch extension permit? According to the Bach,[20] all the thirty-nine Melachot are Biblically permitted on Yom Tov, because they could all potentially be performed in connection with the preparation of food. In fact, as pointed out by Tosafot,[21] even building a house on Yom Tov is Biblically permitted, because the Melachah of building is sometimes performed in connection with the preparation of food, such as in the process of forming hard cheese in a mold. So why, asks Tosafot, should a person not be able to build a house on Yom Tov to protect him from the heat of a sandstorm as he eats his Yom Tov meal? According to the Bach and Tosafot, the only reason one may not build a house on Yom Tov is because the Rabbis forbid Uvda Dechol activities. The Rambam, on the other hand, rules that only two of the 39 Melachot, namely, lighting a fire and carrying, can be extended to non-food related activities on Yom Tov.[22] According to Rashi,[23] based on the principle of Mitoch, work that is unrelated to the preparation of food is Biblically permitted on Yom Tov, even if it is entirely unnecessary for Yom Tov. The Rabbis forbade such work, however, in order to preserve the atmosphere of Yom Tov. According to Tosafot,[24] such work is only Biblically permitted to the extent it enhances the pleasure of Yom Tov, even if only a little - צורך יום טוב קצת -Tzorech Yom Tov Ketzat, or is in connection with the performance of a Mitzvah, - צורך מצוה - Tzorech Mitzvah. In practice, we follow the opinion of the Mishnah Berurah and permit the following activities on Yom Tov, even if not related to the preparation of food.[25] They are, carrying, slaughtering and kindling fire from an existing flame.

Although the Mitoch extension permits lighting fire from an existing flame, it does not permit the creation of fire by striking a match or rubbing together two stones.[26] Some authorities[27] are of the opinion that the creation of a new flame is Biblically prohibited under the category of - מוליד - Molid, which means the creation of something out of nothing - יש מאין - Yesh Meayin. Other authorities[28] are of the opinion that igniting fire is Biblically permitted on Yom Tov, but the Rabbis forbade it because the flame should be lit before Yom Tov as a source of fire for Yom Tov.

If the principle of Mitoch permits the use of fire on Yom Tov for activities unrelated to food preparation but necessary for enhancing Yom Tov pleasure, or for the performance of a Mitzvah, why is one not allowed to drive to Shul on Yom Tov? Rabbi Ovadia Yosef[29] explains that the creation of sparks from the battery and the application of brake lights violates the Biblical prohibition of creating fire, Molid, on Yom Tov. According to those authorities that maintain that the creation of fire is only a Rabbinical prohibition, driving is still prohibited even if in connection with Yom Tov pleasure or the performance of a Mitzvah. The reason, explains Rav Ovadia Yosef, is because of Uvda Dechol.

TURNING ON THE LIGHTS ON YOM TOV
הדלקת וכיבוי מנורת חשמל ביום טוב

Has your hand ever hovered over the electric light switch on Yom Tov as you ask yourself what is wrong with turning the light on? After all, before the invention of electricity, it was permitted to kindle lights from an existing flame to illuminate a room for Yom Tov needs, such as meals.[1] So why is turning the electric light on any different?

The answer to this question depends more upon an analysis of electricity than on any analysis of Halachah. The Halachic situation is clear. On Yom Tov one may not create fire.[2] One may only light fire from existing fire.[3] Two reasons are offered for the prohibition of creating fire on Yom Tov. Rashi[4] explains that creating something out of nothing - מוליד - Molid is so close to the concept of "Melachah"- creative work- that it is prohibited. The Rambam,[5] explains that the Rabbis forbade those Melachot performed for the preparation of food that could have been prepared before Yom Tov without compromising the taste of the food. Clearly, a flame could have been lit before Yom Tov to act as a source of fire on Yom Tov and fire cannot, therefore, be initiated on Yom Tov. All agree, then, that one may not create fire on Yom Tov. The question, therefore, is whether turning on an electric light is creating fire.

According to many Halachic authorities,[6] turning on an electric light on Yom Tov is permitted because it involves neither creation nor fire. The fire, they explain, already exists in the electric current, which flows through the wires. When the switch is turned off, the wire, through which the electricity flows, is temporarily cut, and the electricity flow is temporarily halted. Conversely, when the switch is turned on, the wires are reconnected and electricity flows through as before, just like water, when the tap is turned on again. Turning on the electric light is not similar to rubbing two stones together and creating a spark and is not Molid. Rather, they argue, it is similar to lighting fire from existing fire. Furthermore, turning on the light bulb does not create fire but merely produces "fire-like light" in the tungsten filament. If it were real fire, the filament would burn up instantly. The filament, says the Maharsham, is like the burning bush that was not consumed. Turning on the switch simply releases power latent in the wire, just as breaking open a stick of incense releases fragrance latent in the stick and is permitted on Yom Tov.[7]

Nonsense, fumes the Tzitz Eliezer.[8] The Maharsham studied with the wrong electrician. Electricity produces real fire. Entire neighborhoods burn down when electrical wires overheat. That is why homes are equipped with fuse boxes threaded with thin heat sensitive wires that blow when the heat rises and interrupt the flow of electricity. As for the tungsten "burning bush," the reason it does not burn up immediately is because it is encased in glass from which all oxygen has been extracted. Eventually, however, the filament does burn out. And the Maharsham's theory that fire already exists in the wires is equally false. There is as little latent fire in the wire as there is in flintstones. The wires are merely conduits of electrical current. The electrical power is not in the wire. It is in magnetic fields produced in the generator that drive electrons through copper wires. When you turn on the switch you allow the magnetic field to flow through the wire into the light bulb. That is forbidden on account of Molid. It is similar to inverting a cup of incense over a silk garment for the purpose of infusing the garment with fragrance. The Talmud[9] prohibits this on account of Molid.

The Chazon Ish has a novel approach to the problem. He explains[10] that the prohibition of turning on the light on Yom Tov is not Molid but rather - בונה - Boneh, building. The Melachah of Boneh, he explains, is not only constructing or adding to substance but also empowering substance. Turning on the light empowers the bulb with the power of electricity it did not possess before and is, therefore, prohibited on account of Boneh.

Rabbi Pesach Zvi Frank, the former Chief Rabbi of Jerusalem, and Rabbi Yechiel Epstein,[11] the author of the Aruch Hashulchan, permit turning on the light on Yom Tov for a different reason. They maintain that turning on the switch is not the direct cause but only the indirect cause of creating fire. By turning on the switch, you are not igniting fire but merely causing the connection of two wires that, in turn, ignite fire. Lighting fire indirectly is not prohibited on Yom Tov.[12] Rav Chaim Ozer Grodzinski,[13] Rav Isser Zalman Melzer and Rabbi Shlomo Zalman Auerbach[14] disagree and consider turning on the switch a sufficiently direct cause and, therefore, prohibited on account of Molid.

Rabbi Ovadia Yosef summarizes the opinions of most of the modern day Poskim on the issue and concludes that the majority prohibits turning on lights on Yom Tov. Based on the Halachic rule of the majority, he concludes that it is prohibited.

CHOL HAMOED. AN OXYMORON
חול המועד

hol Hamoed, the weekday of the Festival, is the term used to describe the five days sandwiched between the first two days and the last two days of the Festival of Succot or Pesach. The word - חול - Chol, by itself, means weekday, on which work is permitted. The word - מועד - Moed, by itself, means a Festival day, on which most work is prohibited. The phrase - חול המועד - Chol Hamoed seems a contradiction in terms. What are these five days, Festival or weekday? The blessing we make at Havdalah, to distinguish between the first two days of Succot or Pesach and the onset of Chol Hamoed, - ברוך המבדיל בין קודש לחול - Baruch Hamavdil Bein Kodesh Lechol,[1] suggests that Chol Hamoed is weekday. Yet, the Torah[2] refers to Chol Hamoed by the term "Moed," a term reserved for days on which work is forbidden. But then again, as if to add to the confusion, the Torah[3] declares, "On the first [and second, outside Israel] day [of Succot], you shall not do any work," clearly implying that on the five days of Chol Hamoed one may perform work. Nowhere, perhaps, is the confusion more visible than in the matter of Tefillin on Chol Hamoed, where those that consider it Chol wear Tefillin, and those that consider it Moed do not.[4]

In fact, the truth is somewhere in the middle. On Chol Hamoed, some work is prohibited and some work is permitted. According to some opinions, the work prohibition is Biblical, and according to others, the work prohibition is Rabbinical.[5] Whatever the source of the prohibition, all agree that the Rabbis decide what work may and may not be done on Chol Hamoed.[6] For the Chayei Adam, the starting point for prohibited work on Chol Hamoed is Yom Tov itself. With the exception of a few Melachot, including lighting a fire, the Chayei Adam lists the same Melachot as being prohibited both on Yom Tov and Chol Hamoed.[7] Others maintain that it is impossible to define what work is prohibited on Chol Hamoed. All agree, however, on what work is permitted on Chol Hamoed. Before listing the various permitted categories of work on Chol Hamoed, one should be cognizant of the special status the Rabbis ascribe to Chol Hamoed, which is best summed up in the following phrase - "One who disrespects Chol Hamoed is compared to an idol worshipper." The overriding principle is that work becomes prohibited if it has the effect of rendering Chol Hamoed just another working day.

Work is permitted on Chol Hamoed which falls within one of the following five categories. The first, and perhaps broadest permitted category, is known as - צורך המועד - Tzorach Hamoed, meaning work which enhances the joy of Chol Hamoed.[8] Examples of activities which are permitted if they are performed in order to enhance the enjoyment of Chol Hamoed include driving,[9] turning lights on and off,[10] (which according to the Chayei Adam were never prohibited on Chol Hamoed in the first place), repairing a leaking roof,[11] erecting a Succah,[12] sewing torn clothes needed for immediate wear[13] and writing shopping lists required for Chol Hamoed. Indeed, the determination of what falls into this first category is quite subjective and dependent on individual tastes and preferences. The only restrictions that apply to this first category are that work (other than work involved in preparing food) must not be performed in an artisan fashion and work may not be deliberately postponed to Chol Hamoed.[14] The second permitted category is - דבר האבד - "Davar Ha'aved," meaning work which, if not performed on Chol Hamoed, would result in financial or other loss.[15] This important category includes conducting business or going to work, where failure to do so would cause irretrievable loss of principal.[16] Whether loss of profit is considered Davar Ha'aved is a point of debate. Clearly, if such profit is required and used to cover Chol Hamoed expenses, work generating such profit would be permitted.[17] Again, any work deliberately postponed to Chol Hamoed will not qualify as Davar Ha'aved. According to those who maintain that the source of prohibited work on Chol Hamoed is Rabbinical, any doubt whether a desired activity falls within either of these two permitted categories should be resolved in favor of permitting such work.[18] The third permitted category is work required for - צרכי רבים - Tzorchei Rabim, public welfare, such as repairing public roads or water pipes.[19] The fourth permitted category is that any work, otherwise prohibited on Chol Hamoed, may be performed by a worker who needs the wages from such work to cover his daily living expenses.[20] None of the above-mentioned restrictions (namely not performing the work in an artisan fashion and not deliberately postponing the work to Chol Hamoed) apply to the third and fourth categories.[21] The fifth permitted category is all work required to cure the sick, including the not dangerously sick.[22]

In order to ensure that people will honor Yom Tov by shaving and washing their clothes before the arrival of Yom Tov, the Rabbis prohibit these activities on Chol Hamoed with certain exceptions.[23] Most marriages may not be celebrated on Chol Hamoed, so as not to lose the focus of the Chol Hamoed celebration.[24] Engagements, however, are permitted.

Paradoxically, many of the Chol Hamoed restrictions, (no shaving, no washing clothes, restricted work, no teffilin, no weddings) are common to - אבילות - Aveilut, mourning the dead. Depression is the flip side of happiness, or, as the prophet Amos puts it,[25] - והפכתי חגיכם לאבל - "I will turn your feasts into mourning." Indeed, Tractate Moed Katan, which sets out the laws of Chol Hamoed, also focuses on the laws of Aveilut. The Talmud in Shabbat[26] tells us that for a period of time after death, the lost soul wanders back and forth between heaven and earth, trying, alternately, to penetrate the lifeless body and the space under God's heavenly throne. And the laws of Aveilut, by focusing on the departed, accommodate this desire of the soul. Perhaps too, Chol Hamoed is trying to penetrate the holiness of the Festivals that surround it on either side. And the laws of Chol Hamoed, by focusing on the joy of the festival, accommodate that desire. Perhaps also, the message is that in

Judaism, outward appearances can be misleading and investigation of the soul is more telling.

CELEBRATION AND SERENITY
נשמה יתירה ביום טוב

Its 12:30 on a Yom Tov, Monday morning. You are about to leave the Synagogue for the third day in a row. As you look around, you notice, even as you try to ignore it, a certain wilting of the spirit. A belabored pace. How good you felt on Friday night, with the onset of Shabbat. An effortless serenity set in then. But ever since the departure of Shabbat and the onset of Yom Tov, your soul feels heavier inside you. It does not soar to its Sabbath heights. And as you walk past the apartment building next to the synagogue on your way home, dressed in your finest clothes and wearing a three day shadow, you are aware of the curious gaze of the night guard. "Do these people ever work?" he must be thinking. "How much longer will they be parading between these matinee and evening performances?" And yes, you wonder, perhaps you should be at work. What's going on there, anyway? And will the office be calling when you get home? Oh, banish the thought! It's Yom Tov. Let's celebrate.

Perhaps, we repress these thoughts and never articulate them. But the Rabbis, in their honesty and sensitivity, openly address them. "Which Havdalah blessing do we recite when Shabbat leaves and Yom Tov arrives?," asks the Talmud.[1] - המבדיל בין קודש לקודש - Hamavdil Bein Kodesh Lekodesh, "Blessed are You God, who separates between holy [Shabbat] and holy [Yom Tov]," suggests the Tanna Kamma. "No," responds Rabbi Dosa, המבדיל בין קודש חמור לקודש חול - Hamavdil Bein Kodesh Chamur Lekodesh Chol, "Blessed are You God, who separates between concentrated holiness and diluted holiness."

We awaken to this world with the breath that God first breathed into man on Friday afternoon. - ויפח באפיו נשמת חיים - "Vayipach Be'apav, Nishmat Chaim."[2] And each Friday afternoon, with the onset of Shabbat, God breathes into our souls again. The Kabbalists call this the - נשמה יתרה - "Neshamah Yeterah," the Extra Soul. But this Divine bonus is ephemeral. Cinderella-like, it evaporates on Motzaei Shabbat. As it departs, our surviving soul feels faint and lonely and needs to be revived with - בשמים - Besamim, smelling salts.

But as we bid farewell to Shabbat and welcome in Yom Tov, we do not use Besamim. "Why not?," asks the Rashbam.[3] Because, he suggests, Yom Tov has its own Neshamah Yeterah, so that our weekday soul is not left alone. Not true, say the Tosafists.[4] If that were the case, then we would use Besamim on Monday night, when Yom Tov departs. But we do not. No, there is no Neshamah Yeterah on Yom Tov, insist the Tosafists. But still, they explain, we do not use Besamim when Shabbat departs and Yom Tov arrives, because we comfort the grieving soul instead with food and drink - שמחת יום טוב - Simchat Yom Tov.

Not surprisingly, the Chasidic Masters side with the Rashbam. They are not prepared to give up on the existence of a Yom Tov Neshamah Yeterah. Why, then, do we not use Besamim on Motzei Yom Tov? Because, explains the Sefat Emet,[5] the Yom Tov Neshamah Yeterah does not depart. It remains with us after Yom Tov leaves. In that respect, explains the Sefat Emet, the Neshamah Yeterah of Shabbat differs from the Neshamah Yeterah of Yom Tov. Like Shabbat itself, the Neshamah Yeterah of Shabbat is a gift from God which comes and goes automatically, with no effort on our part. The Neshamah Yeterah of Yom Tov, however, like Yom Tov itself, does not come unless and until we, through the Sanhedrin, (Jerusalem Court of Law) announce its arrival. And we work at it by cooking, eating, drinking and celebrating. The Neshamah Yeterah of Yom Tov is the product of our investment. And what we earn, we keep.

CELEBRATION, SERENITY AND MOURNING
אבילות בשבת ויום טוב

S he returned from the cemetery on Friday afternoon, Erev Succot, just before sundown, after bidding him a final farewell. She took off her shoes and sat down on the living room floor. Then she got right up again. She went to the table and lit the Yahrzeit candle, the Yom Tov candles and the Shabbat candles. She welcomed in the Yom Tov and the Shabbat. On Monday, Chol Hamoed Succot, she dragged herself to work. She missed him terribly. And she missed the Shiva.

The - שבעה - Shiva is the seven day mourning period immediately following the burial of a deceased relative, during which one stays at home, sits on a low chair, wears no shoes, and is comforted by a stream of visitors.[1] After the Shiva one goes to work.[2] A second period of mourning sets in for 23 days. This period is called the - שלושים - Shloshim during which time certain restrictions observed during the Shiva continue to apply, including not shaving,[3] not cutting one's hair, not marrying[4] and not attending celebrations.[5]

The arrival of Yom Tov terminates the Shiva that a relative began to observe before Yom Tov.[6] Similarly, the arrival of Yom Tov terminates the period of Shloshim that a relative began to observe before Yom Tov.[7] In a situation where the deceased died on Erev Yom Tov, Shiva may last for only a few short moments before Yom Tov, and there will be no continuation of the Shiva following Yom Tov. Similarly, if Yom Tov arrives after the relative began to observe the Shloshim, there is no continuation of the Shloshim after Yom Tov, unless the deceased is a parent.[8] The arrival of Shabbat, however, does not cancel the Shiva or the Shloshim.[9] If Shabbat would cancel the Shiva, there would never be a Shiva.[10] On Shabbat, the mourner may leave his house to attend synagogue[11] and mourning is conducted in private.[12] Although Yom Tov has the power to cut short the Shiva and the Shloshim, it does not have the power to cancel them entirely, so that they are never experienced at all. One must have observed Shiva or Shloshim, even for only a moment, in order for Yom Tov to cut them short. If, however, there was no opportunity to observe even a moment of Shiva or Shloshim before the arrival of Yom Tov, such as, where the relative died during Yom Tov, the full Shiva and Shloshim are observed after Yom Tov,[13] and the Shloshim are counted from the day of the burial.

Why does Yom Tov cut short the Shiva and Shloshim? According to Rabbi Eliezer,[14] it is because the eight days of Succot and Pesach overlap the days of the Shiva. Where, however, Yom Tov lasts for less than seven days, as in the case of Shavuot, Rosh Hashanah and Yom Kippur, Rabbi Eliezer rules that the Shiva is not cut short but resumes after Yom Tov.

Rabbi Gamliel disagrees. The power of Yom Tov to cut short the Shiva has nothing to do with the overlap of days. It is more fundamental. On Yom Tov, explains Rabbi Gamliel, we are commanded to celebrate, - ושמחת בחגך - Vesamachta Bechagecha, "You shall rejoice on your festivals."[15] Celebration and mourning are incompatible. Although people have been known to laugh and cry at the same time, one cannot be commanded to do so. Not only would this be an impossible task, it would also be disrespectful to the deceased. Therefore, since we are required to celebrate all the Yamim Tovim and since all the Jewish festivals are called - מועדים - Mo'adim,[16] they all have the power to cut short the Shiva, irrespective of whether they are seven day or one day Festivals. Accordingly, the arrival, respectively, of Pesach, Shavuot, Rosh Hashanah, Yom Kippur and Succot cut short the Shiva. And that is the Halachah.[17]

Just as Yom Tov has the power to cut short a Shiva, it has the power to cut short the Shloshim, provided that the relative began to observe the Shloshim, even momentarily, before Yom Tov. Accordingly, if the relative sat through the complete Shiva, and the seventh day of the Shiva was Erev Yom Tov, he may shave and cut his hair in honor of Yom Tov. In this situation, unless the deceased is a parent, the Shloshim will not be resumed after Yom Tov. This is because, at least for a moment in time on Erev Yom Tov, between getting up from the Shiva and shaving, the relative observed the Shloshim. Although Yom Tov does not have the power to cancel the Shloshim that was not begun before Yom Tov, it does have the power to shorten it. This is because the days of Yom Tov are considered part of the Shloshim. Accordingly, if the deceased died on Erev Pesach and a moment of Shiva was observed before Yom Tov, only 15 days of Shloshim will be observed after Pesach. This is because the moment of Shiva observed before Yom Tov, for which one gets 7 days credit, plus the 8 days of Yom Tov itself, are deducted from the Shloshim.[18] If the deceased died on Erev Shavuot and a moment of Shiva was observed before Yom Tov, only 15 days of Shloshim will be observed after Shavuot.[19] If the deceased died on Erev Rosh Hashanah and a moment of Shiva was observed before Yom Tov, only seven days Shloshim will be observed after Rosh Hashanah. This is because the arrival of Yom Kippur cancels the remainder of the Shloshim observed between Rosh Hashanah and Yom Kippur. Accordingly, in such a situation, the relative may shave on Erev Yom Kippur.[20] If the deceased died on Erev Succot and a moment of Shiva was observed before Yom Tov, only eight days of Shloshim will be observed after Succot. This is because the moment of Shiva observed before Yom Tov, for which one gets seven days credit, plus the eight days of Succot, plus Shemini Atzeret, a Festival all of its own, for which one gets seven days credit, plus one day Simchat Torah are deducted from the Shloshim.[21] The reason why Shemini Atzeret, an independent Festival in its own right, does not cancel the Shloshim but only shortens it, is because no Shloshim was observed before Yom Tov. You must experience the mourning of the Shloshim, even for a moment. If you did not, Yom Tov cannot cancel it.

If mourning is incompatible with Yom Tov, why is it not incompatible with Shabbat? Yom Tov is about outward manifestation of joy, "Simcha," whereas Shabbat is about inward serenity, "Oneg." On Shabbat we celebrate creation. Both life and death are part of creation. Oneg Shabbat is the attempt to come to terms with the way God created the universe.

TWO INTO ONE DOESN'T GO
העוסק במצוה פטור מן המצוה

A s you are disembarking from an El Al flight, you notice that the friendly neighbor who sat next to you has left the plane and forgotten his bag under his seat. You pick it up and run after him. But you are blocked by nine gentlemen who beg you to complete a Minyan, a quorum of ten men, for Minchah. Does your friend lose his bag or do the gentlemen lose their Minyan? Next morning, while praying in the Synagogue, you are approached by a poor man who solicits a donation. Do you disregard the Mitzvah of charity because you are busy praying? You are carrying your mother's heavy suitcase as an old lady, hunched over with shopping bags, shuffles by. Do you have to carry her bags too?

The answer to all these questions depends upon the interpretation of the Talmudic dictum - העוסק במצוה פטור מן המצוה - Ha'osek Bamitzvah Patur Min Hamitzvah, which means that if you are busy performing a Mitzvah you are exempt from performing another Mitzvah.[1]

Does the Osek Bamitzvah exemption apply only in circumstances where it is impossible to perform both, as in the lost bag/lost Minyan/ Impossible Case? Does it also apply where it is easy to perform both as in the "I'm praying, don't bother me" /Easy Case? Does it apply where it is difficult yet still possible to perform both, as in the suitcase/shopping bag/ Difficult Case?

According to Tosafot[2] and the Rosh,[3] the Osek Bamitzvah exemption applies only in the Impossible Case. Clearly, argue Tosafot, one is not exempt from Mitzvot just because one wears Tzizit, fringes, all day or because one is warehousing somebody's lost property. According to Rashi, the Osek Bamitzvah exemption also applies in the Easy Case. Accordingly, a person travelling by day on Succot to perform the Mitzvah of visiting his Rabbi is, according to Rashi, exempt from the Mitzvah of eating and sleeping in the Succah when he sojourns at night.[4] According to the Ran,[5] the Osek Bamitzvah exemption does not apply in the Easy Case but does apply both in the Impossible Case and in the Difficult Case. The Ran cites several proofs for the application of the Osek Bamitzvah exemption in the Difficult Case, as follows. In Talmudic times, a bridegroom was exempt from - קריאת שמע - reciting "Hear O Israel the Lord our God the Lord is one" on account of his preoccupation with his wedding night. Similarly, cites the Ran, a person performing the Mitzvah of guarding the unburied dead or digging them a grave is exempt from all Mitzvot. In all these cases, it is possible, although difficult, to recite Kriyat Shema while preoccupied with the first Mitzvah. Yet, says the Ran, the exemption applies. In explaining the reason for the application of the Osek Bamitzvah exemption in the Impossible Case and the Difficult Case, as opposed to the Easy Case, the Ran points out that the Talmudic dictum is - העוסק במצוה - Haosek Bamitzvah, one who is busy with a Mitzvah and not "המקיים מצוה" Hamekayem Mitzvah, one who is merely fulfilling the Mitzvah. The Halachah, as expressed by the Shulchan Aruch, adopts the approach of the Ran.[6]

The Osek Bamitzvah exemption requires one to complete the Mitzvah one first started, even where the second Mitzvah is more important, carries a harsher penalty for non-performance and will be impossible to perform later. Thus, the duty to sacrifice the Korban Pesach, the Paschal Lamb, in the Temple was postponed in the event of a death requiring a surviving relative to become Tameh, ineligible to enter the Temple.[7] This was the case even though the punishment for unjustifiably ignoring the Korban Peasch is premature death and even though the Korban Pesach is time sensitive. Similarly, a person busy with pressing communal affairs is exempt from reciting Kriyat Shema, even though the Shema contains the credo of every Jew and cannot be recited after a certain hour.[8]

Does the Osek Bamitzvah exemption apply in a case where the second Mitzvah has the independent power to override the first Mitzvah? For example, may a Mohel who is asked to perform a Brit Milah on Rosh Hashanah in an outlying district, refuse to leave his family on the grounds that he is already busy with the Mitzvah of celebrating the holiday with his family? Based on the case of Korban Pesach, the Avne Nezer rules that, even though Milah is time sensitive and carries a penalty of premature death if ignored, the Mohel may refuse.[9] The Minchat Yiztchak is not so sure. After all, he argues, the Mitzvah of performing a Brit Milah on the eighth day overrides Shabbat itself. Certainly, therefore, it should override the Mizvah of Oneg Shabbat, and the Mohel is obliged to go.[10]

THE HOLY THIEF
מצוה הבאה בעבירה

When our son came home from school one day and complained that his Tefillin had been removed from his locker, we wondered how the culprit would ever be able to use those Tefillin. Is it not like stealing somebody else's key to get into one's own front door? How could one possibly perform a Mitzvah with stolen goods?

In the case of certain Mitzvot, the Torah itself makes it perfectly clear that the Mitzvah can only be performed with one's own property. Thus, for example, the Torah[1] explicitly informs us that on the first day of Succot, the Lulav must belong to you. If it is borrowed or stolen from someone else, it cannot be used on the first day. Similarly, the Mitzvah of Challah, separating a portion of dough when kneading it into bread, can only be performed with dough that belongs to you.[2] But on the second day of Succot, the Torah does not insist that the Lulav belong to you. Neither does the Torah insist that the Matzah you are required to eat on the first day of Pesach belong to you. Neither does the Torah insist that the Tefillin you don or the book you study Torah from belong to you.

Where the Torah has not been so explicit, the Rabbis have stepped in and restricted the use of stolen goods in the performance of a Mitzvah. Thus, for example, even though the Torah does not prohibit it, the Rabbis prohibit the use of a stolen Lulav on the second day of Succot because it is a - מצוה הבאה בעבירה - "Mitzvah Haba'ah Be'aveirah," which means that it is a Mitzvah which has no independent existence without the Aveirah, the violation.[3]

Similarly, based on the dictum of Mitzvah Haba'ah Beaveira, the Rabbis prohibit the use of stolen Tefillin,[4] stolen books,[5] stolen Matzah[6] or a synagogue built on stolen land.[7] The application of the Mitzvah Habaah Beaveira rule is restricted, however, to the situation where the Mitzvah has no independent existence without the Aveirah, or, put another way, where the Aveirah, so to speak, resides within the Mitzvah. Accordingly, the Mitzvah of Lulav on the second day of Succot cannot be performed with a stolen Lulav, where the Lulav itself, as opposed to its monetary value, has to be returned to its original owner. As long as the original owner has the right to take his Lulav back, that Lulav may not be used. Where, however, the original owner no longer has the right to take back his stolen Lulav and has only the right to monetary compensation, the stolen Lulav may be used, even on the first day of Succot.[8] There are many situations[9] where the original owner loses his right to the physical return of his stolen goods and can only receive monetary compensation. One such situation occurs where the thief transforms the stolen goods into something else. The thief who steals flour and bakes Matzah cannot return the flour but only its value. Accordingly, the Mitzvah Haba'ah Beaveirah rule will not apply and the Matzah baked from the stolen flour may be used to fulfill the Mitzvah of Matzah on the first day of Pesach.[10] If, however, the Matzah is stolen, the Mitzvah Haba'ah Baeveirah rule would prohibit its use.[11] Another situation where the owner's only remedy is compensation and where the Mitzvah Haba'ah Beaveirah rule would not apply is the case of "Shinui Shem," i.e. where the designation of the stolen good has changed in the hands of the thief. Thus, where a person steals a palm tree branch and transforms it into Kosher Lulavim, the change of designation from a "palm branch" to a Kosher "Lulav" denies the original owner the right to take it back.[12] The reason for this is that the Torah requires the thief to return the same goods that he stole - והשיב את הגזלה אשר גזל - Veheisheev Et Hagezeila Asher Gazal,[13] and not different ones. If they are different, he need not return them but must pay their value instead. Another situation where the owner's only remedy is compensation and where, accordingly, the Mitzvah Haba'ah Beaveirah rule would not apply, is the case of - ייאוש - Yiush, where the owner has verbally renounced the hope of ever retrieving his stolen goods and, in addition, the goods have been transferred to a third party.[14] Accordingly, one who purchases a stolen Lulav or stolen Tefillin need not give the Lulav or the Tefillin back to the owner and may use them for their respective Mitzvot. Whether a blessing may be recited over the Lulav or Tefillin in such circumstances is a matter of Halachic debate. Some authorities[15] consider reciting a blessing in such circumstances to be in bad taste, whereas other authorities[16] see nothing wrong with it.

Is the Mitzvah Haba'ah Beaveirah rule itself of Biblical or Rabbinical origin?[17] If it is only of Rabbinical origin, then stolen goods in the hands of a thief could be used to perform a Mitzvah whose origin is, likewise, only Rabbinical, because the Rabbis never superimpose one Rabbinical enactment over another. Thus, on the second day of Succot, the thief himself could use the stolen Lulav, even where the original owner has the right to take it back. This is because the requirement to use the Lulav on the second day of Succot is itself only of Rabbinical origin.[18] If, however, the Mitzvah Haba'ah Beaveirah rule itself is of Biblical origin, the rule would apply, in such circumstances, even on the second day of Succot.[19]

As for the missing Tefillin, let us assume that the person who took them is just borrowing them. In that case, he may use them and even recite a blessing over them as long as he has in mind to return them. The Halachic presumption is that a person is happy for another to fulfill a Mitzvah with his property.[20]

THE GREAT ESCAPE
חנוכה

In June 1967, even skeptics and agnostics admitted that the people of Israel who, only days before, were preparing their own graves, were saved by nothing short of a miracle. And in May 1982, as the mechanized artillery platoon rolled out from its camouflaged position near the Beirut Damascus road, unscathed by a barrage of Syrian shelling, the nonobservant tank commander exclaimed, "Eize Nes!," "What a miracle!" Years later, however, in conversations with the same people, the miracle, so obvious when it occurred, was camouflaged in a shroud of strategic, military terms.

Clearly, the victories of the outnumbered Maccabean freedom fighters over the vast Syrian armies of Antiochus, Lysias and their allies could only be explained in terms of a miracle. Indeed, the Book of the Maccabees, as well as the Al Hanisim prayer, portray the military victories as miracles. Yet the Talmud,[1] in a seven line summary of the meaning of Chanukah, makes no mention of the military miracles. Rather, the Talmud focuses on the miracle of that small jar of pure oil, untouched by the Syrian invaders, which burned for eight days, even though it contained oil sufficient for only one. Why does the Talmud emphasize the miracle of the oil over the miracle of the military victory?

The Talmud[2] tells us that a lamp is lit over the head of each unborn child in its mother's womb, enabling the child to perceive all the ways of God throughout the world. When the child enters this world, however, it leaves the lamp behind and has to discover the ways of God without it. And, in the jostle and struggle for physical survival, the divine spark that remains to guide us is often threatened with extinction. Life becomes so reasoned and vision so tunneled that even the flare of a miracle can go unrecognized. Enter the Chanukah lights. This miracle of the jar of oil sufficient in quantity for one day, which burned for eight, is a נס גלוי - Nes Galui, inexplicable in natural terms. The Rabbis tell us that the purpose of the Chanukah lights is to illuminate the miracle of the military victory which could, perhaps, be a נס נסתר - Nes Nistar explained in natural terms. They also tell us that the time to light is at sunset,[3] when the light in this world is about to die and that the Chanukah lights must remain burning - עד שתכלה רגל מן השוק - Ad Shetichle Regel Min Hashuk, till the streets become empty.[4] The Berditchever Rebbe points out[5] that the word - רגל - Regel, which means foot, is the same as the word - הרגל - Hergel, which means habit. And so, he explains, the lights of Chanukah should remain burning until they remove the habit of reason from our spiritual vision and allow us to behold the Nes Nistar. Furthermore, although the Maccabean battles for the rededication of the Temple were won, the war was ultimately lost with the destruction of the Temple some 200 years later.[6] The pure oil of the Temple Menorah was extinguished until this day. But not the oil of the Chanukah Menorah. Like the miracle of the burning bush of Moses, the Chanukah lights have withstood, for centuries, the fires of persecution. Like the Jewish people themselves, the Chanukah lights, we are assured, will never die. That was God's promise to Aaron in response to his complaint that the Tribe of Levi was not invited to participate in the dedication of the Sanctuary. The lights of the Sanctuary, God warned, would eventually be extinguished, but the Chanukah lights of Aaron's Maccabean descendants will shine forever.[7]

Unlike during the week, when the Chanukah lights are lit after sunset, on Erev Shabbat, Friday afternoon, they should be lit within one half an hour before sunset.[8] The same Berachot are recited when lighting the Chanukah lights on Erev Shabbat as during the rest of the week. Unlike during the week, when the Chanukah candles should not be lit before Minchah, the afternoon service, on Erev Shabbat one may light them first and then go to the Synagogue to recite Minchah.[9] On Motzaei Shabbat, the Chanukah candles are lit in the Synagogue after reciting the Havdalah in the Amidah but before lighting the Havdalah candle.[10] At home, on Motzaei Shabbat, there is a difference of opinion among the Poskim whether the Havdalah candle should be lit and whether Havdalah should be recited before or after lighting the Chanukah lights.[11] In this matter, one should follow one's family custom.[12] During the week, the optimum time for lighting the Chanukah candles is within half an hour after Sunset I, when the sun sets below the horizon and is no longer visible.[13] If one is detained at work, the candles may be lit with a Berachah until midnight. After midnight, they may be lit with a Berachah, if members of the household are awake and without a Berachah until dawn if they are asleep.[14] Women are obliged to light candles[15] and men and women can light for one another, as long as they have in mind to fulfil the Mitzvah for each other. In view of the equal Halachic status of men and women in connection with Chanukah, Rav Ovadiah Yosef rules that if a man is detained at work while his wife is at home, he should request his wife to light for him at sunset rather than wait until he arrives home.[16] There is a Halachic dispute whether the Mitzvah of lighting Chanukah lights is a - חובת גברא - a personal obligation, similar to wearing Tefillin, or whether it is a - חובת חפצא - an obligation which applies to the house, such as Mezuzah.[17] The practical difference would be whether a person who has no house must light Chanukah candles[18] and whether one can appoint an agent to light candles on one's behalf. The most accepted answer is that lighting the candles is a "house Mitzvah,"[19] whereas acknowledging the miracle by reciting the blessing of שעשה ניסים and שהחיינו is a personal Mitzvah.[20] Accordingly, a hotel room over which you pay for sole, albeit temporary, possession is considered your house and you should light Chanukah candles there, if possible,[21] even if your family is lighting at home. Although an electric light bulb qualifies for Havdalah, it does not qualify for Chanukah lights, because the miracle we celebrate occurred with oil and wicks.[22]

The Midrash identifies seven Chanukot in history, which include: the Chanukah of Creation, when God lit the lights of the world, the Chanukah of the Sanctuary, the Maccabean

Chanukah, and the Chanukah of the Messiah. On Shabbat Chanukah, we celebrate two Chanukot, the Chanukah of Creation and the Chanukah of the Maccabees. Which do we light first? The Shabbat and the Havdalah candles, which celebrate the Chanukah of Creation, or the Chanukah candles, which celebrate the Chanukah of the Maccabbees? The answer of reason and numbers would dictate, - תדיר ושאינו תדיר תדיר קודם - Tadir Vesheino Tadir, Tadir Kodem, which means do first what you do more frequently. And since Shabbat is celebrated each week and Chanukah just once a year, light the Shabbat candles first. But the Chanukah lights defy the logic of numbers and reason. Their message of - פרסומי ניסא - Pirsumei Nissa, publicizing the miracle, takes precedence to remind us that creation and daily existence are miracles which cannot be explained in natural terms. That is perhaps one of the reasons why most agree that the Chanukah lights are lit before the Shabbat candles[23] and why most agree that the Chanukah lights are lit at home, before the Havdalah candles, after reciting Havdalah in the Amida.[24]

MEGILLAH ON THE INTERNET
קריאת מגילה

Why is the Megillah read in Jerusalem on the 15th day of Adar, in New York on the 14th day of Adar and in Sefat and Chevron on the 14th and the 15th of Adar? On what day does an American tourist read the Megillah in Jerusalem, and when does an Israeli tourist read the Megillah in New York? Why is the Megillah read twice during the same day, once at night and once during the day? If one can only attend one reading of the Megillah, which one should one choose? Why does Purim outside of Israel never occur on Shabbat? When Purim in Israel occurs on Shabbat, why is the Megillah read on Friday? Can the Megillah be recited in English? Can the Mitzvah of listening to the Megillah be fulfilled over the telephone or the radio? Can a loud speaker be used?

Those who reside in a city, such as Jerusalem, which was surrounded by a wall in the days of Joshua, recite the Megillah on the 15th day of Adar.[1] Those who reside in cities regarding which there is uncertainty whether or not they were surrounded by a wall in the days of Joshua, such as the cities of Yaffo, Acco, Aza, Lod, Tiveria, Shechem, Chevron, Tsefat and Haifa,[2] are required to read the Megillah both on the 14th and the 15th days of Adar.[3] Residents of all other cities recite the Megillah on the 14th day of Adar.[4] The reason for this distinction is that in the city of Shushan itself, the battle of the Jews against their enemies continued on through the 14th day, and Purim was celebrated on the 15th.[5] Because Shushan was a walled city in Mordechai's day, all other walled cities celebrate Purim on the 15th day of Adar. Out of deference, however, to the cities of Israel, most of which had been destroyed before Mordechai's time, the relevant time chosen by the Sages to determine whether a city was surrounded by a wall or not was the time of Joshua.[6]

A tourist in Jerusalem who originally planned to leave Jerusalem prior to the 15th day of Adar, recites the Megillah in Jerusalem on the 14th day of Adar, even if, contrary to his original plans, he still finds himself in Jerusalem on the 15th of Adar. If, however, such a person originally intended to be in Jerusalem on the 15th of Adar, he recites the Megillah in Jerusalem on the 15th. Conversely, a resident of Jerusalem visiting New York, who, originally, planned to return to Jerusalem prior to the 14th day of Adar, recites the Megillah in New York on the 15th day of Adar, even if, contrary to his plans, he still finds himself in New York on the 14th day of Adar. If, however, such a person originally intended to be in New York on the 14th of Adar, he recites the Megillah in New York on the 14th of Adar.[7]

The Megillah must be recited both on the night of Purim and on Purim day.[8] However, reciting the Megillah on the day of the fifteenth has greater significance than reciting the Megillah at night on the eve of the fifteenth.[9] This is because the day-time reading was instituted by Mordechai and Esther, whereas the night time reading was instituted, subsequently, by the Rabbis. Accordingly, if circumstances force one to choose one reading over the other, most authorities agree that one should attend the day time reading.[10] Others argue that the rule of - אין מעבירים על המצות - Ein Ma'avirin Al Hamitzvot, do not offend a Mitzvah by postponing it, requires that one choose the night-time reading.[11] To fulfill the Mitzvah of listening to the Megillah, each word must be heard. If a word is missed, the listener should read it quietly to himself from the text in his hand.[12] The principal purpose of reciting the Megillah is to publicize the miracle of Purim. Accordingly, many Poskim permit the Megillah to be read in English if the reader does not understand Hebrew.[13] Because Yom Kippur can never occur on a Friday, the 14th day of Adar can never occur on a Shabbat. If the 15th day of Adar occurs on a Shabbat, the Megillah is read in Jerusalem on a Friday.[14] This is out of the dual concern that people would carry the Megillah in the streets on Shabbat[15] and would not be able to give money to the poor on Shabbat.[16]

One can fulfill the Mitzvah of listening to the Megillah as long as one hears the voice of the person reciting the Megillah on one's behalf.[17] Most Poskim agree, therefore, that listening to a live broadcast of the Megillah over the radio or the telephone is unacceptable, because you are listening to an electronic transmission of the reader's voice rather than the voice itself.[18] According to Rabbi Ovadia Yosef, a microphone is unacceptable.[19] This is because, according to his understanding, the membrane of the microphone absorbs the human voice and then emits an electronic version of it. According to Rabbi Moshe Feinstein,[20] however, a microphone is acceptable because the transmission is simultaneously activated by the human voice. Rabbi Ovadia Yosef concedes, however, that a microphone may be used to amplify the reader's voice in a case where the reader's voice would still be audible without it.

PRIME-TIME PRAYER
חודש אלול

1. Rashi, Deuteronomy 9:18 s.v. ואתנפל. Rosh to Rosh Hashanah 35, (in Rosh 40b) Tosafot, Shabbat 89a s.v. לסוף; Tur, Orach Chaim 581.
2. Song of Songs 6:3.
3. Exodus 21:13.
4. Esther 9:22.
5. Tur, Orach Chaim 581.
6. Kitzur Shulchan Aruch 128:2.
7. Numbers 30:3.
8. Kitzur Shulchan Aruch 128:16; Kaf Hachaim, Orach Chaim 581:19.

—⚬—

SELICHOT
ימי הסליחות

1. Yalkut Shimoni to Exodus 34, paragraph 398; Rosh Hashanah 17b.
2. Exodus 34:6-7.
3. Shulchan Aruch, Orach Chaim 581:1, and Mishnah Berurah 6 thereon.
4. Ibid.
5. See note 3
6. Berachot 3b.
7. Avodah Zarah 3b.
8. Shulchan Aruch, Orach Chaim 47:13
9. Shulchan Aruch, Orach Chaim 581:1 and Mishanah Berurah 6 thereon.
10. Mateh Efraim 11.
11. Mishnah Berurah 4 to Shulchan Aruch, Orach Chaim 581:1; Sotah 33.
12. Tur, Orach Chaim 581.

—⚬—

HAPPY BIRTHDAY
מוסף של ראש השנה
(ראש השנה לב.)

1. Midrash Rabbah, Leviticus 29:1.
2. Genesis 2:3 as interpreted by the Chatam Sofer.
3. Rosh Hashanah 16a.
4. In accordance with the opinion of Rabbi Akiva in Talmud Rosh Hashanah 32a.
5. Samuel I:2:1-10.
6. Rosh Hashanah 32a, (4b in Maharsha).

7. Genesis Chapter 1.
8. Rosh Hashanah 32a.
9. These ten verses are taken from Exodus 15:18; Numbers 23:31; Deuteronomy 33:5; Deuteronomy 6:4; Psalms 22:29; Psalms 93:1; Psalms 24:7; Isaiah 44:6; Ovadiah 1:21 and Zechariah 14:9.
10. The ten verses included in Zichronot are taken from Genesis 8:1; Exodus 2:24; Leviticus 26:42; Leviticus 26:45; Psalms 111:4; Psalms 111:5; Psalms 106:45; Jeremiah 2:2; Ezekiel 16:60 and Jeremiah 31:19.
11. The ten verses included in Shofarot are taken from Exodus 19:16; Exodus 19:19; Exodus 20:18; Numbers 10:10; Psalms 47:6; Psalms 98:6; Psalms 81:4; Psalm 150; Isaiah 18:3; Isaiah 27:13 and Zechariah 9:14.

SHOFAR
שופר
(ראש השנה לב - לג)

1. Numbers 29:1.
2. Psalms 47:6.
3. Rosh Hashanah 34:2. Tur, Orach Chaim 590:1; Rambam, Hilchot Shofar 3:1.
4. Shulchan Aruch, Orach Chaim 588:1.
5. Shulchan Aruch, Orach Chaim 585:1, and Mishnah Berurah 1 thereon; Shulchan Aruch, Orach Chaim 585:4, and Rema thereon; Rambam 3:10.
6. Shulchan Aruch, Orach Chaim 592:1, and Mishnah Berurah 2 thereon.
7. Ibid. 592:1, and Mishnah Berurah 4 thereon; Pri Megadim 592.
8. Shulchan Aruch, Orach Chaim 585:1, and Mishnah Berurah 4 thereon.
9. Rosh to Rosh Hashanah 33b (in Rosh 39b).
10. Responsa Avnei Nezer, Orach Chaim 40:6 discussing the Rambam.
11. Kidushin 29a; Rambam, Hilchot Shofar 2:1.
12. Rosh Hashanah 33a. רבי יוסי ורבי שמעון אומרים נשים סומכות רשות Tosafot s.v. הא רבי יהודה והא רבי יוסי.
13. Pirkei DeRabbi Eliezer, 31.
14. Isaiah 27:13.
15. Rabbi Mirski, Hegioneh Halachah volume 2, p.51.

WHERE'S THE SHOFAR?

ראש השנה שחל להיות בשבת
(ראש השנה כט:)

1. Talmud Yerushalmi, Rosh Hashanah 4:1; Rashi, Leviticus 25:9.
2. Numbers 29:1.
3. Leviticus 23:24.
4. Ran to Rif, Megillah 4b (2b in Rif) s.v. פורים.
5. Rosh Hashanah 29b.
6. Shabbat 131b.
7. Rosh Hashanah 29b; Megillah 4b; Succah 42b.
8. Rosh Hashanah 29b, Rashi s.v. גזירה שמא יטלנו.
9. Rosh Hashanah 29b; Rambam, Hilchot Shofar 2:9.
10. Rabbi Eliezer, Rosh Hashanah 29b.
11. The second opinion in the Mishnah, Rosh Hashanah 29b.
12. Milchamot Hashem on Rif to Rosh Hashanah 29b. (8a in Rif) s.v. אמר.
13. Ran to Rosh Hashanah 29b (8 in Rif) s.v. והיינו טעמא.
14. Tosafot, Megillah 4b s.v. ויעבירנה. See also answer of Taz, Hilchot Rosh Hashanah 588:5 s.v. אין תוקעין בשופר that whereas Shofar can be blasted on the day of Rosh Hashanah which is not Shabbat, Milah, if postponed because of Shabbat, could never be performed on the eigth day.
15. Taz, ibid.
16. Rabbi Mirski, Hegione Halachah Vol II, p.45.
17. Rabbi Zevin, Hamoadim Behalachah volume 1, p.59.

—∞—

TWO DAYS ROSH HASHANAH, ERUVIN AND EGGS

ראש השנה. יומא אריכתא
(ראש השנה ל:)

1. Beit Yosef to Tur, Orach Chaim 601 s.v גרסינן, who explains that the reason for this is that if the witnessess who testify to sighting the new moon would arrive after Minchah, then even in Jerusalem two days would be observed; See also Beitzah 4b and 5; See Minchat Chinuch Mitzvah 301.
2. Rambam, Hilchot Kidush Hachodesh 3:11.
3. Rosh Hashanah 30b; Beitzah 5a.
4. Rashi, Beitzah 5a s.v. עד המנחה.
5. Ibid.
6. See "Second Day Yom Tov, Eruvin and Eggs," below, for an articulation of the argument that permits the extension of the Techum Shabbat in both directions and that permit an egg laid on the first day Yom Tov, to be eaten on the second.

7. Beitzah 5a.

8. Rashi, Beitzah 5a s.v. מתקנת רבן יוחנן בן זכאי.

9. Rif quoted in Beit Yosef, note 1 above.

10. Beitzah 4b.

—〜〜—

YOM KIPPUR
יום כפור
(יומה ע.)

1. Exodus 33:20.

2. Yoma 70a.

3. Mishnah Yoma 5:1 s.v. ולא היה מאריך בתפילתו שלא להבעית את ישראל, and Bartenura thereon.

4. Leviticus 10:1-7.

5. Rambam, Hilchot Avodat Yom Hakipurim 1:1-2.

6. Ibid. 2:2

7. Yoma 70a.

8. Shulchan Aruch, Orach Chaim 619:2, and Mishnah Berurah 2 thereon.

9. Shulchan Aruch, Orach Chaim 621:6.

—〜〜—

SUCCOT
סוכות
(סוכה כז - כח:)

1. Leviticus 23:34.

2. Rashi, Deutoronomy 9:18.

3. Rashi, Leviticus 9:1.

4. Exodus 35:1, 36:6, Baal Haturim.

5. Sefer Hatoda'ah, page 91.

6. Opinion of Rabbi Eliezer, Succah 11b.

7. Opinion of Rabbi Akiva ibid. But see Mechilta, Exodus 14, where the opinions of Rabbi Eliezer and Rabbi Akiva are reversed. See also Maharitz Chayot, Succah 11b.

8. Tur and Beit Yosef, Orach Chaim 625 and Rashi, Leviticus 23:43 adopt the opinion of Rabbi Eliezer in Succah 11b.

9. Ha'amek Davar, Numbers 10:34.

10. Shulchan Aruch, Orach Chaim 629:1.

11. Ibid. 635:1, and Rema and Mishnah Berurah 9 thereon.
12. Succah 27a; Shulchan Aruch, Orach Chaim 639:3.
13. Shulchan Aruch, Orach Chaim 640:3.
14. Ibid., 639:5, and Mishnah Berurah 35 thereon in the name of Eliah Rabbah and Pri Megadim.
15. Mishnah Berurah 35 and 36 to Shulchan Aruch, Orach Chaim 639:5
16. Succot 28b.

---ᘉᘓᘉ---

UNDER THE OAK TREE
תעשה ולא מן העשוי
(סוכה י - יא:)

1. Shulchan Aruch, Orach Chaim 626:1, and Mishnah Berurah 1 thereon who points out that בסכת תשבו is written in the singular. There can be no more than one protective layer of shade.
2. Succah 11b; Shulchan Aruch, Orach Chaim 626:1+2, and Mishnah Berurah 13 thereon.
3. Deuteronomy 16:13.
4. Succah 11b.
5. Shulchan Aruch, Orach Chaim 626:2, and Mishnah Berurah 13 thereon.
6. Ibid. 626:1, and Rema thereon.
7. Ibid. 626:2, and Mishnah Berurah 17 thereon.
8. Ibid. 626:3, and Rema and Mishnah Berurah 18 thereon.
9. Deuteronomy 22:12.
10. Succah 11a.
11. Menachot 33b.

---ᘉᘓᘉ---

THE BROKEN STEM
ארבע מינים
(סוכה לב - מד)

1. Leviticus 23:40.
2. Succah 35a.
3. Succah 32b.
4. Shulchan Aruch, Orach Chaim 651:1.
5. Ibid. 651:2.
6. Succah 37b; Shulchan Aruch, Orach Chaim 651:9.
7. Succah 37b; Rashi, Menachot 62a s.v. מוליך ומביא.
8. Megillah 20b; Shulchan Aruch, Orach Chaim 652:1.

9. Pesachim 117a.
10. Succah 37b.
11. Succah 41a.
12. Shulchan Aruch, Orach Chaim 648:22.
13. Ibid. 648:18.
14. Ibid. 649:5, and Mishnah Berurah 45 thereon.
15. Ibid. 648:2.
16. Ibid. 648:20, and Mishnah Berurah 65 thereon.
17. Ibid. 648:7-8, and Mishnah Berurah 30-33 thereon.
18. Succah 32b; Shulchan Aruch, Orach Chaim 650:1.
19. Shulchan Aruch, Orach Chaim 645:3, and Rema in the name of יש מפרשים.
20. Shulchan Aruch, Orach Chaim 646:1+5, and Mishnah Berurah 18 thereon.
21. Shulchan Aruch, Orach Chaim 650:1. The range takes into account the various opinions regarding the definition of a Tefach.
22. Ibid. 646:1+10 and Rema thereon.
23. Ibid. 647:1.
24. Succah 29b, 32b and 33a; Shulchan Aruch, Orach Chaim 649:1+5.
25. Chayei Adam 149:6.
26. Succah 29b; Shulchan Aruch, Orach Chaim 649:3.
27. Shulchan Aruch, Orach Chaim 649:2, and Mishnah Berurah 15 thereon.
28. Magen Avraham to Shulchan Aruch, Orach Chaim quoted in Mishnah Berurah 15 to Shulchan Aruch, Orach Chaim 649:2 - even without such an explicit stipulation a Lulav may be borrowed on the first day because it is presumed that the lender wants the borrower to fullfill the Mitzvah.
29. Chayei Adam 148:10.
30. Shulchan Aruch, Orach Chaim 651:5, and Mishnah Berurah 24+25 thereon.
31. Succah 41a and 44a; Shulchan Aruch, Orach Chaim 658:2.

—ɯ—

WHOLE HALLEL, HALF HALLEL, NO HALLEL
הלל
(ערכין י; פסחים קיז.)

1. Erachin 10a+b; Pesachim 117a; Taanit 28b.
2. Isaiah 30:29.
3. Shulchan Aruch Harav, Orach Chaim 473:47; Shulchan Aruch, Orach Chaim 480:1, and Mishnah Berurah 1 thereon.
4. Shulchan Aruch, Orach Chaim 644:1, and Mishnah Berurah 5 s.v. המנהג לברך לקרוא את ההלל.
5. Erachin 10b.
6. Sanhedrin 39b; Shulchan Aruch, Orach Chaim 490:4, and Mishanah Berurah 4 and Beit Yosef

to Tur, Orach Chaim 490 s.v. כל, quoting Shibulei Leket in name of מדרש הרנינו. Another reason for not reciting whole Hallel on the last two days of Pesach is that the days of Pesach share the same קרבן and are not differentiated by different קרבנות. See Erachin 10b דפסח אין חלוקין בקורבנותיהן. See Mahrsha 22a to Sanhedrin 38b s.v. ומי for an explanation why both reasons are necessary.

7. Mishanah Berurah 4 to Shulchan Aruch, Orach Chaim 490:4.
8. Shulchan Aruch, Orach Chaim 422:2, and Mishnah Berurah 12 thereon.
9. Ibid.
10. Tosafot, Succah 44b s.v. כאן במקדש.
11. Rambam, Hilchot Chanukah 3:7.
12. Tosafot, Berachot 14a s.v. ימים.
13. Responsa Yabia Omer, Orach Chaim Chelek 6, Siman 41, p. 137.

ומעתה נראה שהואיל והנסים שנעשו לנו במלחמת הקוממיות שהצילנו השי"ת מידי אויבינו ושונאינו...
כיון שלא היה נס לכל ישראל, אפשר שנכון לומר הלל, אבל בלי ברכה. ומעתה במלחמת הקוממיות שהנס היה דרך
הטבע, כי כזו וכזו אכלה החרב, וכמה נפשות יקרות נפלו במערכות ישראל, אם כי בסופו של דבר תהלות לאל
יתברך... וגבר ישראל מ"מ אין הדבר חורג מדרך הטבע ולכן אין לקבוע ע"ז הלל הלל בברכה.

14. נצר מטעי, קול מבשר, cited by Rav Ovadia Yosef, Yabia Omer, ibid.

15. Responsa Igrot Moshe, Orach Chaim Chelek 2, Siman 94, p. 287. It should be pointed out that this responsum was written in the context of Hallel in Synagogue on Pesach night, but the principle is the same.

—✴—

SECOND DAY YOM TOV, ERUVIN AND EGGS
יום טוב שני של גלויות
(ראש השנה כה.)

1. Rashi, Exodus 12:2.
2. Rosh Hashanah 25a; Rambam, Hilchot Kiddush Hachodesh 6:3.
3. Numbers 11:20; Megillah 5a.
4. סדר לעשות לוח קצרה, Mishnah Berurah at end of Hilchot Rosh Chodesh.
5. Rambam, Hilchot Kiddush Hachodesh, 5:1-3.
6. Ibid. 1:3-4.
7. Rosh Hashanah 22b.
8. Identity of the Cutheans is described in Kings II, Chapter 17.
9. Beitzah 4b.
10. For an explanation of Eruvei Techumim, see Chapter 2 "Eruvei Techumim Ships, Planes and Moshiach."
11. Eruvin 39a; Rashi, Beitzah 4b s.v. שריא נפשך וממה הוא חול מיניהו דחד בזה: מותרת.

ERUV TAVSHILIN
ערוב תבשילין
(פסחים מו: ; ביצה טו:)

1. Exodus 12:16; Shulchan Aruch, Orach Chaim 495:1.
2. Shulchan Aruch, Orach Chaim 503:1. See also Beitzah 2b.
3. Pesachim 46b.
4. Rashi, Pesachim 46b s.v. מדאורייתא.
5. Leviticus 23:15, וספרתם לכם ממחרת השבת - שבת here refers to חג המצות.
6. Tosafot, Pesachim 46b s.v. רבה, see also Magen Avraham to Shulchan Aruch, Orach Chaim 527:1.
7. Shulchan Aruch, Orach Chaim 527:1-2, and Mishnah Berurah 1-3 thereon.
8. Opinion of Rav Ashi, Beitzah 15b.
9. Opinion of Rava, Beitzah 15b as explained by Rashi s.v. זכרהו מאחר שבא להשכיחו.
10. Exodus 16:23.
11. Mishnah Berurah 5 to Shulchan Aruch, Orach Chaim 527:2.
12. Shulchan Aruch Harav, Orach Chaim 527:18.
13. Shulchan Aruch, Orach Chaim 527:19; Responsa Minchat Yitzchak Chelek 7, Siman 36, p. 85.
14. Rabbi Simcha Rabinowitz, Piskei Teshuvot Chelek 5, p.417, note 4 to Shulchan Aruch, Orach Chaim 527:4.
15. Shulchan Aruch, Orach Chaim 527:13.
16. Ibid. 527:2, and Mishnah Berurah 4 thereon; 527:16, and Mishnah Berurah 48 thereon.
17. Rabbi Simcha Bunim Cohen, The Laws of Yom Tov p. 285, note 46.
18. Shulchan Aruch, Orach Chaim 527:7.
19. Ibid. and Mishnah Berurah 25 thereon.
20. Ibid. 527:1 and Mishnah Berurah 3 thereon.

—⚬—

WHAT YOU CAN DO ON YOM TOV
THAT YOU CAN'T ON SHABBAT
אוכל נפש
(ביצה יב)

1. Exodus 12:16.
2. Shulchan Aruch, Orach Chaim 518:1.
3. Ibid. 595:1.
4. Ibid. 511:1.
5. Ibid. 514:5, and Mishnah Berurah 30 thereon.
6. Shemirat Shabbat, volume 1, Chapter 12:4 provided such dishes are used on Yom Tov.
7. Shulchan Aruch, Orach Chaim 511:2.

8. Ibid. 503:1.
9. Ibid. and Mishnah Berurah 7 thereon.
10. Shulchan Aruch Orach Chaim 502:1 אין מוציאים אש לא מן העצים ולא מן האבנים.; Beitzah 33a.
11. This is the opinion of most Poskim including the Magen Avraham to Shulchan Aruch, Orach Chaim 502:1 s.v. אין מוציאין; Shulchan Aruch Harav, Orach Chaim 502:1; Chayei Adam 95:12; Mishnah Berurah 4 to Shulchan Aruch, Orach Chaim 502:1.
12. Rambam, Hilchot Yom Tov 4:1. The Raavad explains that the Rabbis prohibit it on account of Moliyd, the creation of something out of nothing.
13. Shulchan Aruch Harav, Orach Chaim 307:12; Shulchan Aruch, Orach Chaim 316:8, and Mishanah Berurah 33 thereon.
14. Shulchan Aruch, Orach Chaim 514:1, and Rema and Mishnah Berurah 7; Shemirath Shabbath 13:10.
15. Responsa Igrot Moshe, Orach Chaim Chelek 1, Siman 115, p.177
16. The majority of Halachic opinions prohibit turning off an electric light to enable one to sleep on Yom Tov. The Tzitz Eliezer Chelek 1, Siman 20, Perek 5, p.108 however, permits it as part of Ochel Nefesh.
17. Shulchan Aruch, Orach Chaim 511:1, and Mishanah Berurah 1 thereon; Ketubot 7a.
18. Those that prohibit smoking based on the reason that smoking is not שווה לכל נפש include Magen Avraham to Shulchan Aruch, Orach Chaim 514:1 and Chayei Adam 95:13. See also Rashi, Ketubot 7a בעילה שווה לכל, אבל מוגמר אינו אלא למפונקים; Shulchan Aruch, Orach Chaim 511:4, Biur Halachah s.v. אין עושים מוגמר, who cites the authorities that permit smoking and the conditions under which it is permitted.
19. Rabbi Simcha Bunim Cohen, The Laws of Yom Tov p.109.
20. Beitzah 12a; Shulchan Aruch, Orach Chaim 518:1 and Mishnah Berurah 1 thereon.
21. Rabbi Simcha Rabinowitz, Piskei Teshuvot p.307, note 1 to Shulchan Aruch, Orach Chaim 494:1, and to Mishnah Berurah 1.
22. Shemirat Shabbat 44:2-3.

—

MITOCH. A YOM TOV DRIVING LICENSE?
מתוך שהותרה לצורך הותרה נמי שלא לצורך
(ביצה יב)

1. Exodus 12:16.
2. Shulchan Aruch, Orach Chaim 518:1, and Mishnah Berurah 1 thereon.
3. Rambam, Hilchot Yom Tov 4:1.
4. Shulchan Aruch, Orach Chaim 495:2, and Mishnah Berurah 11, ibid 497:1, Rashi, Beitzah 23b s.v. אין צדין דגים.
5. Chayei Adam 80:4.

6. Beitzah 12b s.v. מתוך שהותרה הבערה לצורך, הותרה נמי שלא לצורך, Shulchan Aruch, Orach Chaim, 511:1, and Mishnah Berurah 1 thereon.

7. Beitzah 19a.

8. Beitzah 12a.

9. Birkat Avraham, Beitzah 14a, quoted by Rabbi Simcha Bunim Cohen in The Laws of Yom Tov, p. 18, Note 1.

10. For other examples of הואיל ואישתרי, see Menachot 45a and Yevamot 7b.

11. Rashi, Beitzah 12a s.v. אלא מדלא איפלוג באבנים. See also Tosafot clarifying Rashi's position s.v. ה"ג. See also Magid Mishnah on Rambam, Hilchot Yom Tov 1:4. See also Shita Mekubetzet, Ketubot 7, in name of שיטה ישנה s.v. כל אותן מלאכות שהותרו לצורך אכילה לא היו בכלל לא תעשה.

12. Ramban, Leviticus 23:7.

13. Exodus 20:10.

14. Leviticus 23:7.

15. Ramban Leviticus s.v. ומלאכה שהיא באוכל נפש היא מלאכת הנאה לא מלאכת עבודה.

16. Sefer Yerayim, Siman 304, p. 170.

17. Exodus 12:20.

18. Pesachim 21b.

19. Sefer Yeraim, Siman 304, p. 170, מתוך אותו מקרא עצמו שאתה למד היתר הנאת הגוף אתה למד היתר הנאת הנשמה.

20. Tur, Orach Chaim 495, Bach s.v. - ומ"ש: ופשיטא דה"נ בכל שאר מלאכות שהרי כולן היו בכלל לא תעשה כל מלאכה, והותרו לצורך אוכל נפש,ומתוך שהותרו לצורך הותרו נמי שלא לצורך.

21. Tosafot, Shabbat 95a. s.v. והרודה.

22. Rambam, Hilchot Yom Tov 1:4.

23. Rashi, Beitza 12a, See note 11.

24. Tosafot Beitzah, 12a s.v. דלמא and see Tosafot, Ketubot 7a s.v. מתוך שהותרה לצורך.

25. Shulchan Aruch, Orach Chaim 518:1, and Mishnah Berurah 1 thereon.

26. Shulchan Aruch, Orach Chaim 502:1; Beitzah 33a.

27. Rav Bartenura, Beitzah 4:7. Taz, to Shulchan Aruch, Orach Chaim 502:1, s.v. אין מוציאים; Raavad notes to Rambam Hilchot Yom Tov 4:1; See also Rashi Beitzah 23a s.v.: דקמוליד ריחא שהמוליד דבר חדש, קרוב הוא לעושה מלאכה חדשה.

28. Rambam, see note 22.

29. Responsa Yechaveh Daat Chelek 3, Siman 36, p.111.

TURNING ON THE LIGHTS ON YOM TOV
הדלקת וכיבוי מנורת חשמל ביום טוב
(ביצה לג.)

1. Shulchan Aruch, Orach Chaim 514:5, and Mishnah Berurah 30+31 thereon.

2. Shulchan Aruch, Orach Chaim 502:1; Beitzah 33a.
3. Rambam, Hilchot Yom Tov 4:1.
4. Rashi, Beitzah 33a s.v. ואין מוציאין את האור.
5. Rambam, Hilchot Yom Tov 4:1. But see Raavad there who agrees with Rashi.
6. Responsa Rabbi Shimon Grunfeld, Mahrshag Chelek 1, Siman 64; Responsa Even Yekarah Chelek 3, Siman 168; Rabbi Zvi Pesach Frank, all quoted in Yechaveh Daat Chelek 1, Siman 32, p. 95.
7. Beitzah 33b.
8. Responsa Tzitz Eliezer Chelek 1, Siman 20, Perek 6, p.112.
9. Beitzah 23a.
10. Chazon Ish, Orach Chaim, Hilchot Shabbat 50.
11. Cited in Yechaveh Daat, see Note 6 above.
12. Shabbat 120b.
13. Responsa Achiezer Chelek 3, Siman 60.
14. Cited in Yechaveh Daat, see Note 6 above.

— ᘓᘉᘓ —

CHOL HAMOED. AN OXYMORON
חול המועד
(מועד קטן יד)

1. Shulchan Aruch, Orach Chaim 491:1.
2. Leviticus 23:37.
3. Leviticus 23:35.
4. Shulchan Aruch, Orach Chaim 31:2. The position of the Mechaber is that the Mitzvot of Succah and Matzah on Chol Hamoed Succot and Pesach are in themselves an אות - a sign, and therefore the אות of Tefillin is redundant. The position of the Rema is that since work is permitted on Chol Hamoed, Tefillin must be worn with a blessing.
5. Biur Halachah to Shulchan Aruch, Orach Chaim 530:1 s.v. ומותר במקצתן lines up those ראשונים, including Rashi, who maintain that the prohibition of work on Chol Hamoed is Biblical and those, including the Rambam, who maintain it to be of Rabbinic origin.
6. Chagigah 18a.
7. Chayei Adam 80-96 and 97-112.
8. Shulchan Aruch, Orach Chaim 530:1, and Mishnah Berurah 1 thereon.

9. Shemirath Shabbat volume 2, 66:59, note 224 quoting Rabbi Shlomo Zalman Auerbach that driving is permitted on Chol Hamoed because it only involves the potential Melachah of lighting a fire which is anyway permitted on Chol Hamoed.

10. Shemirath Shabbat 68:26, note 106.

11. Shulchan Aruch, Orach Chaim 540:3, and Mishnah Berurah 8 thereon.

12. Shulchan Aruch, Orach Chaim 637:1.

13. Shulchan Aruch, Orach Chaim 541:5, and Rema thereon.

14. Mishnah Berurah 1 to Shulchan Aruch, Orach Chaim 540:1:1; See Chayei Adam 106:2 who permits postponing cooking to Chol Hamoed.

15. Shulchan Aruch, Orach Chaim 537.

16. Ibid. 539:4.

17. Ibid.

18. Magen Avraham to Shulchan Aruch, Orach Chaim 537:1 s.v. ספק דבר האבד מותר.

19. Shulchan Aruch, Orach Chaim 544:1.

20. Ibid. 530:1, and Mishnah Berurah 1 thereon.

21. Ibid. 542:2 and 545:2.

22. Ibid. 532:2, and Mishnah Berurah 5 thereon.

23. Ibid. 531:1 and 534:1.

24. Ibid. 546:1.

25. Amos 8:10.

26. Shabbat 152b.

—⟋⟋⟍—

CELEBRATION AND SERENITY
נשמה יתירה ביום טוב
(פסחים קב:)

1. Hullin 26b.

2. Genesis 2:7.

3. Pesachim 102b.

4. Tosafot, Pesachim 102b s.v. רב.

5. Quoted by Al Hadaf, Pesachim 6/27, note 52.

—⟋⟋⟍—

CELEBRATION, SERENITY AND MOURNING
אבילות בשבת ויום טוב
(מועד קטן יט.)

1. Shulchan Aruch, Yoreh Deah 380-393.

2. Ibid. 395.
3. Ibid. 390.
4. Ibid. 392.
5. Shulchan Aruch, Yoreh Deah 391. For parents the prohibition against attending weddings and other celebrations is twelve months, See also Shulchan Aruch, Orach Chaim 548:9.
6. Shulchan Aruch, Yoreah Deah 399:1. Moed Katan 20a following the opinion of the חכמים. See also Shulchan Aruch, Orach Chaim 548:7, and Mishnah Berurah 26 thereon.
7. Shulchan Aruch, Yoreh Deah 399:3.
8. Ibid. 399:4.
9. Ibid. 400:1.
10. Tur, Yoreh Deah 400; Moed Katan 19a.
11. Penei Baruch 33:5.
12. Shulchan Aruch, Yoreh Deah 400:1.
13. Ibid. 399:1. See also Shulchan Aruch, Orach Chaim 548:1, and Mishnah Berurah 1 thereon.
14. Moed Katan 19a.
15. Deuteronomy 16:14; See also Tosafot, Moed Katan 23b s.v. מאן: גבי יום טוב אין עולים לגמרי לא למנין ולא לאבילות משום שמחה.
16. Leviticus 23:44.
17. Shulchan Aruch, Yoreh Deah 399:1:7-11; See also Shulchan Aruch, Orach Chaim 548:11-17.
18. Shulchan Aruch, Orach Chaim 548:12 and Yoreh Deah 399:7.
19. Shulchan Aruch, Orach Chaim 548:13 and Yoreh Deah 399:8.
20. Shulchan Aruch, Orach Chaim 548:14 and Yoreh deah 399:9+10.
21. Shulchan Aruch, Orach Chaim 548:16 and Yoreh Deah 399:11.

—∿—

TWO INTO ONE DOESN'T GO

העוסק במצוה פטור מן המצוה

(סוכה כה)

1. Berachot 11a; Succah 25b.
2. Tosafot, Succah 25a s.v. שלוחי מצוה.
3. Rosh, Succah 25a (in Rosh 61b).
4. Rashi, Succah 25a s.v. פטורין מן הסוכה.
5. Ran to Rif, Succah 25b (in Rif 11) s.v. ואיכא למידק.
6. Shulchan Aruch, Orach Chaim 71:3, and Mishnah Berurah 13 thereon; See also ibid, 38:8, Rema s.v. דכל העוסק במצוה פטור ממצוה אחרת אם צריך לטרוח אחר האחרת, אבל אם יכול לעשות שתיהן כאחת בלא טרח, יעשה שתיהן.
7. Numbers 9:10; Succah 25a+b, Rashi s.v. שחל שביעי שלהן: אלמא מצוה קלה הבאה לידך אינך צריך לדחותה מפני חמורה העתידה לבוא.

8. Rambam, Hilchot Kriat Shema 2:5; Kesef Mishneh s.v. וכתב.

9. Responsa Avnei Nezer, Orach Chaim 2:392.

10. Responsa Minchat Yitzchak Chelek 2, Siman 56, p.153.

—∞—

THE HOLY THIEF
מצוה הבאה בעבירה
(סוכה ל· + מא·)

1. Leviticus 23:40.

2. Numbers 15:20; Pesachim 38a.

3. Chayei Adam 152:12; Shulchan Aruch, Orach Chaim 649:5, and Rema and Mishnah Berurah 32 thereon.

4. Shulchan Aruch Harav, Hilchot Tefillin 25:35.

5. Responsa of Rashba 6:286.

6. Pesachim 38a.

7. Talmudic Encyclopedia Kerach 3, p.191.

8. Shulchan Aruch Harav, Orach Chaim 649:5.

9. Shulchan Aruch, Choshen Mishpat 352:1.

10. Shulchan Aruch, Orach Chaim 454:4.

11. Ibid.

12. Shulchan Aruch Harav, Orach Chaim 649:5 and Shulchan Aruch, Choshen Mishpat 352:1.

13. Leviticus 5:23.

14. Shulchan Aruch, Choshen Mishpat 353:3 and 356:3; Shulchan Aruch Harav, Orach Chaim Hilchot Tefillin, 25:36.

15. Biur Hagra, Shulchan Aruch, Orach Chaim 649:1 s.v. ומיהו לא and Taz there, based on Bava Kamah 94a.

16. Magen Avraham, ibid.

17. Succah 30a, dispute between Rabbi Yochanan and Rabbi Yitzchak.

18. Succah 41a.

19. Tosafot, Succah 30a s.v. מתוך.

20. Shulchan Aruch Harav, Orach Chaim 25:35; Shulchan Aruch, Orach Chaim 649:5, and Rema thereon.

—∞—

THE GREAT ESCAPE
חנוכה
(שבת כא·)

1. Shabbat 21b.

2. Niddah 30b.
3. Shulchan Aruch, Orach Chaim 672:1 and Mishnah Berurah 1.
4. Ibid.
5. Kedushat Halevi, חמש קדושות בעניני חנוכה, קדושה חמישית.
6. Chanukah was declared in 138 BCE. The Second Temple was destroyed in 69 CE.
7. Midrash, quoted by Rabbi Lieberman in Yemei Chanukah, p. 331.
8. Shulchan Aruch, Orach Chaim 679:1 and Simcha Rabinowitz, Piskei Teshuvot Chelek 6, p.502 note 1 to Shulchan Aruch, Orach Chaim, 679:1.
9. Siddur of the Shelah, Sheney Luchot Habrit and Pri Megadim qouted by Rabbi Lieberman in Yemei Chanukah 11:5, note 10. Note, however that the Shaarei Teshuva to Shulchan Aruch, Orach Chaim 679:1 s.v. מדליקין quotes authorities, the Maharash Abuhav among them, who require that one recite Minchah before lighting the Chanukah candles. The accepted practice however is the reverse. This is because of the fear that if one recites Minchah first, there will be insufficient time to light both the Chanukah lights and the Shabbat lights. Furthermore, it is considered more important to recite Minchah with a Minyan than to pray alone as would be required if the Minchah prayer had to be completed first. See Responsa of Rabbi Abraham Jacob Horowitz, Zur Yaacov, Chelek 1, Siman 136.
10. Shulchan Aruch, Orach Chaim 681:2.
11. Shulchan Aruch 681:2 and Biur Halachah 681:1 s.v. מדליקין וכו' קודם הבדלה, for a line up of the Poskim on either side of the issue.
12. Mishnah Berurah 3 to Shulchan Aruch, Orach Chaim 681:2.
13. For an explanation of the term "Sunset I" see Candle Lighting Time Chapter 1 -- above. See also Responsa Rabbi Moshe Shternbukh, Teshuvot Vehanhagot Chelek 2:334.
14. Shulchan Aruch, Orach Chaim 672:2, and Mishnah Berurah 11 thereon.
15. Ibid. 675:3, and Mishnah Berurah 9 and Biur Halachah s.v. אשה מדלקת.
16. Responsa Yechaveh Daat Chelek 3, Siman 51 p.156.
17. Sefat Emet, Shabbat 21b.
18. Tosafot, Succah 46a s.v. הרואה; Rabbi Simcha Rabinowitz, Piskei Teshuvot Chelek 6, p.488, note 3 to Shulchan Aruch, Orach Chaim 675:3.
19. Rambam, Hilchot Chanukah 4:1; Biur Halachah, Shulchan Aruch, Orach Chaim 675:3 s.v. אשה מדלקת: ועיקר החיוב מונח על הבית.
20. Bach on Tur, Orach Chaim 676 s.v. ומ"ש ואין מדליקין.
21. Chovat Hadar, Ner Chanukah Chapter 2, Note 39, p. 112.
22. Shaarim Metzuyanim Behalachach Chelek 3, p.287, note 5 to Kitzur Shulchan Aruch 139:4,
23. Shulchan Aruch, Orach Chaim 679. But see Responsa of Rashba who rules that Shabbat candles are lit before Chanukah lights because Shabbat is more frequent and Shabbat does not commence with the lighting of the candles if one had in mind to light the Chanukah lights following the Shabbat candles. See also Mishnah Berurah 1 to Shulchan Aruch, Orach Chaim 679:1.
24. See Note 12 above.

MEGILLAH ON THE INTERNET
קריאת מגילה
(מגילה ד)

1. Shulchan Aruch, Orach Chaim 688:1, and Mishnah Berurah 1 thereon; Megillah 2b; Rambam, Hilchot Megillah 1:4.

2. Rav Shlomo Yosef Zevin, Hamoadim Behalachah Page 236; Megillah 5b.

3. Shulchan Aruch, Orach Chaim 688:4.

4. Ibid. 688:3.

5. Esther 9:18.

6. Rambam Hilchot Megillah 1:5.

7. Shulchan Aruch, Orach Chaim 688:5, and Mishnah Berurah 12 thereon.

8. Megillah 4a.

9. Shaarei Teshuvah to Shulchan Aruch, Orach Chaim 687:1 s.v. קריאת :חייב אדם.
הלילה דרבנן וקריאת היום מדברי קבלה. See also Tosafot, Megillah 4a, s.v. חייב.

10. Chacham Zvi quoted in Shaarim Hametzuyanim Behalachah Chelek 3, p.303 note 7 to Kitzur Schuchan Aruch 141:7.

11. Radvaz quoted in Shaarim Hametzuyanim Behalacha ibid. discussing the case of a soldier who is given the choice of leave Purim night or Purim day. See also below, "Mitzvah Shopping."

12. Chayei Adam 155:19.

13. Shulchan Aruch, Orach Chaim 690:9, Biur Halachah s.v. באיזה כתב כתובה. Rambam, Hilchot Megillah 2:4.

14. Shulchan Aruch, Orach Chaim 688:6.

15. Megillah 4b, opinion of Rabbah.

16. Ibid., opinion of Rav Yosef there.

17. Shulchan Aruch, Orach Chaim 689:2.

18. Shaarim Hametzuyanim Behalachah p.303, note 6 to Kitzur Shulchan Aruch 141:7; Rabbi Simchah Rabbinovitz, Piskei Teshuvot p.645, note 3 to Shulchan Aruch, Orach Chaim 689:2.

19. Responsa Yechaveh Daat Chelek 3, Siman 54, p.165.

20. Responsa Igrot Moshe, Orach Chaim Chelek 2, Siman 108, p.298.

Chapter Five

The Three Weeks and Tisha Be'av

THE THREE WEEKS AND THE NINE DAYS
בין המצרים

One does not have to be superstitious to recognize facts. It is a historical fact that the period between the seventeenth of Tamuz and the tenth of Av was plagued by recurring tragedies. The door to our troubles first opened on that seventeenth day of Tamuz, when Moses walked in on the worshippers of the Golden Calf and shattered the tablets of the law.[1] On the same date, both in the era of the First Temple and Second Temple, the daily sacrifice, known as the - תמיד - Tamid, which expunged the sins of the Jews and granted them divine amnesty, was brought to a halt. On the seventeenth of Tamuz, the walls of the Second Temple were breached by the enemy that ultimately razed the Temple to the ground on - תשעה באב - Tisha Be'av. Again, on the same date, the city of Beitar was captured and Apustomus, (circa 150 B.C.E), one of the Syrian leaders, with whom the Hellenists collaborated in the persecution of religious Jews in Israel, publicly torched a Sefer Torah. And on the seventeenth of Tamuz, Menasheh, king of Judah, erected an idol in the Temple.[2] For these reasons, this period is called - בין המצרים - Bein Hametzarim - Between the Straits, based on the verse in Lamentations,[3] "all [Israel's] persecutors overtook her between the straits."

Thus, based on the laws of personal mourning, the Three Weeks, from the seventeenth of Tamuz to the tenth of Av, are observed as a period of national mourning.[4] In the case of a personal tragedy, such as the death of a relative, the mourning commences after the death, with the observance of the most severe restrictions of the Shiva,[5] followed by the less severe restrictions of the Shloshim,[6] followed by the least severe restrictions of the eleven months. In the case of Tisha Be'av, the reverse is true. The mourning commences before the event, with the observance of the least severe restrictions (akin to the eleven months) during the First Period between the seventeenth of Tamuz and Rosh Chodesh Av. Stricter restrictions of mourning follow during the Second Period, between Rosh Chodesh Av and Tisha Be'av. The strictest restrictions of mourning are observed on Tisha Be'av itself.

Accordingly, commencing with the First Period, between the seventeenth of Tamuz and Rosh Chodesh Av, the first day of the month of Av, the following are some of the activities which should be avoided. They are, weddings,[7] playing musical instruments for pleasure,[8] and reciting the blessing - שהחיינו - Schehecheyanu, for new things, in connection with the wearing of new garments, or the tasting of new fruit.[9] Some practice the custom of refraining from shaving or cutting hair, even during the First Period.[10] The following activities may be indulged in during the First Period. They are, engagements, with or without a festive meal, until Rosh Chodesh Av,[11] - פדיון הבן - Pidyon Haben, ceremony of redemption of a first born[12], even after Rosh Chodesh Av and attending a - ברית - Brit with a festive (milk or meat) meal up to noon on Erev Tisha Be'av.[13] According to Rav Moshe Feinstein, the First Period commences on the morning of the Seventeenth of Tamuz, rather than the night following the sixteenth of Tamuz. Accordingly, Rav Feinstein permits weddings and haircuts on the evening preceding the fast of Shiva Asar Betamuz.[14]

Commencing with the Second Period of the nine days, between Rosh Chodesh Av and Tisha Be'av, the following are some of the additional activities which should be avoided. They are, consumption of meat and poultry, drinking wine,[15] laundering or wearing freshly laundered clothing,[16] swimming,[17] house painting or other forms of home decorating,[18] planting flowers and plants,[19] as well as any risky activity (such as lawsuits, scheduled surgery, and travel, to the extent that they can be postponed without adverse effect).[20] On Shabbat during the nine days, one may don freshly laundered clothes, eat meat and drink wine, including Havdalah wine.[21] Similarly, the usual Shabbat songs should be sung both in the synagogue and at home. The Munkatcher Responsa criticize the Ashkenazi custom, followed by some, of singing Le'cha Dodi to the dirge of Eli Zion. A commonly employed and permissible device regarding the prohibition of wearing fresh clothes during the nine days is to don them for a moment or two before the nine days.

Tradition has it that the Temple was destroyed due to petty hatred. Accordingly, it is particularly important during the Bein Hametzarim, as always, to set the record straight with kindness and consideration.

WHEN TISHA BE'AV or EREV TISHA BE'AV OCCURS ON SHABBAT
תשעה באב או ערב תשעה באב שחל להיות בשבת

Five tragedies occurred on Tisha Be'av. It was decreed that those who left Egypt would not enter the land of Israel, the first and second Temples were destroyed, the city of Betar was captured with thousands massacred and Turnus Rufus plowed the site of the razed Temple. Consequently, Tisha Be'av was declared a day of national mourning and a fast day.

The fast of Tisha Be'av, like the fast of Yom Kippur, begins at sunset on the night preceding the fast day itself.[1] In order to prepare oneself for the fast, the accepted custom on a weekday is to eat a regular meal without meat and wine before Minchah.[2] Following Minchah, the last meal before the fast, called the - סעודה מפסקת - Se'udah Mafseket, is eaten. This meal, eaten sitting on the floor, consists of bread, water and an egg dipped in ashes.[3] The Se'udah Mafseket may not be eaten as a family meal but rather as an individual meal, each person in his or her own corner and - ברכת המזון - Grace after meals is recited by each person for himself or herself without Mezuman.[4]

When Tisha Be'av occurs on Shabbat, the fast is postponed. It begins on Motzaei Shabbat and ends on Sunday night. When the fast is postponed to Sunday, in this way, or when Erev Tisha Be'av occurs on Shabbat, the final meal before the beginning of the fast is the - סעודה שלישית - Se'udah Shlishit, the third meal of Shabbat. Since it is still Shabbat, during which mourning is prohibited, none of the restrictions of the Se'udah Mafseket that we have described above apply. Accordingly, one may eat meat and drink wine, sit around the table and recite Bitkat Hamazon with Mezuman, and there is no requirement to dip an egg in ashes. The only difference between this Se'udah Shelishit and others eaten during the year is that this one must terminate before the sun sets and the fast begins.[5]

Because the words of the Torah gladden the heart,[6] studying Torah is forbidden when Tisha Be'av is on a weekday, except for passages in Scripture that deal with the destruction of the Temple and other calamities.[7] When Erev Tisha Be'av or Tisha Be'av itself occurs on Shabbat, Torah may be studied, without restriction, on Shabbat morning and, according to many opinions, also on Shabbat afternoon.[8] At Minchah on Shabbat Tisha Be'av, or Shabbat Erev Tisha Be'av, the prayer - צדקתך -Tzidkotchah is omitted,[9] as well as - פרקי אבות - Pirkei Avoth.[10]

When Erev Tisha Be'av or Tisha Be'av itself occurs on Shabbat, the prayer - ויהי נואם - "Vehe Noam," is omitted on Motzaei Shabbat, because it was composed for recital at the inauguration of the Tabernacle, whereas Tisha Be'av commemorates the destruction of the Temple. The prayer of ויתן לך - Veyiten Lecha, is also omitted. קדיש שלם - Kaddish Shalem on this Motzaei Shabbat is recited without - תתקבל - Titkabel.

The procedure with - הבדלה - Havdalah, the blessing marking the departure of Shabbat, is as follows. For those who are fasting, first the Havdalah blessing, - אתה חוננתנו - Ata

Chonantanu, is recited in the Amidah. Then, before reciting - מגילת איכה - Megillat Eichah, Lamentations, the blessing - בורא מאורי האש - Borei Meorei Haesh, is recited over candle light but other blessings, usually recited at Havdalah, are omitted.[11] No wine or Besamim are used on this Motzaei Shabbat. On the evening following the fast, Sunday night, the Havdalah blessing that was omitted on Motzaei Shabbat is recited over wine, but no Besamim or candle light are used. Those who are not required to fast recite Havdalah on Motzaei Shabbat, but use a Chamar Medinah beverage, such as tea, coffee or beer.[12]

When Tisha Be'av occurs on a weekday, leather shoes are removed before sunset. When Erev Tisha Be'av or Tisha Be'av occurs on Shabbat, in order not to display signs of mourning on Shabbat, individuals remove their leather shoes at Ma'ariv after reciting Barchu. The Chazan first recites "Baruch Hamavdil Bein Kodesh Lechol" and then removes them before Barchu.[13]

When Tisha Be'av occurs on a weekday, תחנון- Tachanun is omitted at Minchah on Erev Tisha Be'av and on Tisha Be'av day itself, [14] just as it is not recited on a day of celebration. This is because we believe that the Temple will eventually be rebuilt on Tisha Be'av, which will then become a day of celebration.[15]

THE THREE WEEKS AND THE NINE DAYS
בין המצרים

1. Taanit 26b; Rambam Hilchot Taanit 5:2.
2. Schulchan Aruch, Orach Chaim 549:1, and Mishnah Berurah 2 thereon.
3. Lamentations 1:3.
4. Chayei Adam 133:8.
5. Schulchan Aruch, Yoreh Deah 381-393.
6. Schulchan Aruch, Yoreh Deah 390-395.
7. Schulchan Aruch, Orach Chaim 551:2, and Rema and Mishnah Berurah 15 thereon.
8. Ibid. and Mishanah Berurah 16 thereon.
9. Ibid. 551:17.
10. Ibid. 551:3 and Rema thereon; 551:12 and Mishnah Berurah 82 thereon.
11. Ibid. 551:2.
12. Ibid. 551:17.
13. Rema, Schulchan Aruch, Orach Chaim 551:10.
14. Responsa, Igrot Moshe, Orach Chaim Chelek 1, Siman 168, p.291
15. Schulchan Aruch, Orach Chaim, 551:9, and Mishnah Berurah 58 thereon.
16. Ibid. 551:3 and Rema, and Mishnah Berurah 21 thereon.
17. Ibid. 551:16 and Aruch Hashulchan, Orach Chaim 551:35.
18. Schulchan Aruch, ibid. 551:2, Mishnah Berurah 12.
19. Ibid.
20. Ibid. 551:1.
21. Schulchan Aruch, Orach Chaim 551:9, and Mishnah Berurah 59 thereon; Rema, Schulchan Aruch, Orach Chaim 551:10.

—ɯ—

WHEN TISHA BE'AV OCCURS ON SHABBAT
תשעה באב שחל להיות בשבת

1. Schulchan Aruch, Orach Chaim 553:2.
2. Ibid. 552:9, and Rema.
3. Ibid. 552:6, and Mishnah Berurah 16 thereon.
4. Ibid. 552:8.
5. Ibid. 552:10, and Mishnah Berurah 23 thereon.
6. Psalms 19:9.
7. Schulchan Aruch, Orach Chaim 554:1.
8. Ibid. 553:2, and Mishnah Berurah 9-10 thereon.
9. Ibid. 552:12, and Rema.
10. Ibid. 553:2, and Mishnah Berurah 10 thereon.

11. Ibid. 556:1, and Mishnah Berurah 2+3 thereon.
12. Ruling of Rabbi Moshe Feinstein, quoted by Rabbi Shimon Eider in Halochos of the Three Weeks p.19
13. Schulchan Aruch, Orach Chaim 553:2, and Rema.
14. Ibid. 552:12.
15. Based on Megilat Eichah 1:15.

Chapter Six

Shekalim

FIRST COME FIRST SERVED?
בענין דין קדימה בצדקה

Y ou've been too busy to open your mail. When you finally do, it is overflowing with bills and letters. Solicitation letters from the Jewish hospital, a Gemach (interest free loan fund), the Yeshiva and the Synagogue. As you walk into the great resplendent Synagogue, you are approached by a downtrodden, hungry beggar who solicits you for money. And as you look at the name plaques on the wall, you wonder, perhaps that money should have gone to the needy and the sick. Should charity be prioritized according to the perception of need or is it first come first served ?

All Poskim agree that if you are as wealthy as King Solomon, you should respond gen-erously to all worthy solicitations.[1] But, if you have limited financial resources, then accord-ing to many authorities,[2] the first check should go to those who are both poor and danger-ously sick. This takes precedence not only over the building of a Synagogue, but even over the building of the Temple. Why did King Solomon not use King David's gold and silver to build the Temple? Why did he lock it up in the Temple treasury and use his own money instead? Because, explains the Midrash,[3] a famine had ravaged the land of Israel during the three years that King David accumulated money to build the Temple. King Solomon felt that this money, which should have gone to save the lives of the hungry, was tainted. He did not want to build a Temple on the backs of the poor and hungry. Rabbi Chama and Rabbi Hoshia were strolling past the beautiful synagogue[s] of Lod.[4] "Look up," said Rabbi Chama. "See how much capital my family has invested in this splendid Synagogue!" "And how many bod-ies has your family buried here?" responded Rabbi Hoshia. "Were there no sick people dying in hospital corridors, or poor Torah scholars who needed help?" "And Israel forgot its Maker and built palaces,"[5] he chided. It is noteworthy that, despite his opinion that the first check goes to those whose lives are at risk, the Maharam of Rothenburg, who was incarcerated for seven years in a German fortress because of his religious beliefs, refused to accept ransom money raised by his community.[6]

The second check should go to the Yeshivot, and the third to the Synagogue.[7] If, how-ever, the Gamach is soliciting on behalf of poor but healthy people, or poor people who, though surviving, could do with more, then, according to the same Poskim, the Synagogue gets paid before the poor, so that the order would be, first the Yeshivot, then the Synagogue and lastly, the poor. The Vilna Gaon[8] disagrees, however, and maintains that the poor, even the healthy poor, always come ahead of the Synagogue, so that the order would be first the Yeshivot, then the poor and lastly, the Synagogue. The Aruch Hashulchan, however, suggests that where there is no Synagogue in town, all would agree that building a Synagogue takes precedence over charity to the poor but healthy .[9]

Rabbi Shmuel Landau, the son of the Noda Beyehuda, in his work, Ahavat Zion, suggests that Moses sought guidance on this very issue from God. "If we are to look after the poor," asked Moses, "how will we have enough money to pay for Your Sanctuary?" "By splitting your funds," God responded, - העשיר לא-ירבה...ממחצית השקל - "the rich may not give more than this half Shekel." In this way, there will be enough money for God's house and enough for the poor. Yes, you must build a Synagogue, suggests Rabbi Landau, but it is your duty to look after the poor. Neither has precedence over the other. The beauty of the Synagogue lies not only in the splendor of its structure but also in the comfort of its congregants.

THE MESHULACH
התורה כמקצוע

Finally, at the end of an exhausting day's work, the family gathers around the dinner table, comforted by each other's presence, the smell and taste of hot food and the buzz of friendly conversation. A knock on the door! Outside, in the frosty, December air, stands a stooped, lonely, bearded figure, huddled in a black frock-coat, under a wide, black hat that has seen better days. "A Nedovo," he pleads, "for Yeshivas Toiras Moishe Emes." "Come in Reb Meshulach, sit down." And Father's welcoming voice fades into silence, as he writes the check. Then, a shuffle of feet, some friendly murmurs and blessings, the door closes and Father returns to the table. "Him again!," hisses Chanele. "What is this? Sitting in the Yeshivah, learning the day away while we pay! Get a job! Leave us alone!."

The Rambam would agree. So would the sages of Pirke Avot. They warn us, - אהוב את המלאכה ושנא את הרבנות - "Love work, and hate the Rabbinate;"[1] - יפה תלמוד תורה עם דרך ארץ - "It is good to combine the study of Torah with an occupation," - כל תורה שאין עמה ולא קרדום - "Torah without work is useless and sinful;" מלאכה סופה בטלה וגוררת עוון - כל הנהנה מדברי תורה נוטל חייו מן העולם - "The Torah is not a professional tool;"[2] - לחפור בה - "Reward for Torah in this world is like a check drawn on the world to come." "Rather skin the carcass of a non-Kosher animal in the market place for your keep than say, I am a great scholar, a Kohen, and work is beneath me," says the Talmud.[3] "Rather live in dire poverty and engage in the most menial of trades than accept a dime of charity" the Rambam urges.[4] "Be like Hillel, the wood chopper, Rav Sheshet, the porter, Rav Huna, the water carrier, and Rebbi Yehoshua, the smithy." "Is it conceivable," the Rambam asks "that the community turned its back on these legendary Torah scholars?" "Of course not," the Rambam replies. "The community plied them with charity, but, heeding the Ethics of the Fathers, the scholars refused to accept alms. And those scholars that were forced to accept charity did so bashfully, like the great, starving Rabbi Yonathan Ben Amram, who disguised himself as a commoner so as to be able to accept a handout from Rabbi Yehuda Hanasi, the wealthy prince of Israel."

"How can you say such a thing!," says Father sadly. "Nobody agrees with the Rambam on this one." Why, the Rambam himself, as he was writing these very words, was supported by his brother, David, a diamond merchant, whose generous hand-outs allowed the Rambam to devote himself exclusively to the publications we enjoy today.[5]

Besides, from time immemorial, the Jews have always supported their scholars and teachers. The Torah speaks of "The Kohen, who is greater than his brothers."[6] And the Midrash tells us that if he is not greater than his brothers because he is poor, then the communities must make him great by honoring and supporting him.[7] And so the Priests lived off tithes. The Priests' teachers, who taught them the laws and practice of ritual slaughter and trained them in the dexterous ways of the Temple sacrifices, drew wages from the Temple treasury. So did the Judges.[8] The Jews were taxed with half a Shekel to support these communal activities, and these taxes were enforced by the Sheriffs. Why do you think Rabbi Yehuda Hanasi was handing out charity to the scholars in the first place?[9] Because he knew that it is the duty of the wealthy and well-heeled to support the trusting scholars, who choose public service over personal ambition. If every one worked like we do, what would happen to the Torah? It would be forgotten. Why, we hardly have time for one hour's study a week. That is why the Rema insists that the community support its Rabbis, teachers and Torah scholars.[10] And so does Rabbi Moshe Feinstein.[11] Sure, there were great saints like Hillel, the wood chopper, Rabbi Yehoshua, the smithy and Shmuel, the Prophet. But they were in a league all of their own. They took nothing from anybody. Shmuel the Prophet was always on the road, yet he never accepted an invitation. That famous story about Hillel on the rooftop took place when he was just a student. But once his great wisdom was recognized, he was grabbed for public service and supported by the community.[12] In fact, the Maharam of Rothenberg rails, "Just because the Rambam was fortunate enough to be graced with the mind of a genius and supported by wealthy relatives, doting kings and a lucrative medical practice, does that mean that the less fortunate should perish?"[13] Alas, one year after the Commentary to the Mishnah was completed, the Rambam's brother was drowned at sea, together with all his fortune, leaving the Rambam to care for himself and his brother's wife and two children. After a long period of depression, the Rambam, never defeated, got up, took up medicine and wrote the Mishneh Torah.[14]

FIRST COME FIRST SERVED?
בענין דין קדימה בצדקה
(ירושלמי שקלים פרק חמישי, הלכה 4)

1. Ahavat Zion Drush 10, p.16 אם אדם משופע בשפע טובה וה' נתן לו עושר רב... שאין לו גבול וקצבה
לצדקה לעניים ונותן לכל לפי צרכם ויכולת בידו לפזר הרבה, איש כזה יכול לפזר גם כן לבנין בית
למדרש ובית הכנסת לרומם בית אלוקינו בבנין מפואר, אבל אדם אשר יש לו קצבה וגבול בנתינת צדקה
לעניים אינו רשאי לפזר ממון לבנין בית הכנסת ובית המדרש כי פן יבוא עני הצריך פרנסה והוא יאמץ
את לבבו מאחיו האביון וימנע ממנו צדקה באשר כבר נתן קצבתו ולא נשאר בידו ליתן עוד צדקה
לעניים... איש כזה היה טוב לו שלא לשקוע מעותיו בבנין כדי שיהיה שמורים בידו לעת הצורך
לפרנסת עניים.

2. Responsa Mahram of Rotenberg Chapter 692 באדם שנדר לצדקה סתם אם יש לו ליתן לנרות לבית
הכנסת או לחולים, ומסיק שיש לו ליתן קודם לחולים; See also Shulchan Aruch, Yoreh Deah
249:16; Chochmat Adam, 145:7.

3. Yalkut Shimoni, Melachim 1:7:186 ומי שדורש לגנאי על שבא הרעב בימי דוד שלוש שנים וכמה
אוצרות היו לו לדוד צבורין מכסף וזהב, מה שהיה מתקין לבית המקדש היה צריך להוציאו ולהחיות בו
את הנפשות, ולא עשה כן, אמר לו הקב"ה בני מתים מרעב ואתה צובר ממון לבנות בו בנין, חייך, אין
שלמה נצטרך מהם כלום.

4. Talmud Yerushalmi, Shekalim 15a and end of Yerushalmi Peah. This section is translated in
accordance with the version brought by the Aruch Hashulchan, Yoreh Deah Hilchot Tzedaka
249:18.

5. Hoseah 8:14.

6. The Jewish Time Line Encyclopedia 1286 p.160. It should be noted that the requirement to
redeem captives is an entirely separate issue from the requirement to give to charity and has its
own Halachot.

7. Schulchan Aruch and Chayei Adam, see note 2 above; See also Beit Yosef on Tur, Yoreh Deah
249 s.v. ומ"ש.

8. Biur Hagrah note 20 to Shulchan Aruch, Yoreh Deah 249:16. In support of his position, the
Gra cites Tosafot, Bava Batra 9 s.v. שנאמר.

9. Aruch Haschulchan, see note 4 above.

—〰—

THE MESHULACH
התורה כמקצוע
(פסחים קיג.)

1. Avot 1:10.

2. Avot 4:5.

3. Pesachim 113a.

4. Rambam Commentary to Mishnayot, Avot 4 and Mishneh Torah, Hilchot Talmud Torah
3:10+11.

5. Encyclopedia Judaica Volume 11, page 756, "For eight years Maimonides lived a life free from

care. Supported by his brother David, who dealt in precious stones, he was able to devote him
self entirely to preparing his works for publication and his onerous but honorary work as both
religious and lay leader of the community. His commentary on the Mishnah was completed during this period."

6. Leviticus 21:10.
7. Yoma 18a.
8. Tosafot, Ketubot 105a s.v. גוזרי.
9. Rashi, Sotah 21a s.v. שמעון אחי עזריה.
10. Shulchan Aruch, Yoreh Deah 246:21.
11. Responsa Igrot Moshe, Yoreh Deah Chelek 2, Siman 116, p. 190.
12. Responsa Tashbetz 1:147. See also Kesef Mishneh, Rambam Hilchot Talmud Torah 3:11.
13. Tashbetz, ibid - ואם הוא ז״ל עזרו המזל להיות קרוב למלכות ונכבד בדורו מפני רפואתו וחכמתו ולא
נצטרך ליטול פרס מהקהלות, מה יעשו הרבנים והחכמים אשר לא באו לידי מדה זו, הימותו
ברעב או יתבזו מכבודם או יפרקו עול התורה מעל צוארם? אין זאת כונת התורה והמצות והתלמוד.
14. Encyclopedia Judaica p.256.

Chapter Seven

Mezuzah

MEZUZAH: SUPERVISION or SUPERSTITION
מזוזה: מי שומר - המזוזה עצמה או מצות המזוזה

When the grieving father told the Rabbi of the sudden death of his child, the Rabbi responded with words of comfort mixed with words of advice. "Check the Mezuzot," he said. When the widow, who lost her first husband in a plane crash, remarried, the Rabbi personally affixed the Mezuzah to the bedroom door, so it should not happen again. The Rabbi even suggested that for added protection, the scribe write additional verses in the Mezuzah Scroll, such as - ה׳ ישמר צאתך ובואך מעתה ועד עולם - "May God protect your goings and comings forever."[1] He also suggested that the scribe add the names of guardian angels, such as Michael and Raphael.

"Superstition," protested the father and the widow. "The Mezuzah is not a lucky charm." "Besides, you cannot just add verses to the Mezuzah scroll, just as you cannot add verses to the Tefillin scrolls. That would violate the prohibition of - בל תוסיף - Bal Tosif, which prohibits human additions to Mitzvot." The Rambam would agree. "Those who write the names of angels, or verses on the inside of the Mezuzah," writes the Rambam,[2] "do not have a portion in the world to come. Not only do such fools nullify the Mitzvah, but they reduce a great Mitzvah, which reflects the unity of God, into a talisman for their own benefit." It is not the Mezuzah object itself which guards the house, explains the Kesef Mishneh, rather, it is the performance of God's commandment to affix the Mezuzah that protects you. According to the members of the Superstition camp, the Mitzvah of Mezuzah affords the same protection as the performance of any other Mitzvah. No more, no less. The Rosh,[3] also a member of the Superstition camp, agrees.

The Supervision camp argues that it is the Mezuzah object itself which provides protection. The Mezuzah is like other charms worn in Talmudic times, which contained verses from the Holy Scriptures and which had healing powers.[4] Leading the Supervision camp are Rabbi Eliezer of Metz[5] and Rashi. They do not have to look far for support. The Talmud,[6] opening the discussion on Mezuzah, quotes Rabbi Chanina of Sura, who says that the purpose of the Mezuzah is "to protect the entire house." Support for the Supervision camp is also found in the famous story told in the Talmud[7] of Onkelos, the second century proselyte scholar, whose translation of the Torah into Aramaic is read by us to this day. The Roman Emperor sent contingents of soldiers to arrest Onkelos for becoming a proselyte. And each time, Onkelos managed to convince the soldiers not to arrest him and to convert to Judaism themselves. In despair, the Emperor sent a final contingent with strict instructions to abduct him, but not to talk to him. As he was marched through the gates, Onkelos placed his hand on the Mezuzah and asked his captors if they knew what a Mezuzah was. "You tell us," they said. "Well," replied Onkelos, "according to universal custom, the mortal king dwells within, and his servants keep guard on him from without; in the case of the Holy One, however, it is His servants who dwell within whilst He keeps guard on them from without." The Talmud tells us that these soldiers, too, converted to Judaism and the Emperor risked sending no more soldiers. And Rashi[8] points out that the reason the tenant must affix a Mezuzah, and not the landlord, is because the tenant, who lives in the rented premises, requires protection. Accordingly, the Supervision camp has no objection to the insertion of additional protective language in the Mezuzah whenever a person feels the need for enhanced protection.

Indeed, the Rambam[9] himself endorses our own custom to write the name of God, "Shadai," on the outside of the Mezuzah, opposite the word - והיה - "Vehayah," which is written on the inside of the Mezuzah. The purpose of adding the name, "Shadai," which does not form part of the mandatory Mezuzah text, is for additional protection. This practice is condoned by the Rambam as long as the additional word is not added to the Mezuzah text on the inside. Rabbi Moshe Feinstein[10] concludes that even the Rambam agrees that the Mezuzah itself, as an object, adds protection beyond the protection already afforded by the Mitzvah itself. The Rambam, according to Rabbi Feinstein, respects the power of holy scripture charms.[11] However, because the Rambam believes that the main Mitzvah of Mezuzah lies in the written text, adding additional language to the text itself violates the prohibition of Bal Tosif. Adding additional protective language on the outside of the Mezuzah does not.

THIS HOUSE IS PROTECTED BY
MEZUZAH SECURITY SYSTEMS
מזוזה

Y ou have found the house of your choice for the month of August. You were involved in a skiing accident and you are laid up in a private hospital room for months. You built a Succah. You own a garage. Do you need a Mezuzah for any of these?

וכתבתם על מזוזת ביתך ובשעריך - "Write them on parchments affixed to the doorposts of your houses and gates."[1] According to the Rambam,[2] a Mezuzah is only required if the structure in question meets all of the following ten conditions: it has an area of at least seven square feet; it has two door posts; it has a lintel; it has a ceiling; it has a door; it is at least three feet high; it is not used for holy purposes; people live in it; it is respectable; and it is used for permanent residence.

A garage or a storehouse would not require a Mezuzah, according to the Rambam, because it is not lived in.[3] Neither would a Beit Hamidrash, a house of Torah study, because it is a holy place.[4] Not all agree with all of the Rambam's requirements. Thus, according to the Shulchan Aruch,[5] a garage or a storehouse would require a Mezuzah if they are frequented occasionally by the householder. According to the Shulchan Aruch, as interpreted by the Minchat Yitzchak,[6] a garage does require a Mezuzah. If the garage has a door leading into the house, the Mezuzah should be affixed to the doorpost on the right side of the entrance to the house and the blessing - לקבוע מזוזה - "Likboa Mezuzah," should be recited. If the garage has no door leading to the house, a Mezuzah may be affixed to the garage entrance without a blessing. The Shulchan Aruch also disagrees with the Rambam's statement that a Mezuzah should never be affixed to the doorpost of a holy place. Based on the opinion of Rabbi Meir and the Maharam of Rottenberg, the Shulchan Aruch recommends that a Mezuzah be affixed, without reciting the blessing, to the door of a Beit Hamedrash.[7] It should not, however, be placed on the entrance to a Synagogue, unless the Synagogue is also used as living quarters.[8] The protection of a Mezuzah is generally unnecessary in a holy place such as the - בית המקדש - the Temple, or a - בית הכנסת - a Synagogue, because the presence of God or His Torah creates a safe haven. All Poskim agree that a Mezuzah may not be affixed to bathroom or Mikveh entrances.[9]

What obligation does a tenant have to fix a Mezuzah? In Israel, a tenant is required to affix the Mezuzah the moment he takes possession of the home.[10] Outside Israel, the tenant must affix the Mezuzah after thirty days residence.[11] It is the tenant's obligation to affix the Mezuzah, not the landlord, unless he too occupies the leased premises or stores his belongings there.[12] Because the occupancy of a hotel or a hospital room, even for a prolonged period, does not give one exclusive possession of the premises, the occupant has no obligation to affix a Mezuzah.[13] A Succah, which, by definition, is a temporary abode (Dirat Arai) needs no Mezuzah.[14] If, however, the Succah has a detachable roof and is used the rest of the year as a residence or storehouse, it requires a Mezuzah during the rest of the year.[15]

The entrance to a mobile home requires a Mezuzah if the mobile home is inhabited for more than thirty days at a time.[16] According to the Minchat Yitzchak, entrances to elevators in Israeli apartment houses require a Mezuzah.[17] A structure in which one is confined against one's will, such as a prison cell, requires no Mezuzah.[18]

The entrance to a house that is inhabited both by Jews and gentiles is exempt from a Mezuzah. This is because of the concern that it will not be treated with respect or may even be removed.[19]

The Israeli cab driver who hangs a Mezuzah around his neck has a point.[20] The Mezuzah is there to protect us. How different is God from other kings, notes the Talmud.[21] Other kings stay inside while their servants guard outside. God guards outside while His servants stay inside.

MEZUZAH, SUPERVISION or SUPERSTITION

מזוזה: מי שומר - המזוזה עצמה או מצות המזוזה

(פסחים ד.)

1. Psalms 121:7.
2. Rambam Hilchot Tefillin 5:4 and Kesef Mishneh s.v. מנהג.
3. Halachot Ketanot, Hilchot Mezuzah Chapter 18.
4. Shabbat 61b.
5. Sefer Yerayim, Amud Hayirah 18.
6. Menachot 33b.
7. Avodah Zarah 11a.
8. Rashi, Pesachim 4a s.v. חובת הדר
9. Rambam, Hilchot Tefillin, see note 2 above.
10. Responsa Igrot Moshe, Yoreh Deah Chelek 2, Siman 141, p.236.
11. Rambam, Hilchot Sefer Torah 10:5.

—ɯ—

THIS HOUSE IS PROTECTED BY
MEZUZAH SECURITY SYSTEMS

מזוזה

(יומה יא·)

1. Deuteronomy 6:9.
2. Rambam, Hilchot Mezuzah 6:1.
3. Ibid. 6:7 following the opinion of Rabbi Yehudah, the teacher of Rabbi Kahanah, Yoma 11a. See Kesef Mishneh on the Rambam s.v. לפיכך
4. Rambam, Hilchot Mezuzah 6:6.
5. Shulchan Aruch, Yoreh Deah 286:2 following the opinion of Rav Kahanah in Yoma 11a.
6. Responsa Minchat Yitzchak Chelek 10, Siman 96, p.158.
7. Shulchan Aruch, Yoreh Deah 286:10 in the name of יש אומרים.
8. Ibid 286:3.
9. Ibid 286:4; Rambam, Hilchot Mezuzah 6:1.
10. Shulchan Aruch, Yoreh Deah 286:22; Pesachim 4a, Rashi s.v. , חובת הדר: לפי שהיא משמרתו.
11. Shulchan Aruch, Yoreh Deah 286:22.
12. Responsa Igrot Moshe, Yoreh Deah Chelek 2, Siman 141, p.236.
13. Chovat Hadar 3:5, note 16, citing Pnei Moshe and Maharam Chalavah. However, see dissenting opinion in Shulchan Aruch Yoreh Deah 286:22 (הדר בפונדק בארץ ישראל פטור ממזוזה 30 יום). Regarding a hospital room see ruling of Avnei Nezer, Responsa 380 that a Mezuzah is not required.
14. Shulchan Aruch, Yoreh Deah 286:11.

15. Chovat Hadar 4:4.
16. Responsa Minchat Yitzchak Chelek 2, Siman 82, p.166.
17. Responsa Minchat Yitzchak Chelek 3, Siman 93, p.209.
18. Birkei Yosef, Shulchan Aruch, Yoreh Deah 286:4, although not free from doubt. Chovat Hadar suggests fixing a Mezuzah after 30 days in prison without a blessing. See Chovath Hadar 3:10.
19. Rema, Shulchan Aruch Yoreh Deah 286:1.
20. Responsa Igrot Moshe, see note 12 above.
21. Menachot 33b.

Chapter Eight

Other Topics in Seder Moed

MITZVAH SHOPPING
בענין אין מעבירין על המצות

He must be a very important person to get such an important Mitzvah, I heard them say, as Mr. Lowenstein, the local Assemblyman, stepped up to recite the Torah blessing before the reading of the Ten Commandments. And Mr. Kleppish was too embarrassed to tell his wife that he only got third Gelila (binding the ribbon around the Torah scroll) on Shabbat Rosh Chodesh, Chanukah. Meanwhile, in the local Shtiebel (make-shift Synagogue), Maftir (the last section of the weekly Torah reading) was sold for $500 and Peticha (opening the Holy Ark) was sold for $20. Do we know which Mitzvah is more important than another? Should we give priority to an important Mitzvah over an "unimportant" Mitzvah?

Watching the Kohen, the Priest, as he performed the rituals of the daily morning sacrifice, provides us with an illustrative answer. Which Mitzvah was he to perform first? The distinguished task of preparing the Menorah for the evening kindling, or the menial task of sweeping the Altar from yesterday's ashes? First he swept off the ashes and then he prepared the Menorah. Because, explains Resh Lakish,[1] the Altar was closer to the door, through which the Kohen entered the Sanctuary, than the Menorah was, so that the Kohen reached the Altar first. - אין מעבירין על מצות - "Ein Ma'avirin Al Hamitzvot," do not offend a Mitzvah by postponing it, says Resh Lakish. First, do the Mitzvah which first comes your way.

Even if the Mitzvah that first comes your way is considered by the Halachah to be less holy than the second, most agree that the less holy Mitzvah should be performed first. The Tefillin Shel Rosh - Tefillin worn on the head - is holier than the Tefillin Shel Yad - Tefillin worn on the arm - because it has more letters of God's name on it than the Teffilin Shel Yad.[2] Yet, the Tefillin worn on the arm is put on first. This, explains Rashi,[3] is because the arm is closer to the hand than to the head. For the same reason, explain the Tosafot,[4] when replacing the Tefillin back in their bag, the Tefillin Shel Rosh should not be placed on top of the Tefillin Shel Yad, for by doing so one would violate the rule of Ein Ma'avirin Al Hamitzvot. This is because the Tefillin Shel Rosh would have to be put aside the next morning, while the Tefillin Shel Yad is being donned first, in order to comply with the sequence in which the Torah introduces them - וקשרתם לאות על ידך והיו לטטפות בין עיניך - "Bind these words as a sign on your hand and let them be an emblem in the center of your head."[5] Similarly, when reciting the verse - פותח את ידך ומשביע לכל חי רצון - "You open Your hand and satisfy the need of every human being," the Tefillin Shel Yad should be touched first.

The correct order for donning Tallit and Tefillin is Tallit first and then Tefillin.[6] This order respects the rule of - מעלין בקודש - Ma'alin Bakodesh, ascend in the order of holiness.[7] The rule of Ma'alin Bakodesh gives way, however, to the rule of Ein Ma'avirin Al Hamitzvot, in the following situation. If one pulls the Tefillin out of the bag before the Tallit, then, according to the Shulchan Aruch, Tefillin should be donned first, in order not to violate the rule of Ein Ma'avirin Al Hamitzvot.[8] In order to avoid this conflict, the Tallit should be put back in the bag, on top of the Tefillin. The correct order for reading the Torah on Chanukah, Rosh Chodesh Tevet, is first the portion of Rosh Chodesh and then the portion of Chanukah. This order respects the rule of "Tadir Kodem," which means perform first the Mitzvah that occurs with higher frequency.[9] The rule of Tadir Kodem gives way, however, to the rule of Ein Ma'avirin Al Hamitzvot in the following situation: If one mistakenly began reading the Chanukah portion first, then, according to the Taz, one should not interrupt this reading with the Rosh Chodesh reading, in order not to violate the rule of Ein Ma'avirin Al Hamitzvot.[10]

The Radvaz[11] was once asked whether a prisoner who was given one day furlough each year should take it at the earliest opportunity or wait for Yom Kippur. After all, on Yom Kippur one can perform more important Mitzvot. Based on the rule of Ein Ma'avirin Al Hamitzvot, he ruled that the prisoner should take it now, even though it was an ordinary weekday. The Chacham Zvi[12] disagreed. If you can be certain, he says, that the authorities will not change their minds, it is preferable to wait for Yom Kippur.

MORE ON MITZVAH SHOPPING
עוד בעניין אין מעבירין על המצות

It is a matter a dispute, whether the rule of Ein Ma'avirin Al Hamitzvot, (do not offend a Mitzvah by postponing it), means that one should perform a Mitzvah Derabanan, of Rabbinic origin, before a Mitzvah De'oraita, of Biblical origin, just because the Mitzvah Derabanan first came one's way. Take a person who finishes Se'udah Shlishit, the meal eaten before Sabbath ends, at the very moment that Shabbat ends, and he only has one cup of wine. At this point in time, the same cup of wine is needed for two separate Mitzvot, Birkat Hamazon, Grace after meals, and Havdalah, the blessing upon the departure of Shabbat. Birkat Hamazon is a Mitzvah De'oraita,[1] whereas making Havdalah over wine is a Mitzvah Derabanan.[2] In this situation, the order of events is as follows: First, one recites Grace after meals, then Havdalah and then one drinks the wine.[3] Rashi[4] explains that this order is dictated by the rule Ein Ma'avirin Al Hamitzvot, since Se'udah Shlishit precedes the departure of Shabbat. The fact that Birkat Hamazon also happens to be a Mitzvah De'oraita and Havdalah over wine is only a Mitzvah Derabanan is, according to Rashi, entirely irrelevant. Accordingly, it is clear that the origin of the Mitzvah, whether Derabanan or De'oraita, is not a factor to be considered in deciding which Mitzvah to perform first. In fact, the very source of the rule Ein Ma'avirin Al Hamitzvot demonstrates that if a Mitzvah Derabanan comes one's way first, it should be performed before the Mitzvah De'oraita. The source of this rule[5] is that the Kohen, on his daily Temple rounds, had to sweep the altar from yesterday's ashes first and then prepared the Menorah for kindling, even though sweeping the ashes was, according to certain opinions,[6] a Mitzvah Derabanan.

Others argue that the rule of Ein Ma'avirin Al Hamitzvot has no application in a contest between a Mitzvah Derabanan and a Mitzvah De'oraita. What happens, asks the Magen Avraham, when Yom Tov is on Thursday night and Friday and you only have one cup of wine? Do you use it for Yom Tov Kiddush on Thursday night, even though Yom Tov Kiddush is only a Mitzvah Derabanan?[7] Or do you keep the wine for Friday night Kiddush, which is a Mitzvah De'oraita?[8] You keep the wine for Friday night, rules the Magen Avraham.[9]

Does the rule Ein Ma'avirin Al Hamitzvot mean that you must perform the Mitzvah that first comes your way even if, as a result, it becomes impossible later to perform a Mitzvah of greater Halachic consequence? Take, for example, the case of a person who, during the Temple era, was obliged to offer a Korban Pesach, a Paschal Lamb, on the 14th of Nissan. So crucial was the requirement to sacrifice the Korban Pesach on that day that the punishment for unjustifiably failing to do so was premature death at the hand of God, Karet.[10] Nevertheless, if a person was confronted with the Mitzvah of taking care of the dead prior to the fourteenth, he was obliged to do so, even though he would render himself Tamei (due to contact with death or aborted life) and, thereby, unfit to offer the Korban Pesach on the fourteenth.[11] Others (such as the Chayei Adam) disagree and maintain that Ein Ma'avirin Al Hamitzvot does not apply in such circumstances.[12] According to this opinion, one may forgo a Mitzvah of less Halachic importance if performing it first would eliminate the performance of a Mitzvah of greater Halachic importance.

In a leap year, should the Purim Megillah be read in the first month of Adar rather than in the second, based on the rule of Ein Ma'avirin Al Hamitzvot? The answer is that it should, and it would,[13] were it not for the verse in Megillat Esther,[14] which mandates that the Megillah be read in the second month of Adar.

A Mitzvah may be postponed in order to enhance its performance. Accordingly, one who sights the new moon during the week should wait with Kiddush Levana (blessing over the new moon) until Motzaei Shabbat, Saturday night, when he is in festive attire and in a festive mood, unless he is concerned that it will no longer be visible at that later time.[15]

PERSONAL AND NATIONAL REVELATION
באם קיימו האבות תרי"ג מצות

W as the Revelation at Sinai, a Divine graduation ceremony for Torah, already studied and practiced years before? Or was it a Divine introduction to the Book of
Books? Did the Hebrews become Jewish at the time of the Revelation, or were Abraham,
Isaac and Jacob already Jews in their time? Did Abraham observe the laws of the Torah in
all their detail, or was he a monotheist-humanist who practiced God's Natural Laws and
spread human kindness. It all depends on how one interprets the following words: עקב -
אשר שמע אברהם בקלי וישמר משמרתי, מצותי, חקותי, ותורתי - "Ekev Asher Shama Avraham
Bekoli, Vayishmor Mishmarti, Mitzvotai, Chukotai Vetorotai," "All this is because Abraham
obeyed My voice, and kept My charge, My commandments, My decrees and My laws."[1] The
words Mishmarti, (My charge) Mitzvotai (My commandments), Chukotai (My decrees) and
Torotai (My laws), can be given a technical, legal interpretation or a pragmatic interpretation.

It is an ancient debate: "Our father Abraham fulfilled the entire Torah," proclaims Rav.[2]
"Perhaps not," suggests Rav Shimi. "Perhaps, he only observed the seven Noachide laws"
(which prohibit idolatry, adultery, murder, stealing, severing a limb from a live animal, and
blasphemy and which require the formation of a judicial system to enforce such prohibitions). "But Abraham performed circumcision!" responds Rav. "Well, let's say he kept the
seven Noachide laws and circumcision," concedes Rav Shimi. "Not so," insists Rav,
"Abraham kept all the commandments, even the Rabbinical commandments. Why, he even
practiced the laws of Eruvei Tavshilin (a Rabbinical procedure which permits a Jew to prepare food on Yom Tov for a meal on Shabbat)."

And the debate continues throughout the ages. Rashi adheres to the technical, legal, yet
mystical interpretation of the words. Mishmarti, according to Rashi, means protective
Rabbinical legislation, which is intended to keep one from Biblical infringements. Mitzvotai,
according to Rashi, means those natural laws, like robbery and murder, that are self-
explanatory.[3] Chukotai[4] means those laws that can be challenged from a purely rational
point of view, such as the dietary laws and the laws of mixed species, which we ultimately
observe because we are commanded to. And "Torotai,"[5] which is written in the plural,
means both the Written and the Oral Law.

Others[6] prefer the pragmatic approach. According to them, "Mishmarti" means
Abraham kept the Monotheistic faith. "Mitzvotai" means Abraham simply obeyed those
commandments personally given to him, such as the order to leave his land and to sacrifice
his son. "Chukotai" refers to the seven Noachide laws and "Torotai" refers to circumcision.

The Ramban[7] struggles with both interpretations. If our forefathers observed all the
commandments of the Written and Oral law, he asks, why was Jacob married to

Rachel and Leah at the same time? And how could Amram, the father of Moses and Aaron, have married Yocheved, his father's sister? The Torah[8] prohibits both. And how could Moses have erected monuments for the glory of God[9] when the Torah[10] prohibits this? Besides, if the Torah had not yet been revealed, how did Abraham know it? The Ramban gives two answers. A rational one and a mystical one. The rational answer concurs with the Chizkuni, the Rashbam and the Seforno above. The mystical one, which, he admits, appeals to him more, is based on a dictum of Rabbi Shimon, as follows: "Abraham's two kidneys were fashioned like two jugs of water, from which Torah poured." Abraham's personal Torah teacher was God, and he observed the commandments voluntarily. Or, in the words of Philip Biberfeld,[11] [Abraham] "was a Navi, a man inspired by personal, divine revelation." As for Jacob's marriage to two sisters and Amram's marriage to his aunt, Ramban points out that these marriages occurred outside Israel where, according to many opinions, the laws of the Torah had less application. And building monuments was a prohibition enacted after Moses' act. Perhaps, the title of Biberfeld's work, "Universal Jewish History," is an amalgam of the technical and the pragmatic approach.

FOLLOW THE LEADER?

בענין תקדים מחייב בפסיקה התורנית

Whenever I resisted learning Talmud with my father, preferring to study only the Torah, he would respond: "The Written Law is meaningless without the Oral Law, just like the short hand notes of a student who attended a lecture in the hands of a student who did not."

It is a fundamental principle of Judaism that the Divine Lawgiver imparted to Moshe two Codes of Law.[1] The Written Law, consisting of the Five Books of Moses, and the Oral Law, which interprets the Written Law. When the Torah says, "You shall slaughter your cattle in the way I have commanded you,"[2] or "you shall wear Totafot between your eyes,"[3] or "you should take the fruit of the Hadar tree,"[4] it is the Oral Law that tells us what the Torah means.[5] The Oral Law was orally transmitted by God to Moshe during his forty day stay on Mount Sinai.[6] Moshe then taught the Oral law to the rest of Israel through Aaron, his sons and the Elders of Israel. The Oral law consists of two parts. First - הלכה למשה מסיני - Halachah le Moshe Misinai, which are specific laws dealing with more frequently occurring cases. These laws were taught by Moshe himself. Second, rules of derivation, or hermeneutic rules, known as the - י"ג מדות - Yud Gimmel Midot, which are applied to the written text to derive the law as it applies to less frequently occurring cases. The Sages never disagree regarding the exact content of Halachah Le'Moshe Misinai, which was carefully preserved from generation to generation.[7] They often disagree, however, on the result of the application of the Yud Gimmel Midot to the facts of a particular case. "If it is Halachah Le'Moshe Misinai, it must be accepted, but if it is derived from the Yud Gimmel Midot, it can be debated."[8]

Is a contemporary Jewish Court of law permitted to arrive at a different legal conclusion from the Mishnah or the Talmud when applying any of the Yud Gimmel Midot to a specific case under consideration? For example, the Talmud[9] derives that a person who borrows an article must pay the owner if the article is lost or stolen while in the borrower's possession. Although this result is not explicitly written in the Torah, it is derived by the Talmud from a Kal Vechomer, (one of the Yud Gimmel Midot, that if a lenient case has a stringency, the same stringency should apply, a fortiori, to a stricter case). The Kal Vechomer argument is as follows: "If a paid bailee, who is not responsible for the injury or natural death of the animal entrusted to him, is nevertheless liable for its theft or loss, then a borrower, who the Torah explicitly renders liable for such injury or sudden death, should surely be liable for such theft or loss." What if a contemporary court disagrees with this Kal Vechomer and finds a convincing argument why the borrower should be exempt for such theft or loss? For example, the Court may argue that the friendly relationship that gave rise to the free use of the loaned article in the first place should forgive the borrower for such loss or theft. Can a present day court overrule the opinions of the Tanna'im in the Mishnah and the Amoraim in the Talmud?

In response to this question, the Rambam[10] rules that a contemporary court may overrule the decision of a prior court if it believes that the prior court's application of the Yud Gimmel Midot was incorrect. The contemporary court derives this authority from the words of Deuteronomy 17:9, "You shall go to ...the judge who shall exist in [your] days." Even if that judge is less qualified than his predecessors, his decision is binding.[11] The Kesef Mishneh questions the Rambam's general statement. If that were so, he asks, why are the Amoraim (Talmudic sages belonging to the period starting with Rav and Shmuel in 219 C.E. and ending with Rav Ashi and Ravina in 475 C.E.) not allowed to overrule the Tanna'im (sages belonging to the period starting with Hillel and Shamai 61 B.C.E. and ending with Rabbi Yehuda Hanasi, who compiled the Mishnah in 189 C.E.). Why does the Talmud go to such lengths to line up the opinions of Amoraim with Tanna'im? The Kesef Mishneh answers that the license of an Amora to overrule a Tanna ended when the Mishnah (the memorized Oral Law) was reduced to writing by Rabbi Yehudah Hanasi. Similarly, the license of a contemporary Posek (judge) to contradict an Amora ended when Rav Ashi and Ravina reduced the Talmud to writing. There are two reasons for this. One reason, given by the Kesef Mishneh himself, is that the people simply accepted upon themselves the rulings of the Tannaim and Amoraim as binding precedent. The other reason, given by Rabbi Yosef Dov Soloveichik,[12] is that only those sages that participated in the live Halachic debates of the great Babylonian academies were considered part of the Ba'alei Masora (the owners of tradition). In the course of a live debate, the minority has the ability to challenge and persuade the majority. Once the debate is reduced to writing, says the Rav, the ebb and flow of exchange is frozen and the opportunity to turn the tide is lost. The opinion of the Kesef Mishneh, that the rulings of the Mishnah and Talmud are binding precedents, has been adopted as the Halachah. Accordingly, a decision of a contemporary judge inconsistent with such precedent is void.[13]

Are the decisions of the Poskim (judges) who lived after the era of the Amoraim binding on contemporary Jewish courts of law? The period of the Amoraim and their immediate disciples, the Savoraim, was followed by the period of the Gaonim, lasting until 1038 C.E. at which time the great Babylonian centers of learning at Sura and Pumbedita closed their doors. With the disappearance of the great Babylonian academies of learning, there was no longer a universally accepted authority. However, several codes of law based on the Talmud and the decisions of the Gaonim were written by leading Rabbis and became almost universally accepted. Chief among these were the works of the Rishonim (the first codifiers), such as Rabbi Yitzchak Alfasi (Rif; 1013-1103 C.E.) and Rabbi Asher Ben Yechiel (Rosh; 1250-1328 C.E.) as well as the Yad Hachazakah, also known as the Mishneh Torah, by the

Rambam (1135-1204 C.E.) The codifiers of this period are called Rishonim. The code of law that was most widely accepted, however, was the Shulchan Aruch of Rabbi Yosef Karo, (1488-1575 C.E.) which took into consideration almost all of the earlier Rishonim. Following the Shulchan Aruch, the period of the Rishonim ended and the period of the Acharonim began. Because of the almost universal acceptance of the Shulchan Aruch, its decisions, as modified for the Ashkenazi community by Rabbi Moshe Isserles (1520-1527 C.E.), are deemed binding. So are the works of many of the commentators on the Shulchan Aruch. Nevertheless, a court of law of recognized Torah scholars may dispute a decision of the Shulchan Aruch, or any other accepted post-Talmudic, prior Posek, based on persuasive Talmudic proof, or on a tradition that a particular prior decision was not universally accepted.[14] Where there is a dispute between two equally rated authorities, the rule is as follows. If the case concerns a matter of Biblical Law, the stricter opinion is followed.[15] If the case involves a matter of Rabbinical Law, the more lenient opinion is followed.[16] The scholar with the larger following is considered the greater authority.[17] Within the limitations discussed above, when a community accepts a Rabbi as their religious leader, his decisions are considered binding even if they are more lenient than the decisions of his predecessors.[18]

THE FIRST REFERENDUM
בענין תקנות, גזירות וסייגם: תוקפם וביטולם

J og, stop smoking, change your diet, get your blood pressure down. Doctor's orders. Reluctantly, with the threat of sudden death hanging over your head, you obey, even as you yearn for the couch, the cigarette and the chocolate cake. Months or years later you feel so healthy and energized that you cannot conceive of ever living differently. And the next time that they offer you a cigarette or a piece of chocolate cake, you turn them down, doctor's orders or not. The deepest entrenchment of the law is voluntary acceptance.

נעשה ונשמע - Na'aseh Venishma, "Whatever You say," responded the Jews to God's commandments at Mount Sinai. But they did not really mean it. The Midrash tells us that God suspended Mount Sinai over their heads and threatened them with instant death if they declined the Torah.[1] At Sinai, the Jews chose survival. Only later, during the days of Mordechai and Esther, did the Jews, after being saved from annihilation, willingly accept the Torah.[2] Clearly, it was important to the Divine Lawgiver that His commandments be voluntarily accepted by the majority of Israel rather than involuntarily imposed.

If this is true for the Law of God, it is certainly true for the laws of the Rabbis. The Torah[3] gives the Sanhedrin, the Supreme Court and legislature in matters of Torah Law, legislative power to enact - תקנות וגזירות - Takanot and Gezeirot, ordinances and decrees, to address unsettled questions of law and to erect - סייגים - Seyagim, legislative barriers to safeguard against violation of Torah laws.[4] Legislation enacted by the Sanhedrin is referred to as a - מצוה דרבנן - Mitzvah Derabanan, Rabbinical legislation, as distinguished from a - מצוה דאורייתא - Mitzvah De'oraita, a Torah commandment.

Takanot, Gezeirot and Seyagim are unenforceable, however, if the majority of Israel cannot abide by them.[5] Indeed, before the Rabbis enact Takanot and Gezeirot, they must assess the probability of their public acceptance.[6] If such acceptance appears unlikely, the Rabbis have no authority to enact them. And if the Rabbis misjudged the likelihood of their acceptance and enacted Takanot, Gezeirot or Seyagim that are subsequently rejected by the majority of Israel, such Takanot, Gezeirot and Seyagim are void.[7]

Can a Takanah, Gezeirah or Seyag, enacted by the Rabbis of an earlier generation, be repealed by the Rabbis of a later generation? If the Takanah or the Gezeirah is in the nature of a Seyag (preventative legislation to safeguard against violation of Torah laws) and if it has been accepted by the majority of Israel, it cannot be repealed.[8] Thus, the prohibition against drinking wine manufactured or handled by non Jews - יין נסך - Yayin Nesach, legislated by Hillel and Shamai[9] to discourage fraternization that might lead to intermarriage, is a Seyag which has been accepted by the majority of Israel. As such, it cannot be repealed. On the other hand, the prohibition against consuming oil prepared by non-Jews, also a Seyag enacted by Hillel and Shammai for the same reason, was not accepted by the majority of Israel and was, subsequently, repealed. Of course, a Takanah or Gezeirah can be repealed, even if it is in the nature of a Seyag and even if it has been accepted by the majority of Israel, if the Rabbis that originally enacted it explicitly gave future Rabbis the power to repeal it.[10] A Takanah or Gezeira that is not a Seyag but which has been accepted by the majority of Israel, may be repealed by the Rabbis of a subsequent generation, provided that such Rabbis are superior in wisdom and prestige to the earlier Rabbis that enacted it. Thus, the Takanah of - פרוזבול - Pruzbul, enacted by Hillel to preserve the right of a creditor to claim the repayment of his debt during the Shemittah year, was not in the nature of a Seyag, even though it was accepted by the majority of Israel. Accordingly, later Rabbis, greater in wisdom and prestige than Hillel, could repeal it.[11]

Where the rationale for a Takanah or Gezeirah, as expressed by the Rabbis that originally enacted it, no longer applies, then, according to many opinions,[12] such a Takanah or Gezeirah automatically expires, and no formal repeal is necessary. Thus, the stated reason for the Takanah, which requires one to eat some bread or drink some water between meat and fish is that eating fish and meat together is a health hazard.[13] Today, however, this is no longer considered dangerous and, according to the Magen Avraham, this Takanah no longer applies. However, a Takanah enacted without an expressed rationale, though clearly no longer applicable, does not die automatically but must be formally repealed.[14]

Where the very body of religious observance is threatened -הוראת שעה - Hora'at Sha'ah, the Rabbis, like a surgeon who amputates to save a life, have the authority, to suspend temporarily the application of any law, whether Rabbinical or Biblical.[15]

MITZVAH SHOPPING
בענין אין מעבירין על המצות
(יומא לג.)

1. Yoma 33a+b
2. Menachot 34b s.v. ושל ראש אין עושין אותה של יד לפי שאין מורידין מקדושה חמורה לקדושה קלה. The Tefillin Shel Rosh has the letter ש on the בית and ד on the רצועה. The Tefillin Shel Yad only has the ד on the רצועה. See Shulchan Aruch, Orach Chaim 32:52.
3. Rashi, Yoma 33b s.v. עבורי דרעא אטוטפתא.
4. Tosafot, Yoma 33b s.v. עבורי דרעא אטוטפתא giving a different explanation of the circumstances in which אין מעבירין על המצות applies to Tefillin.
5. Deutoronomy 6:8.
6. Shulchan Aruch, Orach Chaim, 25:1.
7. Two other reasons that require this order are that the Tallit is more frequently worn, תדיר ושאינו תדיר תדיר קודם, and that the Mitzvah of Tzizit is equivalent to all the other Mitzvot. see Aruch Hashulchan, Orach Chaim 25:1 and Beit Yosef to Tur, Orach Chaim 25:1 s.v. ואחר
8. Shulchan Aruch, Orach Chaim 25:1
9. Ibid., 684:3.
10. Taz Shulchan Aruch, Orach Chaim 684:3 s.v. ואם טעה.
11. Radvaz, Responsa 4:13.
12. Chacham Zvi, Responsa 107.

—␣␣␣—

MORE ON MITZVAH SHOPPING
עוד בענין אין מעבירין על המצות
(יומא לג.)

1. Deuteronomy 8:10.
2. Rambam, Hilchot Shabbat 29:6.
3. Shulchan Aruch, Orach Chaim 296:3.
4. Pesachim 103a s.v. על המוץ שהוא שבתחלה: כיון דעבד סעודתו בדהא אדיב בי"שא ואין מעבירין על המצות.
5. Yoma 33a+b. The source of Ein Maavirin al Hamitzvot is to be found in the Mechilta Exodus 12, 17 quoted by Rashi on the Torah.
6. Tosafot, Meilah 11b s.v. בשלמא.
7. Mishnah Berurah 1 to Shulchan Aruch, Orach Chaim 271:1; Magen Avraham to Shulchan Aruch, Orach Chaim 271:3 s.v. ודע.
8. Exodus 20:8; Mishnah Berurah, ibid.
9. Magen Avraham, Shulchan Aruch, Orach Chaim 271:3 s.v. ודע.
10. Rambam, Hilchot Korban Pesach 1:2.
11. Rashi, Succah 25a+b s.v. שחל שביעי שלהן: אלמא מצוה קלה הבאה לידך אינך צריך לדחותה מפני חמורה העתידה לבוא.

12. Talmudic Encyclopedia Kerach 1, p.668 quoting the Chayei Adam 68.
13. Megillah 6b in the name of Rabbi Eliezer son of Rabbi Yose.
14. Esther 9:29 "לקים את אגרת הפורים הזאת השנית".
15. Terumat Hadeshen Chelek 1, Siman 35.

—⟊—

PERSONAL AND NATIONAL REVELATION
באם קיימו האבות תרי"ג מצות
(יומה כח:)

1. Genesis 26:5.
2. Yoma 28b.
3. Yoma 67b.
4. Ibid.
5. Yoma 28b.
6. Chizkuni, Rashbam, Seforno in their commentaries to Genesis 26:5.
7. Rambam, commentary to Genesis 26:5.
8. Leviticus Chapter 18.
9. Exodus 24:4.
10. Deut. 16:6.
11. Philip Biberfeld, Universal Jewish History.

—⟊—

FOLLOW THE LEADER?
בענין תקדים מחייב בפסיקה התורנית

1. Thirteen Principles of Faith 8; Exodus 24:12; Berachoth 5a.
2. Deuteronomy 12:21.
3. Deuteronomy 6:8.
4. Leviticus 23:40.
5. Shabbath 31a.
6. Rashi, Leviticus 25:1; Tosafot, Yevamot 77b s.v. הלכה.
7. Tosafoth, Yevamoth 77b; Rambam, Introduction to Mishnah.
8. Mishnah Yevamoth 8:3.
9. Bava Metzia 95a.
10. Hilchot Mamrim 2:1.
11. See Rashi to Deuteronomy 17:9; Rosh Hashana 25b.
12. Nefesh Harav p.36.

13. Shulchan Aruch, Choshen Mishpat 25:1 and the commentary of the Vilna Gaon thereon s.v. לחלוק.

14. Shulchan Aruch, Choshen Mishpat 25:1.

15. Bava Bathra 57b.

16. Shabbath 34.

17. Rambam, Hilchot Mamrim 2:2.

18. Shulchan Aruch, Choshen Mishpat 25:1.

—◊◊◊—

THE FIRST REFERENDUM
בענין תקנות, גזירות וסייגם, תוקפם וביטולם
(שבת פח.)

1. Shabbat 88a.

2. Esther 9:27.

3. Deuteronomy 17:11. Rambam, Mishneh Torah, Hilchot Mamrim 1:2.

4. Leviticus 18:30; Rambam, introduction to Mishneh Torah; Minchat Chinuch Mitzvah 454.

5. Rambam, Mishneh Torah, Hilchot Mamrim 2:5.

6. Ibid.

7. Ibid.

8. Radvaz on Rambam, Hilchot Mamrim 2:3; see also Tosafot, Avodah Zara 37a s.v. ורבנן.

9. Shabbat 17b.

10. Radvaz on Rambam, Hilchot Mamrim 2:2, s.v. היה גדול בחכמה

11. Gittin 36b.

12. Radbaz, Rambam, Hilchot Mamrim 2:2.

13. Shulchan Aruch, Orach Chaim 173:2.

14. Rashi, Beitzah 5a s.v. מנא אמינא לה. Tosafot, Sanhedrin 59b s.v. לכל.

15. Psalms 119:126; Rambam, Mishneh Torah, Hilchot Mamrim 2:9.

BIBLIOGRAPHY

Bechhofer, Rabbi Yosef Gavriel. *The Contemporary Eruv, Eruvin in Modern Metropolitan Areas.* Jerusalem: Feldheim Publishers, 1998, (referred to herein as "The Contemporary Eruv.")

Blau, Yaacov Yeshayahu. *Sefer Chovat Hadar.* Jerusalem: 1975, (referred to herein as "Chovat Hadar.")

Blau, Rabbi Yaacov Yeshayahu. *Sefer Netivot Shabbat, Halachot, Hotza'ah Ve'eruvin.* Jerusalem: Machon Lehoraah Monsi - Jerushalayim, 1998, (referred to herein as "Netivot Shabbat.")

Biberfeld, Philip. *Universal Jewish History.* New York: Philip Feldheim Inc. 1973, (referred to herein as "Universal Jewish History.")

Bodner, Rabbi Yisroel Pinchas. *Sefer Tiltulei Shabbat, The Halochos of Muktza.* New Jersey: Halachah Publications, 1981, (referred to herein as "Halochos of Muktza.")

Cohen, Rabbi Simcha Bunim. *Hilchot Yom Tov, The Laws of Yom Tov, A Comprehensive Halachic guide to the laws and practices of the Festivals.* New Jersey: Mesorah Publications, Ltd, 1997, (referred to herein as "The Laws of Yom Tov.")

Cohen, Rabbi Simcha Bunim. *Hilchot Amirah Leacum. The Sanctity of Shabbos. A comprehensive guide to the laws of Shabbos and Yom Tov as they apply to a non-Jew on behalf of a Jew.* New Jersey: Messorah Publications, Ltd, 1988, (referred to herein as "Hilchot Amirah Leacum.")

Cohen, Rabbi Zvi. *Tevilat Keilim, Halachot Uminhagim Hashalem.* Jerusalem: Hamachon Hotorani Beyisrael Hamercaz Lecheker Hahalachah Uminhagei Yisrael, 1982, (referred to herein as "Tevilat Keilim.")

Cohen, Rabbi Zvi. *Hagalat Keilim, Halachot Uminhagim Hashalem.* Jerusalem: Hamachon Hatorani Beyisrael Hamercaz Lecheker Hahalachah Uminhagei Yisrael, 1981, (referred to herein as " Hagalat Keilim.")

Eider, Rabbi Shimon D. *Sefer Hilchot Shabbat, Halochos of Shabbos.* Jerusalem: Philp Feldheim, Inc, 1989, (referred to herein as "Halochos of Shabbos.")

Eider, Rabbi Shimon D. *Kitzur Halachot Bein Hameitzarim, A Summary of the Halochos of the three weeks.* New Jersey: Feldheim Publishers, Inc, 1993, (referred to herein as "Halochos of the three weeks.")

Eider, Rabbi Shimon D. *Sefer Hilchot Pesach, Halochos of Pesach.* New York: Feldheim Publishers, 1984, (referred to herein as "Halochos of Pesach.")

Goldberg, Rabbi Chaim Binyamin. *Sefer Penei Baruch Avelut Behalachah.* Jerusalem: 1985, (referred to herein as "Penei Baruch.")

Goren, Rabbi Shlomo. *Mo'adei Yisrael.* Jerusalem: Hotza'at Haaidra Rabba Umesurah La'am, 1996, (referred to herein as "Mo'adei Yisrael.")

Grunfeld, Dayan Dr. I. *The Jewish Dietary Laws.* London: The Soncino Press, 1972, (referred to herein as "The Jewish Dietary Laws.")

Grunfeld, Dayan Dr. I. *The Sabbath. A Guide to its Understanding and Observance.* Jerusalem: Feldheim Publishers Ltd, 1959, (referred to herein as "The Sabbath.")

Harari, Rabbi Moshe. *Sefer Mikraei Kodesh Hilchot Lel Haseder.* Jerusalem: Yeshivat Mercaz Harav, 1998, (referred to herein as "Hilchot Leil Haseder.")

Kantor Mattis. *The Jewish Time Line Encyclopedia.* Jerusalem: Jason Aronson Inc, 1989, (referred to herein as "The Jewish Time Line.")

KiTov, Eliahu. *Sefer Hatoda'ah.* Jerusalem: Yad Eliyahu KiTov, 1997, (referred to herein as "Sefer Hatoda'ah.")

Lau, Rabbi Yisrael. *Yahadut Halachah Lema'aseh Devarim Sheba'al Peh.* Tel Aviv: Modan Hotza'ah La'or, 1998, (referred to herein as "Yahadut Halachah Lema'aseh.")

Lieberman, Rabbi Yitchak Meir. *Sefer Yemei Chanukah, Dinim Uminhagim.* Jerusalem: The Center for Promotion of Torah Culture and Research Projects in Israel, 1997, (referred to herein as "Yemei Chanukah.")

Mirski, Rabbi Yitzchak. *Hegione Halachah Beinyanei Shabbat Umoadim.* Jerusalem: Mosad Harav Kook, 1989, (referred to herein as "Hegione Halachah.")

Neuwirth, Rabbi Yehoushuah, Yeshayah. *Shemirat Shabbat Kehilchatah.* Jerusalem: Bet Midrash Halachah - Moriah 1965, (referred to herein as "Shemirat Shabbat.")

Rabinowitz, Rabbi Simcha. *Piskei Teshuvot Lefi Seder Mishnah Berurah.* Jerusalem: 1995, (referred to herein as "Piskei Teshuvot.")

Shechter, Yoseph. *A Lexicon of the Talmud.* Tel Aviv: Dvir Publishing House, 1990, (referred to herein as "Lexicon of the Talmud.")

Shechter, Rabbi Zvi, *Nefesh Ha'rav.* Israel: 1994, collected works of Harav Yosef Dov Halevi Soloveitchick.

Stern, Rabbi Yechiel Michel. *Sefer Melechet Shabbat Al 39 Melachot.* Jerusalem: 1994, (referred to herein as "Sefer Melechet Shabbat.")

Stern, Rabbi Yisroel David. *Sefer Eruv Tavshilin Haaruch.* Israel: Avraham Stern, 1995, (referred to herein as "Sefer Eruv Tavshilin.")

Tabori, Rabbi Yosef. *Moadei Yisrael Betkufat Hamishnah Vehatalmud.* Jerusalem: Magnus Publishing House, The Hebrew University, 1994, (referred to herein as "Moadei Yisrael.")

Zevin, Rabbi Shlomo Yosef. *Hamoadim Behalachah.* Jerusalem: Yad Harav Herzog - Ichud Mifalim Toraniyim - Safruti'im, 1983, (referred to herein as "Hamoadim Behalachah.")

TRADITIONAL AUTHORITIES CITED IN THIS BOOK

Achiezer. Responsa by Rabbi Chaim Ozer Grodzinski (Vilna,d. 1941).

Aruch Hashulchan. Halachic code by Rabbi Yechiel Michal Epstein (Belorussia, 1829-1908).

Avnei Nezer. Responsa by Rabbi Avraham of Sochatchev (Poland,d. 1910).

Ba'al Shem Tov. Rabbi Israel ben Eliezer (Russia, 1700-1760).

Be'er Heitev. Commentary on *Schulchan Aruch* by Rabbi Yehudah Ashkenazi (Germany and Poland. 18th cent.).

Beit Yosef. Commentary on *Tur* by Rabbi Joseph Karo (Israel, 1488-1575).

Birkei Yosef. Glosses to the Shulchan Aruch by the Chida, Rabbi Chaim Yosef David Azulai (Italy,d. 1806).

Bi'ur Hagrah. Commentary on *Schulchan Aruch* by Rabbi Eliyahu ben Solomon (Lithuania, 1720-1797), also known as the Vilna Gaon.

Bi'ur Halachah. Halachic work by Rabbi Israel Meir ha-Kohen (Lithuania, 1838-1933), also known as Chafetz Chaim.

Chacham Tzvi. Responsa by Rabbi Tzvi Hirsh Ashkenazi (Amsterdam 1660 -1718).

Chatam Sofer. Responsa of Rabbi Moshe Sofer (Hungary 1763-1839).

Chayeh Adam. Halachic work by Rabbi Abraham Danzig (Lithuania, 1748-1820).

Chazon Ish. Responsa by Rabbi Abraham Yeshayah Karelitz (1878-1953).

Chochmat Adam. Halachic work comprising the laws contained in Shulchan Aruch, Yoreh Deah, by Rabbi Abraham Danzig (Vilna,1748-1820).

Divrei Menachem. Responsa on Shulchan Aruch, Orach Chaim by Rabbi Menachem Kasher (20th cent. Israel, U.S.).

Ha'amek Davar. Commentary on the Torah by the Netziv, Rabbi Naftali Tzvi Yehudah Berlin (Velozhin, d. 1893).

Igrot Moshe. Responsa by Rav Moshe Feinstein (U.S. 1895-1986).

Kaf Hachaim. Commentary on *Shulchan Aruch* by Rabbi Jacob Chaim Sofer (Iraq, 20th cent.).

Kedushat HaLevi. Halachic commentary by Rabbi Levi Yitzchak of Berditchev (d. 1809).

Kesef Mishneh. Commentary on *Mishneh Torah* by Rabbi Joseph Karo (Israel. 1488-1575).

Kitzur Shulchan Aruch. Summary of the Shulchan Aruch by Rabbi Shlomo Ganzfried (Hungary, d. 1886).

Lechem Mishneh. Commentary on *Mishneh Torah* by Rabbi Abraham di Boton (Salonika, 1545-1588).

Levush. Halachic code compiled by Rabbi Mordechai Jaffe (Poland, 1535-1612).

Ma'aseh Choshev. Responsa by Rabbi Levi Yitzchak Heilperin (Israel, 21st. cent.)

Magen Avraham. Commentary on *Shulchan Aruch* by Rabbi Abraham Gombiner (Poland, 1636-1683).

Maggid Mishneh. Commentary on the Mishneh Torah by Rabbi Vidal Di Tolose (Spain 14th. cent.)

Maharam of Rotenburg. Rabbi Meir ben Baruch Halevy of Rotenburg (Germany, d. 1293).

Maharsha. Moreinu ha-Rav Samuel Eliezer Edels (Poland, 1555-1631). Author of commentary on Tosafot.

Matteh Ephraim. Halachic commentary by Rabbi Ephraim Zalman Margolis (Austria, d.1828).

Minchat Yitzchak. Responsa by Dayan I.J. Weiss (U.K., Israel. 20th. cent.).

Mishnah Berurah. Commentary on *Shulchan Aruch* by Rabbi Israel Meir ha-Kohen (Lithuania, 1838-1933), also known as Chafetz Chaim.

Mishneh Torah (also known as *Yad ha-Hazakah*). Halachic code compiled by Rabbi Moses

Maimonides (Rambam) (Egypt, 1135-1204). Unless otherwise specified, all references in this work to the Rambam are to the *Mishneh Torah*.

Mordechai. Halachic compendium on most of the Tractates of the Talmud by Rabbi Mordechai ben Hillel Ashkenazi (1240-1298).

Noda Beyehudah. Responsa of Rabbi Yechezkel Landau (Prague,1713-1793).

Or Zaru'a. Halachic work by Rabbi Isaac of Vienna (Austria, 1180-1250).

Pitchei Teshuvah. References to responsa works following the Shulchan Aruch by Rabbi Tzvi Hirsch Eisenstadt (Lithuania, 1813-1868).

Pri Megadim. Commentary on *Shulchan Aruch* by Rabbi Joseph Teomim (Poland, 1727-1792).

Ra'avad. Rabbi Avraham ben David of Posquieres (1120-1197).

Rabbenu Tam. Rabbi Jacob Tam (France, 1100-1171).

Radbaz. Rabbi David ben Solomon ibn Abi Zimra (Egypt, 1479-1530).

Radvaz. Responsa by Rabbi David ben Zimra (Eygypt, 1480-1573).

Ran. Rabbi Nissim of Gerondi (Spain, 1310-1375).

Rambam. Rabbi Moses ben Maimon (Maimonides) (Egypt, 1135-1204).

Ramban. Rabbi Moses ben Nahman (Nahmanides) (Spain, 1194-1270).

Rashba. Rabbi Shlomo ben Avraham Aderet, author of commentary on Talmud and responsa (Spain,1235-1310).

Rashbam. Rabbi Samuel ben Meir (France, 1085-1174).

Rashi. Rabbi Solomon ben Isaac (France, 1040-1105).

Rema. Rabbi Moses Isserles (Poland, 1525-1572), author of *Mappah*, glosses to *Shulchan Aruch* reflecting Ashkenazic practice.

Rif. Rabbi Isaac Alfasi, Codifier and Talmudist (North Africa and Spain, 1013-1103).

Ritva. Rabbi Yom Tov Ishbili (Spain, 1250-1327).

Rosh. Rabbi Asher ben Yehiel (Germany and Spain, 1250-1327) author of halachic compilation on the Talmud.

Schach. Sifsei Kohen, commentary on Shulchan Aruch, Yoreh Deah by Rabbi Shabtai Hakohen (Vilna, 1622-1663).

Sefat Emet. Commentary to the Talmud by Rabbi Yehudah Leib Alter of Gur (Poland, d. 1905).

Sefer Hachinuch. Exposition of the 613 commandments by Rabbi Aaron ha-Levi of Barcelona (Spain, 14th cent.).

Sefer Yereim. Commentary on Halachah and ethics by Rabbi Eliezer of Metz (France, d.1161).

Sha'arim Metzuyanim Behalachah. Commentary on the Kitzur Schulchan Aruch by Rabbi Shlomo Zalman Braun.

Sha'ar Hatzion. Notes by Rabbi Israel Meir Hakohen, also known as Chafetz Chaim to his Mishnah Berurah (Lithuania, 1838-1933).

Sha'arei Teshuvah. References to responsa works to the Shulchan Aruch by Rabbi Chaim Mordechai Margolis (Russia).

Shelah. Sheney Luchot Habrit, halachic and ethical work by Rabbi Yeshayah Halevi Horowitz (Amsterdam, 1565-1630).

Shiltei Giborim. Commentary to the Rif by Rabbi Yehoshuah Boaz (Sabbioneta, d. 16th cent.).

Shita Mekubetzet. Collection of commentaries to various tracates of the Talmud by Rabbi Betzalel Ashkenazi (1520-1591).

Shulchan Aruch. Most widely accepted code of Jewish law compiled by Rabbi Joseph Karo (Spain and Israel, 1488-1575).

Shulchan Aruch Harav. Halachic code by Rabbi Shneur Zalman of Lyady (Russia, 18th cent.).

Shoel Umeishiv. Responsa by Rabbi Yosef Shaul Nathanson (Lvov, d. 1857).

Tashbetz. Responsa of the Maharam of Rottenberg written by Rabbi Shimon Ben Tzadok.

Taz (Turei Zahav). Commentary on *Shulchan Aruch* by Rabbi David ben Samuel ha-Levi (Poland, 1586-1667).

Terumat Hadeshen. Halachic commentary by Rabbi Yisrael Isserlein (Austria, d. 1460).

Tosafot. Literally "Additions." Comments on Talmud by students of Rashi and members of French and German yeshivot (12th-14th cent.).

Tosafot Yom Tov. Commentary on Mishnah by Rabbi Yom Tov Lipmann Heller (Moravia, 1579-1654).

Tur (also known as *Arba'ah Turim*). Halachic code compiled by Rabbi Jacob ben Asher, son of the Rosh (Germany and Spain, 1275-1340).

Tzitz Eliezer. Responsa by Rabbi Eliezer Waldenberg (Switzerland and Israel, 20th cent.).

Yabia Omer. Responsa of Rabbi Ovadiah Yosef (Israel, 20th cent.), former Sephardic Chief Rabbi of Israel.

Yavetz. Rabbi Jacob Emden (Germany, 1698-1776).

Yechaveh Da'at. Responsa of Rabbi Ovadiah Yosef (Israel, 20th cent.).

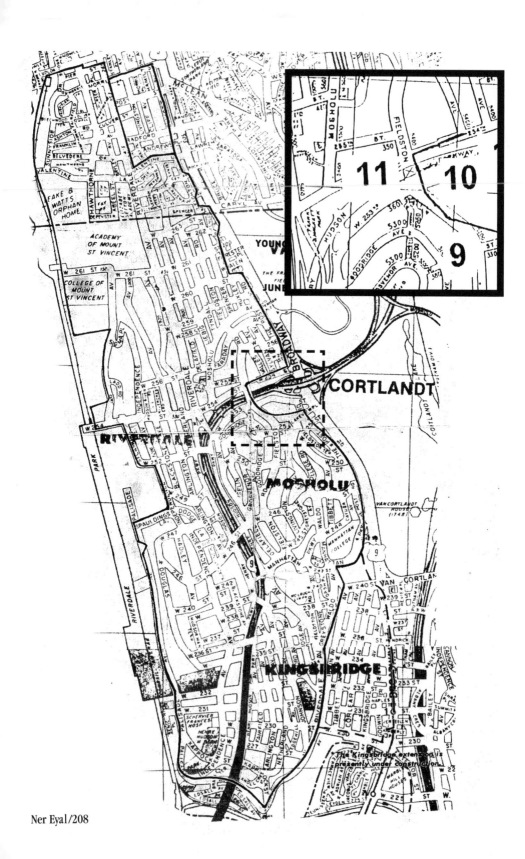